Quality and Equity in Education

Full details of all our publications can be found on http://www.multilin-gual-matters.com, or by writing to Multilingual Matters, St Nicholas House, 31–34 High Street, Bristol, BS1 2AW, UK.

Quality and Equity in Education

A Practical Guide to the Council of Europe Vision of Education for Plurilingual, Intercultural and Democratic Citizenship

Edited by
Michael Byram, Mike Fleming and Joseph Sheils

MULTILINGUAL MATTERS
Bristol • Jackson

DOI https://doi.org/10.21832/BYRAM4020
Library of Congress Cataloging in Publication Data
A catalog record for this book is available from the Library of Congress.
Names: Byram, Michael, editor. | Fleming, Michael (Michael P.), editor. |
    Sheils, Joseph, editor.
Title: Quality and Equity in Education: A Practical Guide to the Council of Europe
Vision of Education for Plurilingual, Intercultural and Democratic Citizenship/
Edited by Michael Byram, Mike Fleming and Joseph Sheils.
Description: Bristol, UK; Jackson, TN: Multilingual Matters, 2023. | Includes
    bibliographical references and index. | Summary: "This book presents a vision
    of plurilingual, intercultural education, demonstrates how it can be realised in
    practice, and does so in a way which is easily and quickly accessible to teachers
    of all subjects and in all educational institutions, as well as to other educationists,
    including policymakers"— Provided by publisher.
Identifiers: LCCN 2022046822 (print) | LCCN 2022046823 (ebook) | ISBN
    9781800414013 (paperback) | ISBN 9781800414020 (hardback) | ISBN
    9781800414037 (pdf) | ISBN 9781800414044 (epub)
Subjects: LCSH: Multilingual education—European Union countries. |
    Multicultural education—European Union countries. | Language and
    education—European Union countries. | Education and state—European
    Union countries. | Council of Europe.
Classification: LCC LC3736.A2 Q35 2023 (print) | LCC LC3736.A2 (ebook) |
    DDC 370.117094—dc23/eng/20221129
LC record available at https://lccn.loc.gov/2022046822
LC ebook record available at https://lccn.loc.gov/2022046823

British Library Cataloguing in Publication Data
A catalogue entry for this book is available from the British Library.

ISBN-13: 978-1-80041-402-0 (hbk)
ISBN-13: 978-1-80041-401-3 (pbk)

Multilingual Matters
UK: St Nicholas House, 31–34 High Street, Bristol, BS1 2AW, UK.
USA: Ingram, Jackson, TN, USA.

Website: www.multilingual-matters.com
Twitter: Multi_Ling_Mat
Facebook: https://www.facebook.com/multilingualmatters
Blog: www.channelviewpublications.wordpress.com

The policy of Multilingual Matters/Channel View Publications is to use papers that
are natural, renewable and recyclable products, made from wood grown in
sustainable forests. In the manufacturing process of our books, and to further
support our policy, preference is given to printers that have FSC and PEFC Chain of
Custody certification. The FSC and/or PEFC logos will appear on those books
where full certification has been granted to the printer concerned.

Typeset by Nova Techset Private Limited, Bengaluru and Chennai, India.
Printed and bound in the UK by the CPI Books Group Ltd.

Contents

Contents

Contributors

Nathalie Auger is Full Professor at University Paul-Valéry Montpellier 3, France. Her principal research interests focus on the inclusion of multilingualism in classrooms as a resource for teaching and learning, in particular in the case of migrant and Roma students. She has written a dozen books on the subject (most recently *Multilingualism and Education*, Cambridge University Press, 2022, with Gail Prasad and Emmanuelle Le Pichon), and has created various websites (SIRIUS, MALEDIVE, LISTIAC) connected to European and Canadian funded projects. She is currently an expert for the European Centre for Modern Languages (Council of Europe), the European Commission and the High Council of Languages at The French Ministry of Education.

Martyn Barrett is Emeritus Professor of Psychology at the University of Surrey, UK. His research examines the development of intercultural, democratic and global competence, and young people's political and civic engagement and global citizenship. He works as a lead expert for the Education Department of the Council of Europe, where he helped to develop the *Reference Framework of Competences for Democratic Culture* and the *Autobiography of Intercultural Encounters*. He also contributed to the development of the conceptual framework and assessments of global competence that were used in the OECD's *Programme for International Student Assessment* (PISA) in 2018. For further details, see www.martynbarrett.com.

Diana-Maria Beldiman is a History and English teacher at two prestigious public schools in Bucharest: Scoala Centrala National College and Petre Ispirescu Secondary School. She holds a PhD in History, an MA in Cultural Heritage and another in Didactics of Philological Subjects. She is interested in identifying new approaches to teaching Languages and History and is carrying out research in Didactics. The results of her work have been published in volumes and articles.

Claudia Borghetti has been Research Fellow in Language Learning and Teaching at the University of Bologna since 2017. She researches intercultural language education, study abroad and multilingualism, teaching L2

Italian, and (academic) writing. Between 2012 and 2015, she was project manager of the European project IEREST (Intercultural Education Resources for Erasmus Students and their Teachers). She has been involved in other international projects focusing on intercultural language education and internationalisation in higher education. Claudia is a member of the management committee of the International Association for Languages and Intercultural Communication (IALIC). For further details see: https://www.unibo.it/sitoweb/claudia.borghetti/en.

Michael Byram is Professor Emeritus at Durham University (UK) and Guest Research Professor at Sofia University, Bulgaria. He studied Languages at King's College, Cambridge, including a PhD in Danish literature, and then taught French and German in secondary and adult education. From 1980, at Durham University, he was involved in teacher training and research on languages and education. He contributed to Council of Europe workshops in the 1990s and in the 2000s he was Adviser to the Council of Europe Language Policy Division. He then became a member of the working group which produced the Council of Europe's *Reference Framework of Competences for Democratic Culture*.

Cecilie Hamnes Carlsen is Professor in Second Language Acquisition at Western Norway University of Applied Sciences. She holds a PhD in language testing and has worked on the development and validation of language tests for adult migrants from 1997 to 2017. Her current research interest relates to the use and misuse of language tests in the migration context, in the labour market and in education, with a particular focus on the impact of language tests on low-literate adult migrants. She is an expert member of ALTE, member of the ALTE Standing Committee and co-chair of the ALTE LAMI project group and the ALTE Social Justice discussion group.

Marisa Cavalli is a teacher-researcher at the former Regional Institute for Educational Research (IRRE) for the Aosta Valley in Italy, and a consultant to the European Centre for Modern Languages of the Council of Europe. She has taken part in activities and projects of the former Language Policy Division (later the Language Policy Unit) of the Council of Europe, notably in the project 'Language in Education – Language for Education' and in three Language Education Policy Profiles. Her field of work is bi-/plurilingual education in relation to the construction of knowledge in the context of policies seeking to preserve minority languages.

Mirjam Egli Cuenat is a researcher in the field of educational linguistics and a teacher educator. She is currently Head of the foreign languages department in primary teacher education at FHNW University of Applied Sciences and Arts Northwestern Switzerland (School of Education). Her research interests include bi- and pluriliteracy, third language learning, plurilingual and intercultural education, learning mobility, curricula and language policy. Since 2001 she has been working as an expert on behalf of the Council of Europe at the former Language Policy Division (later the Language Policy Unit) in Strasbourg and at the European Centre for Modern Languages in Graz.

Jonas Erin is General Inspector for education, sports and research in France. His areas of expertise are integrated youth policies; plurilingual and intercultural education; social cohesion and equity; international cooperation; digital education and change management. Since 2012 he has been working on various projects with the European Centre for Modern Languages in Graz (ECML), e.g. 'Towards whole-school language curricula' (PlurCur) and 'Learning environments where Modern Languages flourish' (EOL). He contributed in 2021 to the 'Recommendation on the importance of plurilingual and intercultural education for democratic culture' (Council of Europe). He has also been involved in the international publication *The Routledge Handbook of Plurilingual Language Education*.

Mike Fleming is Emeritus Professor of Education at the School of Education, Durham University, UK. He has a background in teaching Drama and English. and wide experience in teacher training, research and examining. He has written a number of books and academic papers on aesthetics, drama and arts education, and has published on the relationship between drama and intercultural education. He worked on the 'Languages of Schooling' project at the Council of Europe and authored a number of papers and booklets.

Helmut Linneweber-Lammerskitten was the chair for Teaching and Learning of Mathematics and its Disciplines at the Pädagogische Hochschule Nordwestschweiz (PH FHNW), a professor of mathematics education at the Institut für Bildungswissenschaften der Universität Basel and a private lecturer for philosophy at the University of Bern. He was co-leader of the Swiss national educational standards project (HarmoS) in mathematics and has been involved with the Council of Europe's Language(s) project in all subjects. Together with Marc Schafer from the Rhodes University South Africa he led the project 'Visual Technology for the Autonomous Learning of Mathematics' (VITALmaths).

David Little is a Fellow Emeritus of Trinity College Dublin, Ireland. His principal research interests are the theory and practice of learner autonomy in language education, the management of linguistic diversity in schools and classrooms, and the use of the *Common European Framework of Reference for Languages* to support the design of L2 curricula, teaching/learning programmes, and assessment. He has contributed to the Council of Europe's work in language education since the 1980s, including the European Language Portfolio and Linguistic Integration of Adult Migrants projects. He is currently academic coordinator of the Council's Romani/Plurilingual Policy Experimentation.

Waldemar Martyniuk is Professor at the Institute of Polish Language and Culture for Foreigners of the Jagiellonian University in Krakow, Poland. He holds a PhD in Applied Linguistics and is a teacher trainer and author of several textbooks, curricula and testing materials for Polish as a foreign language. He is a Visiting Professor and lecturer at universities in Germany (Bochum, Giessen, Göttingen, Mainz, Münster), Switzerland (Basel) and in the USA (Stanford University). He was seconded to the Council of Europe, Language Policy Division in Strasbourg, France, 2005–2006, and in 2008–2013 was Executive Director of the European Centre for Modern Languages in Graz, Austria. Since 2019 he has been the Chair of the Board of Trustees at the Association of Language Testers in Europe (ALTE).

María-del-Carmen Méndez-García is a professor at the Department of English Philology, University of Jaén, Spain. She has undertaken research on the cultural component in EFL material, intercultural competence and intercultural communication. She is the author of books, book chapters and articles on intercultural competence and foreign language education. She has participated in international projects such as 'International Competence for Professional Mobility', funded by the European Commission. She has cooperated with the Language Policy Division/Unit of the Council of Europe in the development of the *Autobiography of Intercultural Encounters* and the *Autobiography of Intercultural Encounters through Visual Media*.

Silvia Minardi holds a PhD in linguistics from the University for Foreigners – International University – of Siena, Italy. She is currently teaching English as a Foreign Language at Liceo Statale 'S.Quasimodo' in Magenta and at Università dell'Insubria (Varese). She is the President of the Italian association Lingua e Nuova Didattica and vice-president of Amerigo, the Italian association of US international exchange alumni. From 2016 to 2019 she collaborated with the European Center for Modern Languages (ECML) of the Council of Europe (Graz, Austria) where she was involved as a project team member in the 2016/2019 Programme. She is currently an expert teacher trainer for ECML. She is a member of various committees, councils and advisory boards at national and international level.

Irene Pieper has been a Professor of Literature Education at Freie Universität Berlin since 2020. She previously held a professorship at the University of Hildesheim, Germany. She specialises in literature teaching and learning. Major themes of her research concern verbal interaction and the constitution of subject matter in the classroom, literary development and reading socialisation. She has been involved with the Council of Europe's Platform of Resources for Plurilingual and Intercultural Education and the development of the Literary Framework for Teachers in Secondary Education, LiFT-2. She also served as the first president of the International Association for Research in L1 Education (Languages, Literatures, Literacies), ARLE.

Lorenzo Rocca is, since 2006, responsible for research projects at the national and supranational level focused on connections between teaching and assessment in the migration context; he has published articles, syllabi for language provision and specifications for exams for adult migrants. Rocca has been the chair of LAMI (Language Assessment for Migrants' Integration) in ALTE (Association of Language Testers in Europe) since 2008 and a member of the Council of Europe LIAM project since 2014. In 2020 he was awarded the national academic qualification of Associate Professor. In 2021, Rocca joined the Società Dante Alighieri in Rome where he currently works as manager, responsible for national and international projects.

Florentina Sâmihăian is a lecturer at the Faculty of Letters, University of Bucharest, Romania. She coordinates the master program *Didactics of Philological Subjects*. She has participated in European projects such as LiFT-2 (Literary Framework for Teachers in Secondary Education) and ELiCa (University and School for a European Literary Canon). She also collaborated on the project *Languages of Schooling* initiated by the Council of Europe. Her research interests are in the field of didactics of language and literature. She is a co-author of many textbooks for Romanian language and literature for lower and upper secondary.

Joseph Sheils was a teacher and involved in curriculum development for modern languages in Ireland. He subsequently worked at the Council of Europe in Strasbourg (1992–2011) with responsibility for its intergovernmental language education programmes. He also contributed to the organisation's specific actions to ensure respect for language rights in post-conflict contexts. His work at the Council included initiatives to support the linguistic integration of adult migrants (LIAM). He writes here in a personal capacity. He is currently an Individual Expert Member of ALTE (Association of Language Testers in Europe), and its group on Language Assessment for Migrants' Integration (LAMI).

Eike Thürmann studied languages, phonetics and political sciences in Marburg, Germany and Memphis, USA and has a PhD from Marburg University. He taught phonetics at Cologne University. He trained to become a schoolteacher, transferred to the State Institute for Curriculum Development and In-Service Teacher Training, Soest, where he became Head of the Quality Agency working on behalf of the Ministry of Education and coordinated language policy projects in various areas: heritage language maintenance, CLIL, curriculum development and standards. He worked for the Council of Europe on a variety of projects (e.g. CLIL, national language policy profiles, CEFR, ELP, Languages of/for Schooling) and also for the National Agency for German Schools Abroad (Scientific Advisory Board).

Louise Tranekjær is Associate Professor in Cultural Encounters at the Department of Communication and Arts at Roskilde University. Her research centres on linguistic and cultural encounters in workplace and educational settings and she has worked with global citizenship, intercultural competence and intercultural communication in relation to foreign language and second language learning contexts. She is the editor-in-chief of the journal *Sprogforum*.

Helmut Johannes Vollmer is Professor Emeritus, Faculty of Languages and Literature at the University of Osnabrueck, Germany, where he taught English as a Foreign Language (TEFL) and Applied Linguistics. Earlier positions were at Bremen and Leipzig as well as in England and the US. His research interests include bilingualism and bilingual education as well as subject-matter didactics. He directed the Research Center for Bilingual Education and Multilingualism in Osnabrück. He published widely in Europe and North America (over 230 titles). He was the co-founder of the German Association of Foreign Language Research, of the Association for Fachdidaktik and also of two peer-reviewed journals.

Preface

The Council of Europe has had a major influence on educational policy in Europe for many years. There are many research-oriented, scholarly publications about the Council of Europe and we do not intend to add to that corpus of valuable work. Our purpose in this book is to introduce the values and concepts of the educational vision of the Council of Europe to teachers of all subjects and disciplines, in all levels and sectors of education so that they might more easily adopt and apply them to their own teaching. The Council of Europe has produced many policies and recommendations, guides and practical instruments that need to be interpreted and applied in relation to its underlying principles and values.

The over-arching values of the Council of Europe are prominently displayed on its website and elsewhere: democracy, human rights and the rule of law. Under this umbrella, the Council of Europe has laid great emphasis on equity and quality in education, on enhancing the democratic competences of citizens and on promoting respect for human dignity and diversity without discrimination. 'Equity' is crucial in a continent of great social, cultural and linguistic diversity. It emphasises the right of all learners to have equal access to and be able to profit from educational opportunities. 'Quality' is the guarantee that learners' full potential is realised through their educational experience throughout life. Lifelong learning is the context within which the Council of Europe hopes and expects all who live in Europe to thrive.

Democracy is the foundation on which the education envisioned by the Council of Europe is constructed. Linguistic and cultural diversity is the context within which Europeans live. Intercultural dialogue is the foundation on which Europeans can live together in harmony. Education is the major means through which people living in Europe can acquire the knowledge, skills, attitudes and values necessary to engage in successful dialogue and cooperation, and become plurilingual, intercultural and democratic citizens.

Our purpose as editors has been to bring together authoritative contributors and invite them to distil from the Council of Europe's work the various dimensions of a shared vision of education in such a way that teachers can understand how they can apply that vision of European values in practical ways. We do not presume to provide a comprehensive and detailed guide to the policies of the Council of Europe, although we do provide an introduction to its history and work in an appendix. We draw upon policy and other documents where appropriate and explain and illustrate how they are relevant to teachers in their pedagogical practice.

We hope, too, as editors, that the reach of this book will be beyond Europe. The work of the Council of Europe is known throughout the world. For example, the *Common European Framework of Reference for Languages* has been influential in Asia and South America. We expect that the new *Reference Framework of Competences for Democratic Culture* will be just as influential. We hope therefore that teachers in other continents who share our values and vision, will also find this book useful in their work, for those values and vision are by no means exclusive to Europe, and we make no such claim. Our hope is that this book will support teachers in their efforts to transform values into practice.

Finally, we dedicate this book to Daniel Coste whose influence on, and contribution to, Council of Europe work on language has been immense over many years.

Michael Byram, Mike Fleming, Joseph Sheils

1 Introduction – Quality and Equity in Education: The Council of Europe Vision

Michael Byram and Joseph Sheils

Introduction

For many years the Council of Europe has had a strong and beneficial influence on the education systems of its 46 member states. One main and highly significant element of that influence has been to establish equity and quality as guiding principles and basic tenets of education, and to ensure access to good education for all. It is an influence that may not be noticed by teachers, pupils, students and others in a particular school, college or university, because the influence has been indirect and mediated through ministries of education and related bodies. The purpose of this book is to make that influence known to teachers and others and, more importantly still, to explain how teachers can draw directly on and implement the Council of Europe's vision and philosophy of education in their daily lives as educators.

We aim to explain in an accessible way the implications for schools and classrooms of policies and decisions concerning equity and quality taken at the European and national level, and to show how those implications can be realised in practice. However, it is important to stress here that this is not a matter of showing how policies made 'at the top' can be implemented by those 'at the bottom', for this is not the approach taken at the Council of Europe. There is a long tradition in the Council of Europe of a 'bottom-up', consensual approach to decision making and policy formation. Priority issues are established by representatives of member states which are worked through in practice by networks of education professionals. Programme outcomes are then widely shared, for example as agreed-upon policy guidelines, reference instruments and practical tools to support implementation. A key concept in practical implementation is that the early stages of lifelong education – from pre-primary to tertiary – should help young people to become active citizens in Europe who have the competences they need to be successful, i.e. plurilingual, intercultural and democratic competences. Such competences have been described in Council of Europe policy documents and in its pedagogical tools in ways that make them already part of the resources on which teachers at all levels of education, from primary to higher education, can draw in their daily work.

In this introductory chapter, we present the values of the Council of Europe as the basis on which equity and quality in its educational vision are founded. Secondly, we explain the significance of the 'right to education' in guaranteeing equity and, thirdly, we discuss the concept of quality in education. Finally, we provide an overview of the book and its chapters.

It is a commonplace to say that Europe, and the 46 states of the Council of Europe, is a multicultural space, that it has always been so, and that it continues to become ever more so. The historical and contemporary significance of multiculturalism in Europe is evident from the presence of long-established ethnic minorities in every country, most of which have a language different from the language of the majority. In some countries there are several minorities. In some countries there is more than one majority. Belgium is an example, with its two majorities of Flemish and Walloon groups and a German-speaking minority. In keeping with its values and in an intercultural perspective, the Council of Europe offers support and protection for minority rights and languages through Conventions and Charters.[1] There is no agreed definition of a national minority by all Council of Europe member states,[2] but for our purposes it is useful to refer to such minorities as 'indigenous', although this is a fuzzy term as we shall see below.

There are also other minorities in Europe, and the growing presence of what we can call 'new' minorities, since the 1950s, is a consequence of many factors. Some groups formed as a result of certain European countries inviting workers from other countries in Europe and beyond to become the labour force which the inviting countries needed but could not develop alone. Examples are the invitation of West Germany to Turkish workers, of France to Portuguese and Spanish workers, of Britain to workers from the West Indies and Pakistan. Other groups have formed because of economic migration, for example from Africa, or political events of wars and revolutions, for example refugees and asylum-seekers from the Middle East or South America. The Council of Europe supports the inclusion and integration of such groups with respect to their human rights and has also produced practical tools such as the Linguistic Integration of Adult Migrants project,[3] which builds on its widely recognised foundation work on languages and language teaching, most notably in the *Common European Framework of Reference for Languages* (Council of Europe, 2001).

Such groups can be called 'new' or 'immigrant' minorities, in contrast to 'indigenous' minorities but it is a moot question as to when a 'new' group becomes 'indigenous', after how many years or generations of residence in their new country. 'Indigenous' and 'new/immigrant' are therefore imprecise terms which can be mis-used to imply that 'indigenous' is more positive than 'new/immigrant' and to denigrate the latter, and it is important that this tendency is criticised and avoided.

Conflicts have often arisen both between minority and majority groups, and also among minority groups, whether 'indigenous' or 'new/immigrant'. Politicians and others have recognised that conflict can only be overcome if there is dialogue among groups. Dialogue is a necessary, though not sufficient, condition for creating harmonious societies and harmonious group interaction. In 2008, the Council of Europe and the European Union declared the 'European Year of Intercultural Dialogue'. Among the many activities of the Year, the Council of Europe produced a 'White Paper on Intercultural Dialogue' – a white paper being a policy statement – with the title 'Living Together as Equals in Dignity'. This became the basis for numerous developments, including the *Reference Framework of Competences for Democratic Culture*, which will be introduced below.

The Competences of a Plurilingual, Intercultural and Democratic Citizen in Europe

Before beginning our main task, focused on values and equity and quality, we introduce the competences of a citizen or denizen of Europe as envisioned at the Council of Europe and, in a number of boxes in the text, we present the principal documents and tools in which they appear.

Plurilingualism is a concept which describes how people possess language and languages. Contrary to a widely held view, a 'common sense theory', of how people possess languages, i.e. that their different languages exist separately in the mind, plurilingualism means that languages and varieties of languages – such as dialect variations – are all 'one', are all integrated into one entity, and can work together rather than in competition. This is described both as a 'competence' (Council of Europe, 2001: 4) and as a 'repertoire' (Council of Europe, 2020: 30). People draw upon this competence or repertoire in different ways using their ability to:

- switch from one language or dialect (or variety) to another;
- express oneself in one language (or dialect, or variety) and understand a person speaking another;
- call upon the knowledge of a number of languages (or varieties) to make sense of a text;
- recognise words from a common international store in a new guise;
- mediate between individuals with no common language (or variety), even if possessing only a slight knowledge oneself;
- bring the whole of one's linguistic equipment into play, experimenting with alternative forms of expression;
- exploit paralinguistics (mime, gesture, facial expression, etc.).

(Council of Europe 2020: 30)

Plurilingualism, it is important to note, is not just a matter of different 'languages' but of different 'varieties' of languages. The distinction between a language and a variety is often a matter of socially and politically constructed differences distinguished on what in linguistic terms is a continuum without separations. 'Varieties' are therefore just as important as 'languages'.

People become plurilingual with different languages or varieties from childhood, as they experience languages and varieties in the home, in the society where they live and in contact with other societies (through travel or in schooling). The integration of different languages and varieties into one entity, competence or repertoire, is stronger for those languages experienced earlier. Languages experienced later may remain to some degree separate, but over time become increasingly integrated into a person's plurilingual repertoire.

Council of Europe documents dealing with plurilingualism

The concept of plurilingualism was introduced in the *Common European Framework of Reference for Languages: Learning, Teaching, Assessment*, which is probably the best known of the Council of Europe's publications, especially in countries beyond Europe (Council of Europe, 2001).

This document, often referred to as the CEFR, describes the competences needed in communication, with emphasis on language competences. It includes descriptors of language competences at six levels and is perhaps best known for this, although it presents a vision of language learning, teaching and assessment which is much more complex. It includes chapters on curriculum design, on tasks in learning and teaching and on processes of assessment, for example. In doing so, it supports pedagogic processes which help learners 'to build up attitudes, knowledge and skills they need to become more independent in thought and action, and also more responsible and cooperative in relation to other people. In this way the work contributes to the promotion of democratic citizenship' (Council of Europe, 2001: xii).

The CEFR was published in 2001, after many years of development. In 2020, a *Companion Volume* was published. The *Companion Volume* extends and completes the lists of descriptors and introduces a more complex discussion of the concepts of mediation and pluricultural competence. It also includes reference to sign languages.

From 2005, the Council of Europe turned its attention to 'the languages of schooling' and therefore to the dimensions of plurilingualism which are usually described as 'mother tongue' or L1, although such terms are ambiguous and can be misleading. It deals with the language – sometimes languages – of schooling, which is the L1 of many learners, but it also deals with issues raised by the presence in all education systems of learners with a different L1, such learners often being the children of migration.

The project on the languages of schooling became a *Platform of Resources and References for Plurilingual and Intercultural Education*, where further documents on plurilingualism and other concepts which will be introduced below can be found.[4]

The concept of *pluriculturalism* is introduced in the CEFR and describes a phenomenon of which plurilingualism is a part. Pluriculturalism pre-supposes the concept of 'culture', a term notoriously difficult to define. Groups of all kinds – nations, ethnic groups, cities, neighbourhoods, work organisations, occupational groups, sexual orientation groups, disability groups, generational groups, families, and more – have their own cultures. Yet, because such cultural groups are always internally heterogeneous with diverse practices and norms which are contested, change over time and enacted by individuals in their own ways, it is misleading to reify and talk of 'the' culture of a group; cultures are like languages dynamic. Furthermore, cultural boundaries are often very fuzzy and who is perceived to be within or outside a group may be perceived differently by different group members. Members may, in turn, feel a stronger or weaker identification with the group and its culture.

People experience many different cultures, as they move from home to society and to other societies, and in so doing become pluricultural and plurilingual. However, language is not the only dimension of this experience. It is complemented by other kinds of knowledge and non-verbal competence; cultural learning is not exclusively linguistic. Because pluricultural competence is not tied to language competence, people may have knowledge and skill in the culture of a specific group which is different from their knowledge and skill in the language of that group, whether a small group such as a local community or interest group or a large group such as a society.

Pluricultural people thus have an integrated competence comparable to their plurilingualism and from which they draw in particular situations just as they draw on their plurilingualism:

> in a person's cultural competence, the various cultures (national, regional, social) to which that person has gained access do not simply co-exist side by side; they are compared, contrasted and actively interact to produce an enriched, integrated pluricultural competence, of which plurilingual competence is one component, again interacting with other components. (Council of Europe, 2001: 6)

Council of Europe documents dealing with pluriculturalism

The *Companion Volume* takes up the work of the *Common European Framework of Reference for Languages* in more detail. It describes pluriculturalism as a 'repertoire' of competences. At higher levels this includes competences ranging from ability to evaluate viewpoints, through interpreting and relating documents and events in another culture to those in one's own, to interpreting cultural cues and reflecting on how misunderstandings arise.

Intercultural competence is different from pluriculturalism. It is a concept which defines the knowledge, skills and attitudes that help people to engage with a new group and their culture, to discover and understand the way of living and thinking of the group and individuals within it. People may use their intercultural competence to engage with a new group – small or large – which speaks the same language, or a variety of their language that is comprehensible to them. For example, a person may use their intercultural competence when they join a new interest group in their local society (e.g. a poetry-reading group) in order to learn and understand how the group functions, and to become a member of it. In doing so they may acquire new vocabulary and ways of discussing poetry, a new discourse.

If someone wishes to engage with a group whose language or language variety they do not understand, they need intercultural *communicative* competence, i.e. the skills, knowledge and attitudes of intercultural competence complemented by learning the language of the group.

The importance of intercultural dialogue emphasized in the White Paper of 2008 led to renewed interest in intercultural competence. One result was the creation of the *Autobiography of Intercultural Encounters* (Council of Europe, 2009), which is discussed in more detail in Chapter 2.

Council of Europe documents dealing with intercultural competence

Chapter 5 of the CEFR describes the competences of language users, from the general competences to their specific language competences, and discusses 'intercultural awareness' as a basis for developing intercultural skills. In Chapter 6, there is a section on how non-language specific competences can be taught in language courses.

The *Platform of Resources and References for Plurilingual and Intercultural Education* is an instrument enabling educators to develop their programmes relating to languages of schooling and all language teaching in an integrated approach to language education.

It contains explanations of intercultural competence and intercultural education, and the relationship of these to plurilingualism and plurilingual education.

The *Guide for the Development and Implementation of Curricula for Plurilingual and Intercultural Education*[5] is primarily intended for those responsible for curriculum planning to facilitate improved implementation of the values and principles of plurilingual and intercultural education in the teaching of all languages – foreign, regional or minority, classical, and languages of schooling.

The *Framework of Reference for Pluralistic Approaches to Languages and Cultures – Competences and Resources*[6] presents approaches to teaching which involve the use of two or more varieties of languages or cultures simultaneously, and is above all intended for teachers. It abandons the 'compartmentalised' view of an individual's linguistic and cultural competence(s), and thereby helps to implement the CEFR and its rationale on plurilingual and intercultural competence.

In addition to these documents for anyone responsible for education – whether as policymakers or principals or examiners, for example – there are guides for teachers wishing to introduce the development of intercultural competence in their classrooms.

Council of Europe guides to intercultural competence for teachers

The booklet *Developing Intercultural Competence through Education*[7] is a relatively short document which discusses the characteristics of intercultural competence and provides practical suggestions of how education systems can include it in their purposes and processes.

The *Autobiography of Intercultural Encounters* (Council of Europe, 2009) is a collection of documents for use in formal and non-formal education, and can be introduced by teachers. It is designed to encourage people to think about and learn from intercultural encounters they have had either face to face or through visual media such as television, magazines, films, or through the internet.

The booklet *Developing the Intercultural Dimension in Language Teaching: A Practical Introduction for Teachers*[8] addresses questions teachers often ask when considering the classroom implementation of the intercultural dimension and provides practical examples and further useful sources for helping learners to develop their intercultural competence.

The brochure *Young People Facing Difference: Some Proposals for Teachers*[9] provides an overview of the key issues and concepts for teachers and youth workers, along with a set of practical activities to stimulate discussion with young people on their responses and feelings when confronted with Otherness.

Democratic competence is the ability to use values, attitudes, skills, knowledge and understanding in an effective and appropriate way in democratic situations. It complements intercultural competence which is used in situations where there is intercultural exchange. In those European countries that are multicultural democracies, both intercultural and democratic competences are often needed simultaneously. The Council of Europe has long promoted education for democratic citizenship and linked this to education for human rights, and there is a Charter to underpin this work.

Council of Europe documents dealing with education for democracy

The Council of Europe extended work which combined plurilingual and intercultural education with education for citizenship (a long-established branch of the work of the Council of Europe) to create a framework, following in the footsteps of the CEFR, which describes intercultural and democratic competences: the *Reference Framework of Competences for Democratic Culture (RFCDC)* (Council of Europe, 2018). This document, often referred to as the RFCDC, consists of three volumes, with a total of about 200 pages. The first presents the rationale for producing the framework and a model of intercultural and democratic competences. The second lists descriptors for the competences included in the model, at three levels. The third is a compendium of chapters on how the framework and model can be used by educators in different parts of an education system, from teacher to policymaker, from assessor to teacher educator. There is also a document which presents the RFCDC in brief and another which discusses the importance of recognising the ways in which language and language competence are crucial in acquiring and using competences for democratic culture.

In 2022, a 'Recommendation to member States on the importance of plurilingual and intercultural education for democratic culture' was adopted and thereby puts education for plurilingual, intercultural and democratic competences at the centre of its vision of education.[10] In particular, it states that 'Plurilingual and intercultural education is essential to education for democratic culture' and 'encourages critical reflection on cultural diversity'. An essential element of this recommendation is that those responsible for the education of teachers should promote plurilingual and intercultural education for democratic culture by 'challenging attitudes and beliefs and preconceptions about language, language learning, plurilingualism, culture and intercultural learning'.

The RFCDC contains a model which combines both intercultural and democratic competences (see Figure 1.1). For example, the list of attitudes includes both 'openness to cultural otherness and to other beliefs, world views and practices' and 'civic mindedness'; the list of skills includes both 'empathy' and 'conflict resolution skills'; and the list of competences for knowledge and critical understanding includes knowledge and critical understanding of both 'language and communication' and of 'human rights'.

The model also includes values competences. People who are democratically and interculturally competent in Europe, value human dignity and human rights, cultural diversity, democracy, justice, fairness, equality and the rule of law.

Democratic and intercultural competences are increasingly used in the context of the 'digital revolution' and the Council of Europe recognises the role which education has to play in taking advantage, but also avoiding the pitfalls, of new technologies, including artificial intelligence. This

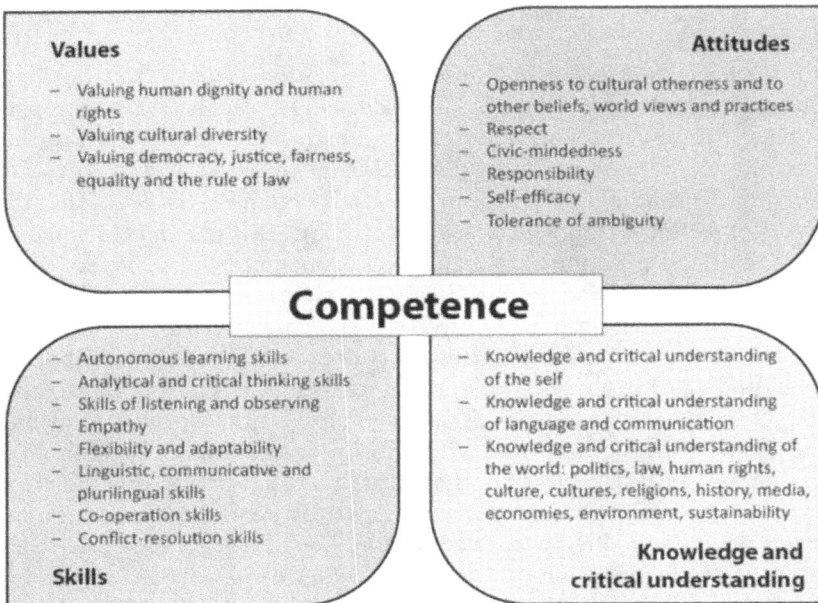

Values
- Valuing human dignity and human rights
- Valuing cultural diversity
- Valuing democracy, justice, fairness, equality and the rule of law

Attitudes
- Openness to cultural otherness and to other beliefs, world views and practices
- Respect
- Civic-mindedness
- Responsibility
- Self-efficacy
- Tolerance of ambiguity

Competence

Skills
- Autonomous learning skills
- Analytical and critical thinking skills
- Skills of listening and observing
- Empathy
- Flexibility and adaptability
- Linguistic, communicative and plurilingual skills
- Co-operation skills
- Conflict-resolution skills

Knowledge and critical understanding
- Knowledge and critical understanding of the self
- Knowledge and critical understanding of language and communication
- Knowledge and critical understanding of the world: politics, law, human rights, culture, cultures, religions, history, media, economies, environment, sustainability

Figure 1.1 Model of competences © Council of Europe
Source: Reference Framework of Competences for Democratic Culture (Council of Europe, 2018: 38).

means that it is a priority of the Council of Europe to ensure that the use of new technologies is 'rooted in democratic values and promotes democratic competence' (Council of Europe, 2021: 137).

In summary, the Council of Europe has created the means to define and develop through teaching and learning the competences needed by a denizen of Europe to be and act as a citizen with the ability to dialogue and live together with others. Success depends on them having intercultural and democratic competences and being plurilingual, in other words being 'plurilingual, intercultural and democratic citizens'. Their competences include the values defined in the *Reference Framework of Competences for Democratic Culture*, values that are explicitly, although not exclusively, European and embraced by the Council of Europe as central to its endeavours.

The Values of the Council of Europe and their Significance for Education

The Council of Europe's web portal[11] displays on its first page three key terms, three 'pillars', in its work: democracy, human rights, rule of law. This is complemented in many other places by reference to the importance of 'dignity' and 'respect for diversity'. As Europe has changed through migration – recognised in the White Paper on Intercultural Dialogue described above – the Council of Europe has increasingly emphasised in its priorities the importance of attention to social inclusion and respect for diversity.

Since its inception in 1947, one of the principal aims of the Council of Europe has been to develop a common democratic and legal area throughout its member states in which human rights are key. The European Convention on Human Rights (ECHR) is the foundation, and is ensured through the work of the European Court of Human Rights (ECtHR). The civil and political rights guaranteed in the ECHR are complemented by the social and economic rights in the European Social Charter (ESC), under the supervision of the European Committee of Social Rights (ECSR). Anti-discrimination, diversity and inclusion are further supported by other standard-setting instruments and monitoring bodies, including the European Commission against Racism and Intolerance (ECRI). There is then a legal, ethical and moral framework within which the people of Europe and Council of Europe states can live together.

With respect to education, the Council of Europe has long taken the view that human rights are not simply part of a legal framework but an integral part of young people's education. For education is central to the effective implementation of the shared values of its member states. For example, in 2006, the Council of Europe's Commissioner for Human Rights said that 'Human Rights values should not only be taught as a separate subject but should permeate the whole education system' (2006,

World Teachers Day – cited in Council of Europe, 2012: 21–22) and in 2021 the Secretary General, Marija Pejčinović Burić, stated that:

> It is not enough for children and young people simply to hold human rights. In order to embed a human rights culture and ensure that our young people understand how to access those rights – and to uphold, defend and promote them – they need an education fit for that purpose.[12]

The Right to Education and Its Significance for Equity in Education

Education is a fundamental right, enshrined in the Universal Declaration of Human Rights (Article 26), the United Nations Convention on the Rights of the Child (Article 29) and in the European Convention on Human Rights (ECHR) and Fundamental Freedoms (Additional Protocol No. 1, Article 2). It is an empowerment right that serves broader societal functions and is necessary for the effective exercise of other human rights in a democratic society.

The protection of this key right has been linked to the prohibition of discrimination (ECHR Article 14), as was demonstrated when Roma children were placed in special schools without objective and reasonable justification, and followed a more basic curriculum than mainstream schools. While the European Court of Human Rights did not assess the components of quality education, which was considered a matter for the government concerned, it found a difference of treatment which discriminated against the right of the children to equity of access to an education of mainstream quality.

The rights of another minority group, migrant children, have been addressed by the European Committee of Social Rights (ECSR) referred to above. The Committee's interpretation of the Charter holds that states are required to ensure that children unlawfully present in their territory have as effective access to education as any other child.

Thus it is that the rights of minority children have led to a situation where equity in access to education is a right for all children. What this means in practice is a matter for practitioners, primarily for teachers, policymakers, principals of educational institutions. Decisions may be difficult. Equity may be interpreted, for example, as meaning:

(1) Every student in a class should receive the same amount of support/attention from their teacher (measured in amount of time).
(2) Every student in a class should receive the amount of support/attention from their teacher necessary to have a real chance to acquire certain competences considered prerequisites for a successful future life, i.e. to achieve a minimal 'threshold' of competences.

(3) Every student in a class not only has a right to receive support/attention from their teacher, they also have some corresponding responsibilities, e.g. they are expected (i) to use the opportunities for learning offered to them and to make efforts to acquire the necessary competences for their future, especially for their future role as democratic citizens, (ii) to feel responsible for every other student in class having a real chance to acquire certain competences, skills, knowledge and experiences as prerequisites for a successful future life.

These distinctions[13] are complex and imply ethical questions which exceed the limits of this book, but it is clear that 'equity', 'equality' and 'fairness', though often used in ordinary language as synonyms and defined in terms of each other in a circular fashion, are matters for careful consideration by practitioners. For example, the first point in the list above is relatively simple but might be considered unfair because, though offering all students 'equality of opportunity' to benefit, it does not take into consideration the different starting points of children, their cultural capital. The second option offers a counter-balance to this but needs clear descriptions of what a 'threshold' might be. The third option extends the complexity because it places the onus on students themselves to be responsible for their peers and to cooperate with them so that everyone can reach the same minimum outcomes (or threshold).

In addition to decisions of this kind concerning equity, it is of equal importance that the education students receive should be of good quality.

Quality in education

The Council of Europe began to turn its attention to the question of quality in education – and to associated terms such as 'quality control' – in the 2000s, as did other governmental and non-governmental organisations. For example, UNICEF in *A Human Rights Based Approach to Education for All* emphasises the right to quality education and seeks a definition:

> Although there is no single definition of 'quality', most attempts to define it incorporate two fundamental perspectives. First, cognitive development is a primary objective of education, with the effectiveness of education measured against its success in achieving this objective. Second, education must promote creative and emotional development, supporting the objectives of peace, citizenship and security, fostering equality and passing global and local cultural values down to future generations. (UNICEF, 2007: 32)

The UNICEF document refers to universally desirable global values – peace, citizenship, security, and equality – but then leaves decisions about which other values should be passed on from one generation to another as a matter of local choice. The Council of Europe also refers to global – using the word 'universal' – and local values but gives a more detailed statement of what the content and purposes of education should be, including the specific values it promotes. Unlike the UNICEF document, the Council of Europe presents a vision rather than an attempt at definition:

> The Council of Europe's vision of a quality education is one that is free from discrimination, providing a secure and non-violent learning environment, in which the rights of all are respected. It develops children's and adults' personality, talents and mental and physical abilities to their fullest potential and encourages them to complete their educational programmes. It promotes *democracy, respect for human rights and social justice* in a learning environment which recognises everyone's learning and social needs. It enables pupils and students to develop appropriate competences, self-confidence and critical thinking to help them become responsible citizens and improve their employability. It passes on *universal and local cultural values* while equipping pupils and students with the faculties to make their own decisions. Certification of the acquired knowledge and competences is carried out transparently, on the basis of a fair assessment and enables further study, employment and other life opportunities.[14] [emphasis added]

The mechanisms by which this vision can be realised in practice include the Council of Europe's intergovernmental programmes which support cooperation between member states in further developing and implementing agreed policy. The results of such European cooperation may then lead to a 'Recommendation' by the Committee of Ministers addressed to education authorities which outlines fundamental guiding principles and recommends specific measures to support their implementation. A 'Recommendation' is a non-binding but consensual and influential policy document which allows each member state to implement effective measures in a principled, context-sensitive manner.

A key Recommendation for our discussion of quality in education is CM/Rec(2012)13.[15] This Recommendation sets out important principles:

> the right to education can only be fully exercised if the education is of adequate quality;

> ensuring that everyone can benefit from a quality education is a matter of individual justice as well as the best possible use of the resources of our societies;

and equal opportunities and equity are crucial:

> in democratic societies, everybody should enjoy equal opportunities so that they can exercise their right to education and benefit from a quality education, commensurate with their aspirations and abilities.

It also ensures that the principles and opportunities for access are linked to the question of quality, with the implication that merely providing education is not enough; it must be of adequate quality:

while access to education is in itself an important right, the true value of this right can only be realised if education is of adequate quality.

The purposes of education include not just preparation of young people for earning their living but also for being democratic citizens in properly functioning democratic institutions and societies:

> education must prepare children and young people for democratic citizenship as well as for economic activity;

> education is crucial to developing the democratic culture that democratic institutions and societies need to function;

and, importantly in the context of our explanation of key concepts above, there is emphasis on intercultural dialogue:

> education must enable pupils and students to develop proficiency in intercultural dialogue.

Finally, returning to the question of plurilingualism and the languages of schooling, it is important to note that learning depends in large part on competence in the language(s) used in education, and even high quality education can be undermined for learners who do not have adequate linguistic competence. This was made explicit in a Recommendation 'on the importance of competences in the language(s) of schooling for equity and quality in education and for educational success', where it was stated that 'the right to education can only be fully exercised if the learners master the specific linguistic rules that are applied in schools and are necessary for access to knowledge'.[16]

Vulnerable learners

The issues raised in ensuring equity and quality in education were in no small part brought to the fore by a concern for access to education for Roma children. The significance of equity and quality in education for all kinds of 'vulnerable learners' is crucial not only for them but, in consequence, for all other learners, and the Council of Europe has paid particular attention to vulnerable learners while emphasising that the linguistic and other assets they already have are fully recognised. Whether learners are vulnerable, for example because of a physical disability, or an initially limited competence in the language of schooling, or lack of access to cultural capital, they need particular attention. The Secretary General made this explicit in her annual report of 2021, emphasising that even in times of crisis, it is crucial to maintain the right to education:

> Making the right to education real, also in time of crisis, is of vital importance to the future of European democracy. In years to come, the Council of Europe will help member states strengthen democracy through education, innovate teaching and learning and *ensure the right to education for the most vulnerable students* [emphasis added]. (Council of Europe, 2021: 13)

One particular group of vulnerable learners which has needed particular attention from the Council of Europe in recent years is the migrants who have entered Europe. They come as refugees from war and other catastrophes, as asylum-seekers fleeing from oppression or as those who seek a better life for themselves and their families, whom they often have to leave behind. There are adults and children, and education systems and governments respond to them in different ways. They too deserve quality and equity in education. We have included two chapters on education for migrants as a major group needing special attention – and making specific calls on education systems – in the present and for the foreseeable future.

Conclusion and Book Overview

In 1996, the 'Delors Report' to UNESCO, *Learning – the Treasure within*, identified four 'pillars' of education: learning to know, learning to do, learning to be, learning to live together, and said of the latter:

> the Commission has put greater emphasis on one of the four pillars that it proposes and describes as the foundations of education: learning to live together, by developing an understanding of others and their history, traditions and spiritual values and, on this basis, creating a new spirit which, guided by recognition of our growing interdependence and a common analysis of the risks and challenges of the future, would induce people to implement common projects or to manage the inevitable conflicts in an intelligent and peaceful way. Utopia, some might think, but it is a necessary Utopia, indeed a vital one if we are to escape from a dangerous cycle sustained by cynicism or by resignation. (Delors, International Commission, 1996: 20)

The competences at the heart of this book are significant means to move towards the necessary utopia. Plurilingual-and-intercultural and democratic competences are necessary in acquiring the understanding and new spirit the Commission wish to see and, perhaps even more so, in facilitating common projects and managing conflicts. The Council of Europe's vision of quality and equity points the way towards this 'necessary Utopia'.

To reiterate our purpose – to provide a guide for teachers and other educationists to the educational values of the Council of Europe and their practical implications – is to reinforce the connection between quality and equity on the one hand, and the teaching and learning of intercultural, plurilingual and democratic competences on the other. It is in the spirit of offering guidance – but nothing more – that the following chapters often open with a question, a question we think teachers will ask about the practical implications.

The questions, and answers, start from the fundamental concepts of 'quality' and 'equity' and in Chapter 2 María-del-Carmen Méndez-García and Mike Fleming emphasise that:

> Quality education is always fundamentally about values and choices. This fact can sometimes be obscured in contemporary writing about education where there is an emphasis on evidence-based approaches, research and scientific methods.

They emphasise that the Council of Europe's recommendations take a broader and richer view of quality to include policy and practice, as well as outcomes and process. Significantly, in the main recommendation on quality there is specific reference to vulnerable and disadvantaged learners which is a theme of later chapters in this book. Méndez-García and Fleming pay particular attention to the importance of language in education and how disadvantaged learners such as migrants may have heightened difficulties because of language issues, a theme that is further developed in later chapters too.

The main focus of Chapter 3 is to bring more depth and detail to the plurilingual, intercultural and democratic competences by emphasising and analysing interaction among young people in an intercultural situation, and then considering how this analysis can help teachers to plan their work. Louise Tranekjær presents an example from interaction among Danish and South Korean young people during an educational exchange. She analyses the power relations reflected and embodied in the use of language and then invites readers to think about how 'particular languages and identities can be used as resources and when they are, alternatively, barriers for understanding and dialogue', and the implications for teaching.

In Chapter 4, the crucial relationship between language and linguistic competences and school-based learning of all kinds, including the teaching of intercultural and democratic competences, which is first raised in Chapter 2, is analysed in depth. For the Council of Europe has long recognised the significance of language in all learning, and made this the focus of its language education activity since the 2000s with the development of the *Platform of Resources and References for Plurilingual and Intercultural Education*. In Chapter 4, therefore, Helmut Vollmer and Eike Thürmann first discuss the various dimensions of language use in schools – whether informal or formal, whether close to learners' everyday language use or distant and therefore problematic – and then concentrate on the specific patterns of classroom language. This analysis is followed by suggestions as to how teachers of all subjects – for this is not just a matter for teachers of first and second languages – can support learners' academic language use.

Then, in Chapter 5, Florentina Sâmihăian and Diana-Maria Beldiman turn the focus onto the ways in which language competence is the foundation for teaching and learning the competences necessary in a multicultural and democratic society, be it at the geographically limited local level or at the level of European society. This is a matter for all teachers, since they all rely on language competence – their own and that of their learners – as the means of teaching their subject, as is shown in Chapter 4, but also as the means of making a contribution to the education of the plurilingual, intercultural and democratic citizen. This chapter suggests and illustrates a range of activities which teachers can use in the specific context of promoting intercultural and democratic competences.

In Chapter 6, three contributors have taken these issues further into the specifics of their own subject. We might have included more detail, but space precludes this and, more importantly, we think that other teachers will quickly see the significance for their own subject and how they can transfer the insights of these three authors to their subject or area of the curriculum. The subjects analysed and illustrated represent different areas of the curriculum.

Helmut Linneweber-Lammerskitten points out that, though mathematicians often think of mathematics as a language for science, there is little awareness of natural language. Although they may recognise the significance of language competence for participation in classroom talk, it is often under-estimated. Yet mathematical reasoning is much more than simply posing problems to be solved, and natural language is a significant element of classroom processes. Furthermore, students need to be able to discuss and communicate with others about social issues that need to be addressed with mathematical solutions, such as climate change or population growth. This is followed by an analysis of the need for equity and quality in mathematics education and how these may be achieved.

Silvia Minardi introduces the language dimension in the teaching of physics. She starts with an example from lessons dealing with magnetic fields and the magnetic north pole. She emphasises that the 'disciplinary literacy' of physics includes reading and writing the language of physics and shows that physics literacy is multimodal. She then presents an approach to embedding multimodal literacy in the context of teaching content, whether in physics or other subjects. A close analysis of how this can be done in teaching the physics of forces then follows which teachers of other subjects too can transfer into their own reflections and pedagogical planning.

Irene Pieper deals with the teaching of 'literature' but emphasises that this includes many different kinds of texts and modes of interacting with them, whether as a book or an internet document. The teaching of literature is therefore a matter of both private and social practices, and of developing literacy in a full and rich sense. She illustrates this with an example from a classroom and then suggests factors which need to be taken into consideration in the choice of texts, whatever the kind of mode.

Teaching is usually accompanied by assessment and, in recent decades, assessment has become ever more important, not least in the eyes of policymakers and politicians. In Chapter 7, Claudia Borghetti and Martyn Barrett first discuss the relationship between assessment and equity and quality and then turn their attention to the assessment of plurilingual, intercultural and democratic competences as manifest in Council of Europe approaches such as the *European Language Portfolio*, the *Autobiography of Intercultural Encounters*, and the *Portfolio of Competences for Democratic Culture*. They provide descriptive vignettes to help readers to visualise the ways in which assessment respecting quality and equity can be done in practice.

The work of the Council of Europe on language education began with the teaching of foreign languages but did so in the context of creating a common European space in which citizens can live and communicate freely. The significance of language in education as a fundamental condition for quality and equity in all subjects and for all teachers has been stated in earlier chapters. In Chapter 8, the particular contribution that can be made by teachers of second or foreign languages is the focus, for such teachers are often the best qualified in a school or other educational institution to know how to ensure that the significance of language in learning is understood and becomes an effective aspect of teaching in all subjects. Mirjam Egli Cuenat and Marisa Cavalli analyse and reflect on the role of language and languages in the whole curriculum, the central idea of learners' plurilingual repertoire as a resource, and then consider the specific roles of teachers as individuals and in teams in implementing such an approach. Finally, they discuss methods and modes of implementation and present some innovative tools for use in implementation.

In Chapters 9 and 10, we return to the question of vulnerable learners, in particular learners who are disadvantaged because they are migrants. In Chapter 9, Nathalie Auger and David Little deal with education for children. They address the twin questions of how, in the face of large-scale migration, education systems can help children to acquire at least adequate proficiency in the language(s) of schooling for them to be able to benefit to the full from educational opportunities, and second, how schools can ensure a place for the languages of their homes in schools so that they and also other learners can benefit. They present examples of this kind of work from Ireland and France, with two vignettes in which educational inclusion was pursued in a primary school in Ireland, and the inclusion of literatures in learners' home languages was introduced into work on literature in a secondary school in France.

In Chapter 10, Cecilie Hamnes Carlsen, Lorenzo Rocca and Joseph Sheils concentrate on the case of adult migrants and the important issue of their integration into society and the Council of Europe's vision of a multinational and multicultural society in which migrants have a full and equal role in society as democratic citizens. Education is crucial, particularly for those migrants who may not have had opportunity to complete their education in their society of origin. Adults often live in complex and tension-laden situations where their immediate needs – and those of their family – have to be balanced with their longer-term hopes and ambitions which may depend on a good standard of education. This chapter focuses on the particular characteristics of adult learners and includes four vignettes which illustrate how teachers can act, using both the toolkit designed to provide language support for refugees, and a Reference Guide to support teachers working with adult migrants with low levels of literacy. These practical instruments were created at the Council of Europe in the Linguistic Integration of Adult Migrants project.

Although much of this book is addressed to teachers and their questions, we know that teachers are helped and hindered by the institutional structures in which they work. In the final chapter, therefore, Jonas Erin and Waldemar Martyniuk write for leaders of educational institutions, explain how they can take a whole-school approach to language in education policy and the questions of equity and quality. Having explained the issues in this perspective they provide practical suggestions for supporting learners, for developing school policies, for project approaches and for quality assurance *inter alia*.

Finally, in an appendix, the editors have provided a more detailed explanation of the work and history of the Council of Europe, focusing in particular on the legal and institutional framework for its vision of a Europe where quality and equity in education are fundamental. It includes, too, an account of the Council of Europe's work on a range of language policies and programmes, from minority and regional languages to modern foreign language and languages of schooling.

Notes

(1) See: *Framework Convention for the Protection of National Minorities*, https://www.coe.int/en/web/minorities/home and the *European Charter for Regional or Minority Languages*, https://www.coe.int/en/web/european-charter-regional-or-minority-languages/about-the-charter.
(2) https://www.coe.int/en/web/minorities/fcnm-factsheet
(3) https://www.coe.int/en/web/language-policy/adult-migrants
(4) https://www.coe.int/en/web/platform-plurilingual-intercultural-language-education/home
(5) https://www.coe.int/en/web/platform-plurilingual-intercultural-language-education/
three-fundamental-and-complementary-tools-for-the-implementation-of-plurilingual-education
(6) https://carap.ecml.at/Documents/tabid/2668/language/en-GB/Default.
aspx#:~:text=FREPA%20%E2%80%93%20Competences%20and%20
resources%20A%20systematic%20presentation,approaches%20English%2C%20
French%2C%20Italian%2C%20Arabic%2C%20Slovenian%20and%20Spanish
(7) https://www.coe.int/en/web/interculturalcities/-/
developing-intercultural-competence-through-education
(8) http://rm.coe.int/09000016802fc1c3
(9) https://www.coe.int/en/web/language-policy/selection-of-major-texts-and-reports
(10) https://search.coe.int/cm/Pages/result_details.aspx?ObjectID=0900001680a563ca
(11) https://www.coe.int/en/web/portal/home
(12) https://www.coe.int/en/web/compass/ (accessed 5 May 2021).

(13) We are very grateful to Helmut Linneweber-Lammerskitten for drawing our attention to these points and the formulations of alternatives.

(14) https://www.coe.int/en/web/education/vision-for-a-quality-education

(15) Readers who wish to see the legal formulations can find it online: https://search.coe.int/cm/Pages/result_details.aspx?ObjectId=09000016805c94fb.

(16) CM/Rec(2014)5.

References

Council of Europe (2001) *Common European Framework of Reference for Languages: Learning, Teaching, Assessment*. Strasbourg: Council of Europe. https://rm.coe.int/CoERMPublicCommonSearchServices/DisplayDCTMContent?documentId=0900001680459f97

Council of Europe (2009) *Autobiography of Intercultural Encounters: Context, Concepts and Theories*. Strasbourg: Council of Europe. https://rm.coe.int/context-concepts-and-theories-autobiography-of-intercultural-encounter/168089eb76

Council of Europe (2012) *Compass: Manual for Human Rights Education with Young People*. Strasbourg: Council of Europe. https://www.coe.int/en/web/compass

Council of Europe (2018) *Reference Framework of Competences for Democratic Culture. Volume 1: Context, Concepts and Model*. Strasbourg: Council of Europe. https://www.coe.int/en/web/reference-framework-of-competences-for-democratic-culture/rfcdc-volumes

Council of Europe (2020) *Common European Framework of Reference for Languages: Learning, Teaching, Assessment – Companion Volume*. Strasbourg: Council of Europe. https://rm.coe.int/common-european-framework-of-reference-for-languages-learning-teaching/16809ea0d4

Council of Europe (2021) *State of Democracy, Human Rights and the Rule of Law. A Democratic Renewal for Europe. Report by the Secretary General. Annual Report*. Strasbourg: Council of Europe.

International Commission on Education for the Twenty-First Century (the Delors Report) (1996) *Learning: The Treasure within; Report to UNESCO of the International Commission on Education for the Twenty-first Century*. Paris: UNESCO.

UNICEF (2007) *A Human Rights Based Approach to Education for All*. New York: United Nations Children's Fund.

2 What Do I Need to Know about 'Quality' and 'Equity' in Education?

María-del-Carmen Méndez-García and
Mike Fleming

Introduction

In Chapter 1 of this volume the concepts of 'equity' and 'quality' were introduced in general terms in the context of the Council of Europe's vision and values, 'as guiding principles and basic tenets of education, and to ensure access to good education for all' (p. 1). The aim of this chapter is to focus more specifically on the implications of these concepts for schools and other educational institutions as well as for teaching. It is fairly easy to recognise that the concepts of equality and equity are highly relevant to education policy at a national and regional level. For example, in order to ensure the right to education it is important that there is adequate provision, that resources are distributed fairly, or that admission policies are administered justly, to name but a few. Some of these issues may be beyond the influence of schools and teachers, and it is perhaps less obvious how the concepts of 'quality' and 'equity' are of relevance to everyday practice at the institution and classroom level. Injustices that may prevent access to quality education can all too easily be concealed or remain unnoticed, particularly when it comes to matters related to language and how it impacts on teaching and learning.

The chapter begins by examining the concepts of 'quality' and 'education' and then discusses the significance of language in ensuring that the goals of equity and quality in education are met. The following section widens the perspective to consider the importance of the social environment and its impact on learning, looking specifically at a practical instrument devised by the Council of Europe to help students reflect critically on their own responses and attitudes to experiences of other cultures in visual media. The final section explores the concept of 'mediation' as it has evolved in Council of Europe documents and considers its relationship with equity and quality.

The Concepts of 'Quality' and 'Equity'

The concepts of 'quality' and 'equity' when employed by the Council of Europe are often mentioned together. This is entirely appropriate for they are closely related. The concept of 'equity' (treating people in a way that recognises their particular needs to ensure fair outcomes and processes) can nonetheless be usefully distinguished from some uses of 'equality' (when it implies treating everyone in exactly the same way). Equity has to do with fairness and justice, which is more likely to mean recognising, and taking measures to address, the particular needs of groups and individuals. It means that personal or social circumstances such as gender, ethnic origin or family background, should not be obstacles to achieving educational potential (OECD, 2012). However, a focus on equity in education without attention to quality may result in simply ensuring fair access to poor or inadequate provision. On the other hand, a focus purely on quality measured in outcomes (e.g. test data) may show that the average achievement in a school or education system is high but conceal the fact that some groups are disadvantaged.

Test data, of course, may be very helpful in identifying injustices in the education provision, for example if they reveal that some groups are underachieving in comparison to others. However, the focus needs to be not just on outcomes (important though they are) but also on the education process. It is important to resist a reductive and technicist interpretation of quality education as being only about achievement measured by tests. Quality also refers to pedagogy, and such issues as the ethos and nature of the relationships within an institution or class.

Recommendation CM/Rec(2012)13 of the Committee of Ministers to Member States (see Chapter 1) describes 'quality education' as education which:

(a) gives access to learning to all pupils and students, particularly those in vulnerable or disadvantaged groups, adapted to their needs as appropriate;

(b) provides a secure and non-violent learning environment in which the rights of all are respected;

(c) develops each pupil's and student's personality, talents and mental and physical abilities to their fullest potential and encourages them to complete the educational programmes in which they enrol;

(d) promotes democracy, respect for human rights and social justice in a learning environment which recognises everyone's learning and social needs;

(e) enables pupils and students to develop appropriate competences, self-confidence and critical thinking to help them become responsible citizens and improve their employability;

(f) passes on universal and local cultural values to pupils and students while equipping them also to make their own decisions;

(g) certifies outcomes of formal and non-formal learning in a transparent way based on fair assessment enabling acquired knowledge and competences to be recognised for further study, employment and other purposes;

(h) relies on qualified teachers who are committed to continuous professional development;

(i) is free of corruption.

This list recognises both policy and practice, as well as outcomes and process, and takes a broad view of what quality education should entail. There is recognition of the importance of teaching and learning as a critical factor in the achievement of the goals of quality and equity. In modern classrooms in democratic societies it is highly unlikely that teachers would disagree with the values described here.

Quality education is always fundamentally about values and choices. This fact can sometimes be obscured in contemporary writing about education where there is an emphasis on evidence-based approaches, research and scientific methods. Such findings can help inform policy and practice but important decisions in education are at base normative in nature. Research may inform us what subject pupils prefer to study but it will not determine what subjects should be chosen for the curriculum; it may tell us what methods are best to teach reading but it will not determine why the ability to read should be a priority for all pupils. Most importantly, research may help inform decisions about the aims of education but the final say is always a matter of choice based on values, and this can easily be overlooked.

It is important, therefore, to subject institutional policies and teaching practices to honest scrutiny, asking whether they include, and are a proper reflection of, values. Everyday practice can easily become routinised and taken for granted such that the importance of values is not sufficiently recognised. For example, there are dangers of over-generalising about learners and underestimating the specific needs of individuals or groups. Sometimes the language used to talk about learners, for example, that 'they can't keep up', 'have difficulty concentrating' or 'are easily distracted', may prevent further questions about the appropriateness of the materials or strategies being employed. It is all too easy to underestimate the potential of some learners and not challenge them enough. This can happen for various reasons but one common cause is when the role of language in relation to quality and equity is not fully recognised.

The Importance of Language

Proficiency in language is important for quality education as it is the primary means of communication, and the central medium of teaching. Language is moreover the predominant means by which learners demonstrate their knowledge and understanding, and it is central to most formal assessment. However, the case for the importance of language needs to go further. It needs to recognise the wider role of language not only in communication but also in relation to learning, identity formation and values.

As described in Chapter 1, 'plurilingual and intercultural competence' is a key concept for the Council of Europe in relation to language education. The term has a richer connotation than simply 'speaking more than one language' and, as used in the various Council of Europe documents, implies a more embedded and holistic vision of language, identity and culture (Coste *et al.*, 2009). Language needs to be seen not as a disembodied skill or a mere tool but as an integrated aspect of learning and personal development. The acquisition of additional languages or varieties of language has an impact on the understanding of self and others.

Learners may however also be disadvantaged because of issues related to language, as recognised in the following Council of Europe documents. Recommendation CM/Rec(2014)5 of the Committee of Ministers to Member States on the importance of learners' competences in the language(s) of schooling for equity and quality in education and for educational success highlights the importance of language not just as a separate subject in school, but in all subjects across the curriculum. It emphasises the importance of being aware:

- that the right to education can only be fully exercised if the learners master the specific linguistic rules that are applied in schools and are necessary for access to knowledge;
- that such linguistic competences are one of the factors in educational success and that they are a prerequisite for undertaking further qualifying academic or vocational education and training, and therefore important for participation in society and sustainable inclusion;
- that some learners may be disadvantaged vis-à-vis mastery of these linguistic competences because of social and linguistic inequalities.

The Recommendation also states that it is desirable that those responsible for educational contents and programmes promote effective consideration of the linguistic dimensions of subjects by:

(i) making explicit the specific linguistic norms and competences which learners must be able to master in individual subjects.
(ii) making explicit in the programmes and curricula the learning modalities that should allow all learners, and in particular the most vulnerable among them, to be exposed to diversified language-learning situations in order to develop their cognitive and linguistic capacities;
(iii) highlighting, in the programmes, convergences in the linguistic dimensions of the various subjects, in such a way as to reinforce the effectiveness of the educational project;
(iv) recalling, in the programmes for the language of schooling as a specific school subject, the special place which this language holds because of its cross-cutting effect on all the learning processes conducted in that language;

(v) encouraging authors of educational materials to ensure that such materials explicitly take account of the linguistic dimensions of the different subjects;

(vi) continuing and extending research in this field.

The Recommendation then draws attention to the fact that some groups may be disadvantaged in relation to language. Some pupils are disadvantaged because they have to learn subjects and to think in subject terms at school in a language that is not their first language. Schools and classrooms have a role to play in making sure that the languages that are present in the school but not taught are welcomed and seen as a resource and not a barrier. Other pupils may struggle with the language of schooling not because it is a different language from their own but because it involves a level of formality and complexity that presents particular difficulties. Some pupils can use language informally in their daily lives well enough but struggle when it comes to understanding concepts, issues and relationships within school subjects through 'academic language'. For other pupils this is much easier because they are familiar with more complex, abstract, formally structured language in the home. This means that some learners may be doubly disadvantaged, both by the demands of the academic language and the fact that the language of instruction (or 'language of schooling') is not their first language.

A difficulty can arise if there is a mismatch between the academic language and the academic content familiar to a particular group (e.g. migrants) and the corresponding educational curriculum in the new education context (e.g. their new countries). The curriculum may be significantly different and thus hinder migrants' adaptation to the school and prevent success in their learning. Sensitivity to an issue such as this means being aware that curricula are developed in particular cultural contexts and that language invariably needs to be considered in relation to culture. The close relationship between language and culture is emphasised in the *Common European Framework of References for Languages – Companion Volume* (Council of Europe, 2020: 124), which speaks about a comprehensive plurilingual and pluricultural competence. This includes elements such as the understanding that each society has a series of practices and norms different from each other, the recognition of similarities and differences between communities, tolerance of ambiguity when faced with cultural diversity, including the need to modify and adapt the language, or having the predisposition as a speaker to ask for and offer clarification and anticipate the risks of misunderstanding.

When considering the ways in which conscious reflection on language is important in teaching, it helps to distinguish between spoken and written forms. Spoken language is usually highly contextualised, often with the interlocutors being in the same place and time, and often makes use of non-verbal clues to intended meaning, for example an accompanying smile can change the meaning and connotations of a statement. Written language on the other hand is usually more distant from the potential audience and needs to be more structured and precise in order to replace the context and the non-verbal. Too often it is assumed that learners with good spoken competences will acquire the written form quite naturally, and that learners with a migrant background only need support until they acquire the same level of informal and social communication as others. However, the 'academic language', more based on the written form even when spoken, is not acquired spontaneously; it must be taught to all learners throughout the education stages.

Learners may be judged to be less intelligent or not good at a subject, but it may be a matter of being disadvantaged by the language as a cognitive and conceptual tool. This has implications for the classroom, as teachers may need to adapt their practice, for example: finding ways of making new material engaging and accessible; being more attentive to clarity of explanations; allowing pupils some use of their first language to support their understanding; providing and explaining subject-specific vocabulary; making sure that the language demands of a task (e.g. writing in a specific genre such as describing an experiment/writing a scientific report) are not taken for granted but clearly explained and supported; making imaginative use of digital resources (e.g. by having learners use software packages to present text types such as newspaper articles or scientific reports in more realistic ways).

Another practical approach is to foster visual literacy in combination with textual literacy. Whereas young learners' education is highly visual, the relevance of visual training often declines after two or three years of schooling and shifts to alphabetic or textual literacy until the written text, reading and writing words, gains uncontested predominance in most school programmes. Furthermore, the incorporation of new technologies into education facilitates the use of images at all levels and across disciplines (García Sánchez et al., 2019). Visual literacy may develop on its own to a degree, although pedagogical guidance enhances individuals' appraisal skills of visuals, and activates the skills needed for critical engagement with images. Visual literacy work may thus provide some support for learners who struggle to gain access to the curriculum through the language of schooling.

The importance of language for equity and quality in education, then, is clear. Learners can be disadvantaged if they struggle with the language of schooling, either because it is not their home language or because they are unfamiliar with its format and conventions. Schools have a responsibility to examine their own language context (e.g. language varieties) and take this into account in developing policy, particularly with a view to, ideally, allowing pupils to maintain and develop their existing language repertoires. At the very least, schools should recognise languages that are different from the language of schooling. Subject teachers need to recognise the linguistic demands of their subjects and provide specific support for those pupils who find these challenging. In the classroom the variety of languages present should be seen as an advantage and resource rather than a problem. The importance of language in all subjects is explored in more detail in Chapters 4 and 6 of this volume.

However, a focus purely on language may not be enough. As indicated in the introduction to this chapter, other issues to do, for example, with personal or social circumstances such as gender, ethnic origin or family background, should not be obstacles to achieving educational potential. Language is highly relevant to all of these issues but the focus in relation to equity and quality may need to be broader than an exclusive focus on language. For example, children from an ethnic background that is different from the majority in a class can easily be made to feel unwelcome or out of place; this can happen deliberately or inadvertently. The social environment is crucial in ensuring that all pupils are in the appropriate frame of mind to learn. If they are made to feel out of place this may adversely affect their responses in the class. Teachers have an important role to play in encouraging openness to others, fostering positive attitudes toward difference, and promoting awareness of diversity and intercultural understanding in the class. The following section provides a concrete example of the use of a practical instrument developed by the Council of Europe (the *Autobiography of Intercultural Encounters through Visual Media*) that is aimed at helping students reflect critically on their own responses and attitudes to experiences of other cultures. The fact that the approach uses visual media as its central focus provides an additional source of motivation, as well as support, for learners in their use of language.

Autobiography of Intercultural Encounters through Visual Media

The current pervasiveness of visual representations of reality, due to the widespread use of the internet, enables the teacher to provide mediated encounters with otherness. The concept of 'otherness' in a school context can of course take different forms (such as new disciplines/subjects or new forms of discourse). Here it refers to encountering other groups.

However, analysing images is complex, especially because deeply ingrained values in different societies may inspire a different interpretation of the same image. Therefore, guidance is needed to interpret a variety of aspects from the individuals' cultural background and other cultures rendered through visuals.

Being aware that individuals learn about otherness and other groups, to a considerable extent, through images that appear in the media, the Council of Europe developed the *Autobiography of Intercultural Encounters through Visual Media* (AIEVM) (Barrett *et al.*, 2013) to look into images of how 'the other' is represented. The AIEVM was designed to assist users in exploring a specific image which they have encountered in

---

Description of the image, the context of the image and justification.

The users' feelings and interpretation of the other people's feelings.

Thinking about communication.

Similarities and differences between user and person portrayed.

Thinking further about the image and the person who made the image.

Finding out about things that puzzle or raise users' interest.

Thinking backward and looking forward.

Figure 2.1 Areas of questioning in the *Autobiography of Intercultural Encounters through Visual Media* © Council of Europe

the media and which portrays somebody different from them, guiding their analysis of images for intercultural understanding. Structured according to questions or cues divided into different areas (see Figure 2.1), the AIEVM invites users to reflect on the composition of the image in connection with fundamental fields for intercultural reflection and development, such as their own feelings, the feelings of other people or the similarities and differences between the people represented in the images and the user.

In the following two examples, extracts are provided from the extended responses provided by the students, which address each of the areas of questioning in a structured way. In the first example a student has chosen a screenshot of an Indian wedding in Spain from a television programme. The student (writing in English, the language they are learning) has described the content of the image and the reasons for choosing it. The questions then focus on feelings.

Your feelings	*How did you feel when you first saw the image?*	
	I felt confused because the programme shows a very biased perception of other cultures and personal relationships. Also, that this view was not promoting understanding and tolerance between the Spanish and Indian culture, as only the costs and extravagances are considered.	
The feelings of the other people	*Do you think they would have been preferred to be shown differently? Please explain your answer.*	
	I think they would have the chance to greet their family and their mix of cultures, the values they respect and the traditional ceremony they chose.	
	How do you think other people from the same group or culture as them would feel about the image?	
	I think they would feel like seeing Indian wedding being popular around the world because it would make them feel proud about such a significant thing in India.	

Thinking about communication	*What do you think you could do to make it easier for you to understand each other?*
	I would like to know their reasons to get married so soon and so young.
Same and different	*Thinking about the person/people in the image and yourself, what do you think are the main similarities between them and yourself?*
	I think I am very different from the couple in terms of ethnic background and cultural background, traditions and relationships.
	Are they like anyone that you know in your own life? If so, in what ways do they resemble them? For example, in the way they look, the way they behave, the way they think…?
	They are completely different from anyone I know because of their economic status and culture.

In another example the student describes the content of the chosen image and her responses to it.

The Image	It is a photo found in an online newspaper.
The contents of the image	Two English police women and some people demonstrating against the unfulfilment of the Brexit at the entrance of the Parliament.
	In my opinion the demonstrators seem tired and bored and also I could think they are not very supported.
	They are women and men older than me and they belong to another group of countries, Great Britain where they use another language (English) and various religions. They also have different appearances and different skin colours.
Your feelings	*How did you feel when you first saw the image?*
	I felt confused and I asked myself how could they be there if nobody is going to attend them.
	What do you think caused these feelings? These feelings could appear because I have a different concept of Europe from the one these people on the photo have as I understand it has facilities for my country to go steps forward.
	Would you like to have an image made of you which looked like this? Please give your reasons.
	I wouldn't mind having a photo like this one if it represents and shows the readers of the newspaper the real reasons of standing there in front of the Parliament.
	Would you like to meet the person/people shown in the image in real life? Please give your reasons.
	Yes, of course. I would be pleased to share with them our opinions and points of view. I would like to understand why they are there and why they bet for this to be the most acceptable option for their culture and country. I truly believe it would be an appealing conversation which would oblige me to consider my own culture and pre-conceived ideas.

The feelings of the other people	*How do you think other people from the same group or culture as them would feel about the image?*
	Maybe, they would understand better the reasons of their attitudes or why they seem disinterested and at the same time annoyed.
Thinking about communication	*What do you think you could do to make it easier for you to understand each other?*
	Firstly, not judging them at any point, trying not to dispute but to argue and having made a previous personal reflection about the reasons of their ideas comparing it with other similar situations in my own country.
Same and different	*What do you think are the main differences between them and yourself?*
	We live in different countries, we have different ages and maybe, we haven't lived the same things and probably we don't have the same interests and conception about the world surrounding us.
	Similarities I noticed...
	Their appearances and looks are very similar to the ones in Spain. Also the use of banners and posters is similar.
Thinking further about the image	*Do you think that the image is a stereotype of the person/people shown in the image?*
	If so, why do you think it is a stereotype?
	Yes, I think this photo stereotype the British as people who doesn't want to be part of Europe and who encourage some isolation and self-sufficiency which has always been part of their culture.
	Do you think this image is fair or unfair as a way of showing this person's/ these people's group or culture? Give reasons for your answer.
	I think this is unfair, because the photo does not represent a whole culture. On the other hand, it is fair, as it represents a group of people who share opinions and ideas.

In both examples the writers' sense of ownership and engagement is enhanced by the fact that they have chosen the images themselves. The structured questions are designed to prompt critical reflection so that the images are not taken for granted. The AIEVM is intended to help promote awareness of diversity and intercultural understanding in the class. It can also be used as a technique for giving visibility to migrant pupils' cultural background by analysing images portraying their culture(s) of origin so that they can mediate between their culture(s) of origin and their new cultural environment. The concept of 'mediation' has been an important concept in much of the Council of Europe's work on language. In the following section the evolution of the concept in relation to equity and quality in education is examined.

Mediation

The concept of mediation appears in the first version of the *Common European Framework of Reference for Languages* (CEFR) 'as making communication possible between persons who are unable, for whatever reason, to communicate with each other directly' (Council of Europe, 2001: 14).

Translation and interpretation are given as examples of mediation. Distinctions are also made between mediating 'activities' and 'strategies', and between oral and written mediation (Council of Europe, 2001: 87).

The concept of mediation was further developed in a Council of Europe paper by Coste and Cavalli (2015). Here the term is extended and the more integrated concept makes the relationship with equity and quality clearer, because it goes beyond the individual and stresses the social and cross-cutting nature of the term:

> Defining mediation very generally as the process of reducing the distance between two poles in a state of tension and regarding schooling as a mediation macro-system admittedly constitutes a significant extension in relation to the process of linguistic reformulation described in the CEFR. Similarly, postulating that cognitive mediation and relational mediation closely complement one another and do not simply depend on the initiative of individuals but also on the responsibility of institutions, as regards both education and social inclusion and cohesion, is tantamount to regarding mediation as being of major cross-cutting importance at different levels of the functioning of societies. (Coste & Cavalli, 2015: 62)

The *Common European Framework of Reference for Languages – Companion Volume* (CEFR-CV) (Council of Europe, 2020) presents scales for mediation in three groups: mediating texts, mediating concepts and mediating communication. The accompanying discussion highlights the moral dimension:

> in mediation one is less concerned with one's own needs, ideas or expression than with those of the party or parties for whom one is mediating. A person who engages in mediation activity needs to have a well-developed emotional intelligence, or an openness to develop it, in order to have sufficient empathy for the viewpoints and emotional states of other participants in the communicative situation. (Council of Europe, 2020: 91)

The importance of the concept of mediation conceived in this way indicates an enrichment of the Council of Europe's work on language by placing its values and not just functional tools more clearly at the centre. This reflects an important development in thinking, beyond a focus purely on the individual social actor to recognise the importance of social groups such as migrants and those who are socially disadvantaged.

The CEFR/CV specifies that mediation entails not only passing on information from one language to another (cross-linguistic mediation), but also enabling communication between individuals who are not capable of communicating with one another directly. Even if direct communication is possible, mediation may also be needed when people are not able to understand each other, irrespective of whether or not they share one or several languages.

Mediation constitutes a key element in individuals' language proficiency, being at the heart of communicative language activities and strategies (see Figure 2.2), the activities that enable communication and the

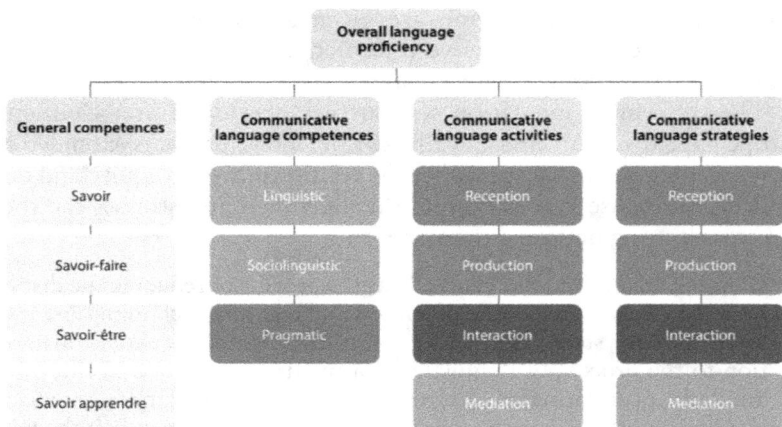

Figure 2.2 Mediation as a key component of overall language proficiency (Council of Europe, 2020: 32) © Council of Europe

strategies that smooth the communication process (e.g. strategies to deal with misunderstandings). Mediation facilitates the act of receiving and producing messages or texts and interacting with another person.

To act as intermediaries, individuals need to be familiar with socio-cultural and sociolinguistic differences, show sensitivity towards other sociocultural and sociolinguistic perspectives and norms, and anticipate, address and repair misunderstandings that arise from these discrepancies. The CEFR/CV (Council of Europe, 2020: 114–115) points to lifelong learning as regards languages and cultures:

> Naturally, the mediator themselves needs a continually developing aware-ness of sociocultural and sociolinguistic differences affecting cross-cul-tural communication. Key concepts operationalised in the scale include the following:
>
> • using questions and showing interest to promote understanding of cultural norms and perspectives between participants;
> • demonstrating sensitivity to and respect for different sociocultural and sociolinguistic perspectives and norms;
> • anticipating, dealing with and/or repairing misunderstandings arising from sociocultural and sociolinguistic differences.

The *Guide for the Development and Implementation of Curricula for Plurilingual and Intercultural Education* (Beacco *et al.*, 2016) also highlights the value of mediation as a cognitive, communicative and intercultural construct entwined with understanding and production in a language, and that implies the implementation of a series of compe-tences (see Figure 2.3).

In a context of intercultural communication, mediation comprises a complex of skills (including the capacities of negotiation, adaptation, mediation and conflict resolution), the construction and development of a

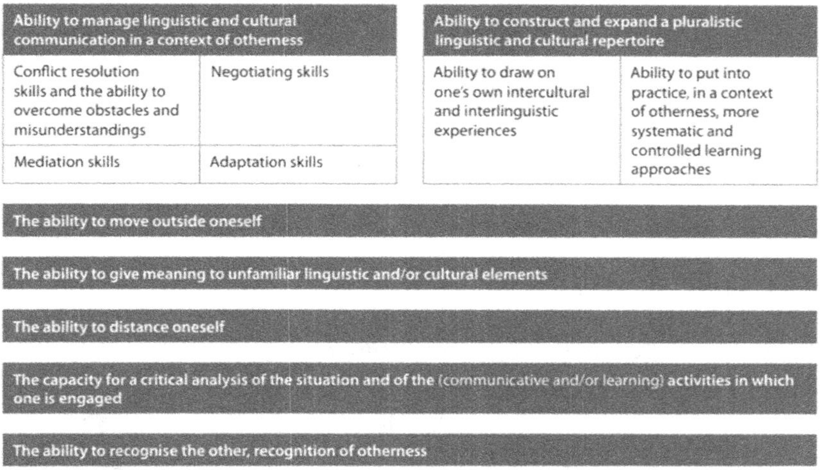

Ability to manage linguistic and cultural communication in a context of otherness		Ability to construct and expand a pluralistic linguistic and cultural repertoire	
Conflict resolution skills and the ability to overcome obstacles and misunderstandings	Negotiating skills	Ability to draw on one's own intercultural and interlinguistic experiences	Ability to put into practice, in a context of otherness, more systematic and controlled learning approaches
Mediation skills	Adaptation skills		

The ability to move outside oneself

The ability to give meaning to unfamiliar linguistic and/or cultural elements

The ability to distance oneself

The capacity for a critical analysis of the situation and of the (communicative and/or learning) activities in which one is engaged

The ability to recognise the other, recognition of otherness

Figure 2.3 Mediation skills (Beacco *et al.*, 2016: 58) © Council of Europe

plural linguistic and cultural repertoire, the skills to go beyond oneself and of distancing oneself from the known and the cultural fact, the capacities to give meaning to unknown linguistic and cultural aspects and to make a critical analysis of them, and the ability to recognise the other and otherness.

Conclusion

One of the perspectives offered by this chapter is that in order to further equity and quality in education, it is not just a matter of adopting particular policies or prescribed practices, but it is also important to address less tangible elements to do with attitudes and ethos. As suggested at the start of this chapter, it may be difficult for schools and teachers to have influence on some practical matters such as the adequacy of resources. Nevertheless, there are other issues on which they can have impact. For that reason, we end this chapter with some questions for consideration to support self-reflection on practices in schools and classrooms.

Questions to consider

At school level

- Has the school specifically analysed its own sociolinguistic context (language varieties present, perceptions of languages, etc.) and taken this into account in developing policy?
- Do teachers of all subjects meet to coordinate and identify synergies between the different language elements in the curriculum?
- Do subject teachers identify the language components shared by other subjects as well as those that are unique to their subject?

- Do policies exist that allow pupils to maintain and develop their existing language repertoires?
- Are steps taken to give relevance to migrant learners' languages (and cultures) when they are different from the language of schooling?

At classroom level

- Do all subject teachers recognise the linguistic demands of their subject and provide explicit teaching of the language elements that are necessary for pupils to learn the subject?
- Are the home languages of migrant pupils seen as a valuable resource rather than as a barrier to success?
- Are steps taken to provide specific support to vulnerable learners in an inclusive way to help them access the curriculum?
- How can visual literacy be used to enhance migrant pupils' textual or alphabetic literacy in the language of schooling?
- Are measures taken to promote awareness of diversity and intercultural understanding in the class?

Acknowledgements

Thanks are due to the two former students who gave permission for the use of their Autobiographies.

References

Barrett, M., Byram, M., Ipgrave, J. and Seurrat, A. (2013) *Images of Others: An Autobiography of Intercultural Encounters through Visual Media*. Strasbourg: Council of Europe. https://www.coe.int/en/web/autobiography-intercultural-encoun ters/images-of-others

Beacco, J.C., Byram, M., Cavalli, M., Coste, D., Cuenat, M.E., Goullier, F. and Panthier, J. (2016) *Guide for the Development and Implementation of Curricula for Plurilingual and Intercultural Education*. Strasbourg: Council of Europe. https://rm.coe.int/16806ae621

Coste, D. and Cavalli, M. (2015) *Education, Mobility, Otherness: The Mediation Functions of Schools*. Strasbourg: Council of Europe. https://rm.coe.int/education-mobility-otherness-the-mediation-functions-of-schools/16807367ee

Coste, D., Cavalli, M., Crişan, A. and van de Ven, P. (2009) *Pluringual and Intercultural Education as a Project*. Strasbourg: Council of Europe. https://rm.coe.int/plurilingual-and-intercultural-education-as-a-project-this-text-has-be/16805a219f

Council of Europe (2001) *Common European Framework of Reference for Languages: Learning, Teaching, Assessment*. Strasbourg: Council of Europe. https://rm.coe.int/CoERMPublicCommonSearchServices/DisplayDCTMContent?documentId=09000 01680459f97

Council of Europe (2020) *Common European Framework of Reference for Languages: Learning, Teaching, Assessment – Companion Volume*. Strasbourg: Council of Europe. https://rm.coe.int/common-european-framework-of-reference-for -languages-learning-teaching/16809ea0d4

García Sánchez, F., Therón, R. and Gómez-Isla, J. (2019) Alfabetización visual en nuevos medios: revisión y mapeo sistemático de la literatura. *Education in the Knowledge Society* 20: 1–44. https://doi.org/10.14201/eks2019_20_a6

OECD (2012) *Equity and Quality in Education: Supporting Disadvantaged Students and Schools*. Paris: OECD Publishing. http://dx.doi.org/10.1787/9789264130852-en

3 What Do I Need to Know about Plurilingual-and-Intercultural and Democratic Competences?

Louise Tranekjær

Introduction

This chapter analyses the notions of plurilingual-and-intercultural competence and democratic competence as they are defined in the various documents published by the Council of Europe and explained in Chapter 1, by applying the concepts to an example of a plurilingual and intercultural encounter. In brief, the chapter seeks to answer the question formulated in the title by explaining that what teachers and others need to know about these competences is how they are needed and manifested in actual encounters and interactions and how this can be used pedagogically. The contexts of practice considered are interactions between high school students from South Korea and Denmark that were videorecorded in South Korea during a study exchange that was part of the Danish students' 'global citizenship' curricular programme.

An Interactional Approach

As stated in Chapter 1, the Council of Europe has made a Recommendation on 'the importance of plurilingual and intercultural education for democratic culture' which places these competences at the heart of its vision of education. The notions of plurilingual-and-intercultural and democratic competences emphasise the competences of the individual which need to be complemented by attention to social interaction and the competences of others. Definitions of plurilingual-and-intercultural and democratic competences of the individual do not necessarily highlight the interactional competences involved and needed for individuals to engage and interact in linguistically and culturally complex interactions where actions and behaviours might be unexpected and unfamiliar to participants. The *Common European Framework of Reference for Languages* (CEFR) puts considerable emphasis on 'interaction' competences (Council of Europe, 2001). The *Companion Volume* to the CEFR (CV) focuses on the notion of mediation and facilitating pluricultural space, which acknowledges the role of interactional resources as a central part of managing potential interpersonal conflicts or misunderstandings (Council of Europe, 2020). The *Reference Framework of Competences for Democratic Culture* (RFCDC) includes skills of cooperation and conflict resolution which emphasises working together with others, finding shared ways of thinking and acting where possible and finding compromises and resolutions where there are difficulties (Council of Europe, 2018a, 2018b, 2018c).

The approach to educational practices taken in this chapter emphasises the interactional, which highlights not only the competences of the individual but the way such competences are actualised and contextualised in interactions with 'the other'. I seek to anchor the discussion of competences in teaching activities and interactions that unfold as part of such activities rather than in learning goal formulations and curriculum documents. The chapter in this way provides input for the operationalisation of the notions of intercultural, plurilingual and democratic competences and seeks to help teachers identify and describe such competences in the practices of their students. The descriptors formulated in the RFCDC specify the Values, Attitudes, Skills and Knowledge and Critical Understanding required of democratic and interculturally competent learners, and this chapter shows how some of these descriptors can be employed and operationalised in relation to students' interactional behaviours.

Intercultural/Plurilingual Competences and Situations

As said in the first chapter of this book, many educational contexts today are culturally and linguistically diverse because of the varied linguistic and cultural backgrounds of students. In this sense, while intercultural and plurilingual competences are not necessarily emphasised or even recognised in all educational contexts, all educational contexts and activities are nonetheless potentially intercultural and plurilingual. This means that only cultural and linguistic resources defined for learners from the majority population are made explicitly relevant through the learning goals, the activities and the orientation of the teachers and students. It is important to bear in mind the needs of learners of minority backgrounds.

When looking at examples from actual teaching situations, it becomes possible to specify the ways in which intercultural, plurilingual and democratic resources and identities play a role in educational contexts, whether they are emphasised or not. Such specification allows teachers to identify the potential to include and emphasise interculturality and plurilingualism as an explicit part of curriculum, learning goals and activities. It is also important to note that when speaking of educational activities in relation to such competences, we need to consider a broad span of activities ranging from formal, classroom-based teaching situations to pedagogically unplanned non-formal linguistic and cultural encounters. In the latter, which are situations that can occur at any given moment within or beyond the classroom, students meet some of the challenges that they have learned about and been prepared for in class and have to employ the resources and competences that they have acquired. Between these two opposite poles of a continuum, we find a range of activities and situations that can be formal, informal or non-formal and involve varying degrees of pedagogic planning and follow-up.

An example of an activity in a formal education context might be a role-play in the classroom where students are to act and think as UN delegates representing different nations. An example of a non-formal encounter could be an educational visit to a food market in a foreign country, where students are expected to learn and enquire about local goods and produce in an informal setting. An informal learning context might be when students are chatting with their host family. Elsewhere, I have described the barriers and potentials of some of these varying types of educational encounters (see Tranekjær, 2019, 2023) but here the point is simply that the application and learning of intercultural, plurilingual and democratic competences takes place in all of these different contexts and that there is potential for paying greater pedagogic attention to those unplannable contexts that otherwise lie outside of the pedagogic scope.

Despite its apparent simplicity, the following extract provides an example of an informal and pedagogically unplanned (unplannable) language and culture encounter that took place as part of a study exchange to South Korea by Danish students at Gymnasium level (upper secondary school). The encounter is shown in Figure 3.1. Given that the study

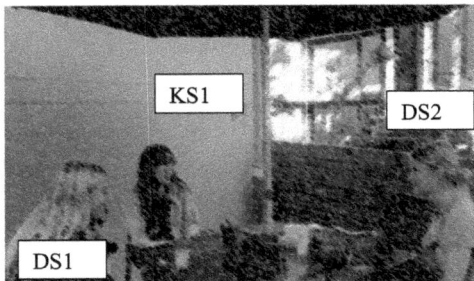

Figure 3.1 The students' encounter

exchange formed a central part of the pedagogic focus of this particular Gymnasium's programme on global citizenship, it could be considered part of the overall educational planning and yet, many of the various encounters including this one, that the Danish students would engage in as part of this trip to South Korea, were unforeseen and unpredictable in terms of focus and interactional dynamics. The purpose of presenting this type of situation in this chapter is to show how any type of encounter can be characterised in terms of the linguistic and cultural complexity it presents and how such complexity calls for a range of different intercultural, plurilingual democratic competences.

Informal student encounter

DS1:   Danish student 1
DS2:   Danish student 2
KS1:   Korean Student 1

DS1:   Diane is coming
KS1:   Yeah
DS1:   yeah know right
DS2:   its (.) but I don't know her name
DS1:   Diane
DS2:   and Laura is coming and I think Emma is coming too
DS1:   Eehm Erm
KS1:   yeah
DS1:   the one who we went shopping with
KS1:   yeah
DS1:   [Thursday] her Korean is coming too
KS1:   [yeah yeah]
KS1:   wow
KS1:   she just told me (0.3)
KS1:   and Laura (.) I don't know who her Korean is
DS2:   me neither
DS1:   it's like (0.2) I can't remember all of their [names]
DS2:   [any names]
DS1:   I can
DS1:   your name and I can [remember] Tone's name because it's Diane
DS2:   yeah [it's very] easy heh Rehm
DS1:   [it's English]
DS1:   and that is all I can
DS2:   yeah (0.3)
DS2:   I have a hard time remembering my own Korean's name

In this exchange, two female students from the Gymnasium are having a chat with a female Korean student during a week-long home stay exchange to Korea. They are meeting on the terrasse of a hostel before heading out together to a social event, and are talking about who will be coming to the event. During this home stay experience, all the Danish students have been 'paired' with South Korean students and stay in their homes during the trip. This is the context for understanding the reference to 'her Korean' and 'my Korean' found in the extract, which were formulations used by the Danish students throughout the exchange. Another part of the context for understanding this way of referring to the South Korean students is the fact that, for the Danish students, the names of the South Korean students are challenging. This is also brought up as a topic of the interaction, and by making references to 'her' or 'his' Korean, the students avoid the problem and potential awkwardness of either not remembering or not being able to pronounce the 'foreign' names. I will save a further discussion of the implications of the form 'my Korean' until the next section and focus here on the intercultural and plurilingual aspects of the encounter and the competences needed for the students to engage meaningfully and respectfully.

In the extract, we see how the students demonstrate plurilingual competence by being able to speak and communicate in English as a lingua franca and by identifying the relevant type of discourse for the occasion, i.e. an informal encounter between students. While this particular extract only shows the use of English, the students would also on occasion, including this particular conversation, demonstrate the ability to switch between English and South Korean or Danish, whenever this was found relevant or useful, thus signalling their memberships of different cultural groups. The extract shows that these different cultural memberships are activated and made relevant at different moments and in different turns within the interaction and that the students unproblematically integrate and move between these various cultural identities.

Another pedagogic potential to take from this example, with respect to plurilingual resources, is reflection about code-switching as a plurilingual competence. Learners' attention can be drawn to moments where code-switching is conducive to intercultural communication and other moments where it works to close down dialogue and exclude 'the other'. Code-switching can work as a resource for securing understanding across language differences and in foreign language learning situations. It can be a useful resource for intercultural communication, in the sense that participants can use the linguistic repertoires that they have at their disposal individually to build understanding collectively. However, choosing to speak in a lingua franca or the language of 'the other' rather than one's native or preferred language can also be a means of explicit inclusion and alignment. This way of employing plurilingual competences was seen in many of the exchanges taking place in South Korea and in the exchange above where the two Danish women stick to speaking English, also in side-sequence moments where they are specifically addressing each other, and where code-switching to Danish could have been an option. However, in other situations, and later in the same exchange, the Danish or the

Korean students would sometimes make code-switches – determined by the topic – from English as lingua franca to their first languages, which immediately created problems in understanding. Sometimes, it would seem, such exclusion or avoidance of the understanding of 'the other' was the goal of the code-switch but in many cases it seemed to be a non-deliberate shifting within complex and diverse linguistic, cultural and social contexts. One pedagogical consequence of helping students to analyse this is to make them aware of the unintended effect of their action.

The point here is not to characterise different types and purposes of code-switching but to point to the complexity in how code-switching may be used as a plurilingual resource for intercultural communication and the potential of addressing such complexity pedagogically. Similar situations might appear in classrooms where learners of different first or preferred languages work together in groups. In both cases, teachers can draw learners' attention to what is happening in a 'meta-analysis' of what they are doing and what the implications are.

With respect to the intercultural dimension of the example above, the students demonstrate awareness and orientation towards not only the cultural memberships that distinguish them from one another, South Korean and Danish respectively, but they also make relevant that they share a cultural group membership as students, brought together to learn from one another. They are also aware that they share another group membership as young women with interests in some of the same activities; shopping and make-up was a frequently shared reference point for the women while spending time together during the week. This notion of cultural group membership can also become the focus of meta-analysis with learners.

Besides the pedagogic potential of reflecting on the resources and competences that are actually brought into play, the extract reveals various potentials for learning critical awareness of plurilingual and intercultural competences that could be pedagogically explored either before the study trip or after. Initially, the students reveal a lack of knowledge and familiarity with South Korean names and their cultural significance, which is a concrete obstacle and which contributes to creating interactional and social asymmetry between the participants within this particular interaction and more generally during the trip. Extracts such as this one can be used as a clear illustration of how a lack of necessary knowledge about an aspect of language and culture has implications for the ability to engage in intercultural communication and the achievement of respectful and equal social relations. I will return to the power aspect of this later. Here, the issue of knowing and learning South Korean names is a central dimension of the plurilingual competence that students would be expected to acquire, following the values of intercultural communication and intercultural understanding described in Council of Europe documents generally and the learning goals and descriptors described in the *Reference Framework of Competences for Democratic Culture* specifically.

Fourthly, this and other exchanges recorded during the study trip revealed differences in the type and amount of interactional contributions from the South Korean and the Danish participants. The Danish students would often take a more proactive and dominant role in the interactions than the South Korean students. They would define the topics of conversation, contribute with longer passages about their opinions and reflections, and initiate and close different topics. While there were definitely variations and degrees of this pattern among different students, it would be safe to say that this was a pattern observable by both students and teachers. Considering that, during this exchange, the Danish students were the guests and the South Korean students were the hosts, this pattern of unequal distribution of talk and interactional roles was perhaps surprising and not necessarily predictable. It might be possible to interpret the imbalance 'culturally', i.e. as a matter of different norms of linguistic behaviour in the two countries, and then to consider the implications of cultural difference for intercultural communication and collaboration.

While it is beyond the scope of this chapter to discuss further potential cultural differences at play here, the extract above and similar data which teachers can collect for themselves make an excellent starting point for discussing cultural matters such as politeness conventions, differences in the educational system, gender roles, social conventions for interaction and so on. Furthermore, it invites reflections on the role and need for intercultural competences in managing such differences in a way that invites and creates space for the voice of 'the other'. The extract is thus an ideal example of the intimate relation between competences in plurilingual and intercultural communication and the extent to which intercultural communication involves reflecting on the often implicit cultural, social and communicative norms of oneself and 'the other', and how the conditions of communication and interaction are defined and negotiated equally among the participants.

The extract could be used pedagogically for discussions about how and whether the Danish students could have changed the dynamic of this particular exchange, for example by inviting the South Korean student to tell them about Korean names, e.g. 'What are typical names in South Korea, are there any particular cultural norms of naming your children, for example naming them after their father or mother' and telling them what the Danish norms are. Or they could ask whether the South Korean students find Danish names difficult as well and why some of the South Korean students have American names like Diane? Again, the point of this is not normative but exemplary, to show how the competences described in Council of Europe documents and the values formulated in relation to intercultural dialogue, intercultural communication and plurilingual competences can be pedagogically operationalised with a point of departure in actual encounters and interactions.

The issue of equality and asymmetry in interaction leads to a discussion of the relation between plurilingual and intercultural competences, intercultural communicative competences and democratic competences because it points to the role of power in plurilingual and pluricultural encounters.

Democratic Competences and Situations

In this section, I take further the discussion of democratic competence and democratic situations, central to many Council of Europe documents, by engaging with the notion of power. In the *Reference Framework of Competences for Democratic Culture*, critical thinking skills are defined as consisting of 'those skills that are required to evaluate and make judgments about materials of any kind' (Council of Europe, 2018a: 47). Analysis of events such as the example from Korea above shows that this needs to be extended from 'materials' to interactions. In other words, while the notion of power is central to the understanding and advocacy of democratic frameworks of education found in the Council of Europe documents, the examples in this chapter seek to operationalise advocacy for democracy, democratic competence and democratic processes in practical teaching situations.

In the example from Korea it is clear how power-relations play out in ways that have implications at an interactional level but also how they have an impact on the students' management of the intercultural and plurilingual situation. Sometimes this works counterproductively and challenges the use of learners' intercultural and plurilingual resources.

First, unequal power relations appear in the uneven distribution of speech and turns at conversation: the Danish students are the ones to initiate and close topics, ask questions and make assessments, whereas the South Korean student is positioned in a responsive role. Secondly, there is an uneven distribution of language competences: the English proficiency of the Danish students is higher than the South Korean students, which enables them to speak more elaborately and contributes, and perhaps significantly so, to the asymmetric distribution of talk. Their lack of competence in speaking South Korean and knowing and remembering South Korean names is topicalised and could potentially even out some of the asymmetry in language competence. However, it is not treated by the participants as problematic or embarrassing but rather as an object of amusement, which in a sense removes responsibility for learning the names and confirms and reinforces the asymmetric power relations. It should be said that the Danish students were not impolite or disrespectful towards the South Korean students, and that the dynamic I am pointing to is working 'behind the scenes' as an effect of more globally anchored asymmetries and power-relations related to hierarchies between nations, cultures and languages.

Reflection on this example suggests that the pedagogic operationalisation of democratic competences should involve questioning the extent to which any interaction or encounter is equal at the onset and, assuming that it is not, examining and discussing the various relations of power that can potentially have an impact on an encounter. When stated in Chapter 1 that democratic competence is 'the ability to use values, attitudes, skills, knowledge and understanding in an effective and appropriate way in democratic situations', acting effectively and appropriately in fact sometimes means acknowledging that situations which are thought to be democratic are not necessarily equal. Democratic competence involves using plurilingual, pluricultural and intercultural communication competences to negotiate, intervene and mediate inequalities and power-asymmetries as they play out on various levels.

There is no easy answer to how this is done, but a useful pedagogic starting point is the critical examination of power-relations and the way they are informed by differences in language, culture, gender, race, sexuality, class, education systems, age and so on. I have already provided examples of such asymmetries in the extract above, and how they could be pedagogically explored and addressed. Another factor in asymmetries, which does not manifest itself in the talk in this extract but which seems to be relevant when looking at the video of the whole conversation, is race. There was a pronounced axis of differentiation and asymmetry between the participants in many of the other interactions too. The South Korean women would continually and explicitly subscribe to the ideals of beauty in 'the West' and would in the interactions with female Danish students talk frequently about whiteness as an ideal. While one could argue that such racialised and gender-based power-asymmetries were not always relevant for the ongoing interactions and activities that the students participated in, it could also be argued that they were working implicitly behind the scenes in a way that had an impact on the extent to which the student interactions were equal.

Working with and activating democratic competences in this case would entail: (1) an examination of how such power-relations potentially and actually have an effect on the educational and informal contexts that the students were engaging in and were supposed to benefit from; (2) taking measures to account for and maybe alleviate the effects of such power-relations; (3) preparatory and retrospective discussions with students about race-relations and their effects, and useful strategies and resources for navigating them. Such discussions should emphasise to students that problems created by power-relations cannot be 'solved' and that the application of plurilingual and intracultural resources may be appropriate and relevant without being fully effective in securing equality.

A democratic situation should be understood as a normative notion that formulates an aspiration towards a goal of equal interactions, relations and encounters where diversity of backgrounds, perspectives and positions is acknowledged and respected. Democratic competences, as described in the *Reference Framework of Competences for Democratic Culture* are the foundation for any attempt to realise this aspiration. Any attempt must be based however on the realisation that equality is unattainable because of the myriad of power-relations that unavoidably affect any context and relation. Democratic competences, and in particular critical understanding, must be seen, and where appropriate assessed, as the ability for critical reflection and appropriate action rather than the guarantee of a successful outcome.

Conclusion

In this chapter, I have taken an interactional approach to operationalising the CoE competences of *plurilingual-and-intercultural and democratic competence*. I have illustrated, by means of an empirical example, how these competences can be exercised and challenged in student encounters and how teachers can identify these competences by observing and analysing encounters for the sake of emphasising or including them in their pedagogical practices. This can be extended directly to any classroom since all groups of students include a range of identities and power-relations, whether gender relations, or race and ethnic relations, or sports affiliations and so on.

The chapter has provided a way for teachers to move from theoretical or curricular descriptions of concepts like plurilingual-and-intercultural and democratic competence to a concrete analysis of how such competences unfold in practice as students interact in both formal and informal, planned and unplanned learning situations. The chapter invites teachers to consider any type of student interaction with fellow or foreign students, teachers or citizens as intercultural and plurilingual to the extent that the various linguistic or cultural resources of the participants are foregrounded and emphasised and to work pedagogically with such foregrounding.

What I have shown is that raising awareness of the implications of diversity in language and culture in the broadest sense, including differences in terms of race, religion, class, sexuality and so on, can be facilitated by a very concrete analytical approach to intercultural situations and encounters. I have provided a step-by-step analysis of the various ways in which students in a particular intercultural home stay encounter, employ and struggle with plurilingual-and-intercultural and democratic competences. I have argued and shown how power-relations in terms of, for example, race and global relations play a central role in determining what differences and similarities are foregrounded and backgrounded.

Readers may wish to reflect further about who determines which differences matter and how they matter; when and how particular languages and identities can be used as resources and when they are, alternatively, barriers for understanding and dialogue. The analysis of such power-relations, and how they can establish barriers in intercultural situations, should be included as part of the 'need to know' and the pedagogical and learning practices related to plurilingual-and-intercultural and democratic competences.

References

Council of Europe (2001) *Common European Framework of Reference for Languages: Learning, Teaching, Assessment* (CEFR). Strasbourg: Council of Europe. www.coe.int/t/dg4/linguistic/source/framework (accessed 18 February 2022).

Council of Europe (2018a) *Reference Framework for Democratic Culture: Vol. 1. Contexts, Concepts and Model*. Strasbourg: Council of Europe.

Council of Europe (2018b) *Reference Framework for Democratic Culture: Vol. 2. Descriptors of Competences for Democratic Culture*. Strasbourg: Council of Europe.

Council of Europe (2018c) *Reference Framework for Democratic Culture: Vol. 3. Guidance for Implementation*. Strasbourg: Council of Europe.

Council of Europe (2020) *Common European Framework of Reference for Languages: Learning, Teaching, Assessment – Companion Volume*. Strasbourg: Council of Europe. https://www.coe.int/en/web/common-european-framework-reference-languages (accessed 18 February 2022).

Tranekjær, L. (2019) Kulturforståelse, kulturmøder og kulturelle kompetencer i praksis. In S. Beck, A. Schultz and M. Blom (eds) *Veje til Verdensborgerskab* (pp. 249–262). København: Upress.

Tranekjær, L. (2023) Intercultural understanding, cultural encounters and cultural competences in practice. In A. Schultz and M. Blom (eds) *Global Citizenship Education in Praxis: Pathways for Schools*. Bristol: Multilingual Matters.

4 What Do I Need to Know and What Can I Do about the Role Language Plays in Supporting Quality and Equity in Education?

Helmut Johannes Vollmer and Eike Thürmann

Introduction

It is widely accepted that language competence plays a key role in the acquisition of knowledge, in the development of general competences and for success at school and beyond, and therefore teachers should be concerned about the language dimension in education. However, more specific questions have to be dealt with, such as 'Which language competences are actually relevant for successful learning at school?', 'How can these be described, taught and learned?' and 'Who is responsible for the development of such competences?' And there is still another important question to be addressed: 'How can *all the learners* be equipped with the necessary language skills and knowledge to profit from schooling and to finish their school career successfully?' The emphasis on *all* learners is important in order to improve equity in the educational provision; it is important not to focus only on those learners for whom language competence comes more easily or who possess it already on an age-adequate level when entering school (see also Chapters 2 and 6).

This chapter takes as its starting point the overarching and well-established ideas on language in learning across the curriculum.[1] However, it goes further because, in its project 'Language(s) FOR schooling – Language(s) IN schooling', the Council of Europe takes an even more comprehensive view of the issue: on the one hand it demonstrates convincingly that language is a central part of learning in every subject, and on the other hand it confirms the link between language and thinking and shows ways of ensuring transfer of learners' cognitive-linguistic skills and competences between different school/curriculum subjects.

Providing adequate language support for all learners in all subjects thus makes a key contribution to the theme of equity. Modern democratic knowledge societies have become aware of the social and economic consequences for a growing proportion of students who do not have a command of the necessary levels of language competence for success in school and in life. This is a factor which puts learners 'at risk', as do other more self-evident factors such as poverty or diverse linguistic biographies. Results of large-scale comparative studies of education (e.g. PIRLS, PISA) provide ample proof of the resulting performance gaps and their impact on quality and equity in education (e.g. OECD, 2018).

Research also shows that this 'vulnerability', as manifested in below-average school performance, exists, perhaps unsurprisingly so, among groups of students from families with a migrant background who have no, or less than, age-adequate skills in the dominant language of schooling. But vulnerability also exists among 'indigenous', monolingual students from families with low economic status and a lower level of parents' education. Although both groups usually have age-adequate competences for everyday interaction, they do not have language competences for solving complex cognitive tasks in school-based learning environments and beyond. A combination of both factors, migrant background plus lower educational status, particularly endangers the linguistic and cognitive development of a learner, social inclusion, entrance to demanding jobs and democratic participation and citizenship (cf. Thürmann, Vollmer and Pieper, 2010).

The individual student's right to education, explained in more detail in Chapter 1, requires practical and effective measures to support personal development and future success. Educational systems in Europe are challenged to ensure this quality and equity so as not to leave any student behind and to do what is necessary for *all* students to develop self-confidence and to leave school with a certified qualification. This has led to enormous efforts by educational systems focusing on the language needs of children with a different language biography, so that they can at least reach a functional level of competence in the principal language of schooling. Such intervention programmes have become commonly accepted and are in most cases administered by staff especially trained for teaching the principal language of schooling as a 'second' language to non-native learners. On the other hand, it has become increasingly clear internationally that educational quality and equity cannot be achieved by relying only on compensatory language support strategies. In order to ensure personal development, success at school and participation in society, language education must be designed more comprehensively: horizontally across school subjects and vertically through the different educational phases, as a central cooperative task of all teachers and not only as that of 'language specialists'.

The aim of this chapter, therefore, is to help teachers and others responsible for ensuring equity and quality in education to acquire a heightened awareness of the connection between language, cognitive operations and educational success (cf. Beacco *et al.*, 2016).

Educational Language or Language for Academic Purposes

In order to identify pedagogical strategies and methods which will help linguistically disadvantaged students to meet the required performance standards and benefit from their educational opportunities in school, it is first important to emphasise that school is a linguistically complex and condensed social space with its own specific discourse conventions. Teaching and learning in school is much more than mastering academic content. It is also very much a question of mastering the language of thinking and using the dominant institutional register for various purposes, of which knowledge acquisition and knowledge construction are most important, but not the only ones. As shown in Figure 4.1, differentiated language use is needed in at least two other areas of schooling, defined as basic discourse domains (Thürmann *et al.*, 2017: 11).

- There is *informal social interaction* among peers during school breaks and even during classes, as well as in the context of extra-curricular activities. Here, language use is informal and mostly oral, that is, very close to the everyday colloquial patterns used by children and adults when they are at ease, communicating with peers, friends and relatives.
- There are also *more formal communicative activities* happening in school relating to administrative, regulatory, pedagogical and organisational aspects of school life. To a considerable extent the language patterns of these speech acts and documents are unfamiliar to students 'at risk' and their families and difficult to understand in detail.
- The third domain of discourse serves an epistemic function (i.e. how to acquire knowledge) of paramount importance for academic achievement, as already indicated above: *it relates to specific patterns of*

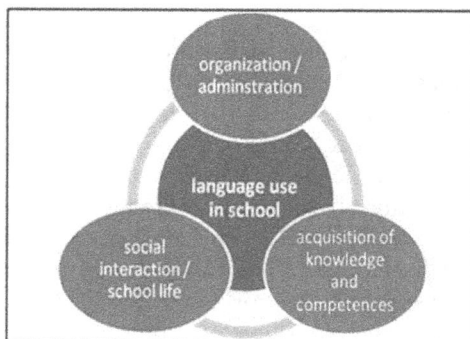

Figure 4.1 Uses of language in schools (Thürmann *et al.*, 2010) © Council of Europe

classroom language use and of verbal thinking *in situations of formal teaching and learning.* The command of the school's dominant language for cognitive purposes is the *sine qua non* for successful learning in all subject areas – and even beyond: for continued learning, for finding a satisfying occupation, for social and political participation, for having a say in shaping the future, not only one's own, but that of society as a whole.

We list all three discourse domains here in order to show the complexities of demands and challenges for students. But the third domain is certainly the most demanding one, yet also the least developed one in many learners. In order to analyse further this third domain, let us look at a typical example of text processing and comprehension with its different layers of cognitive-linguistic meaning-making, taken from a Social Studies course, grade 9 (see Figure 4.2).

The analysis of the academic language features found in this passage shows that, in order to understand the text in terms of the information it carries and the message portrayed, the learner has to do at least five different things, on five different levels, requiring at least five different linguistic and mental operations:

(a) Identify the *content-specific vocabulary/terminology* (example: 'global warming' in Science).
(b) Distinguish *general/essential academic vocabulary* (example: 'prevailing' or 'warrant', applicable in language arts, science, social studies, and other content areas).
(c) Become aware of the specific *grammatical structures* (example: long and complex noun phrases such as 'a conclusion on the issue of global warming').

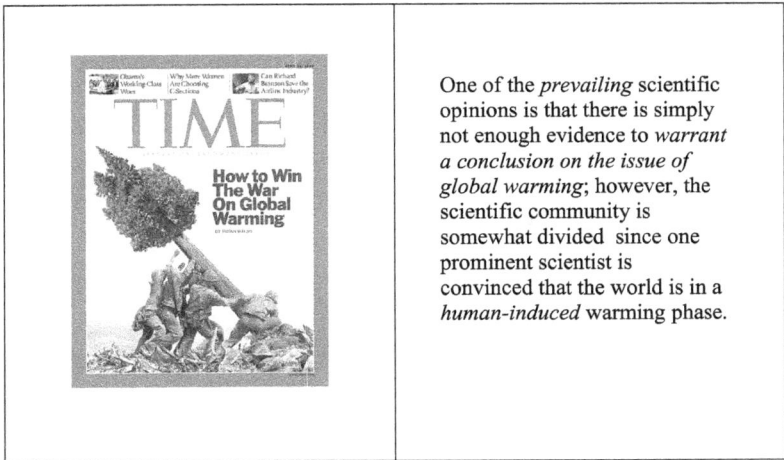

One of the *prevailing* scientific opinions is that there is simply not enough evidence to *warrant a conclusion on the issue of global warming*; however, the scientific community is somewhat divided since one prominent scientist is convinced that the world is in a *human-induced* warming phase.

Figure 4.2 Example illustrating aspects of academic language. Source: Walsh (2008).

(d) Process and understand *academic language functions/discourse functions* to arrive at higher levels of meaning (example: speech acts such as comparing/contrasting, transported through the word 'however', or persuading, conveyed through the structuring of the argument as a whole); more details on this fourth dimension will follow below.

(e) Consider the type of text (*genre*), the medium used, the target group and the purpose of this text or publication with its typical linguistic and structural features.

It is the interaction of these five dimensions, appearing in different surface forms, which constitutes the core of this language variety called 'Academic Language' or 'Language of Schooling'.[2] Through these five processes, the underlying writer-reader interaction is realised. Irrespective of other dimensions, without the performance of at least these five steps and their integration into a holistic understanding, the interpretation of this passage will be incomplete.

The linguistic-cognitive challenges are even greater when a learner tries not only to understand and react, but to form a mental model him- or herself, giving shape to their own perception. For, in order to do this, the learner has to use language productively under contextual and conventional constraints; it has to be done using the language of schooling and within the limits set by the school as a cross-curricular discourse community, the specific curriculum subject and the individual teacher.

In short, academic language and academic language use are highly complex issues and therefore learners need to be trained specifically, mainly within the context of content learning itself, in the comprehension and production of appropriate language on subject-specific topics and how to deal with them.

Tasks like the one above, and the analysis of the cognitive-linguistic demands involved in the task structure, have led to a first characterisation of what academic language is or means (in contrast to everyday language) and how to describe it in qualifying terms (see below). Developing awareness of the characteristic features of the language of schooling is the decisive first step for individual teachers, departments and whole school communities towards modifying conventional teaching practice and setting up programmes for linguistically challenged, vulnerable students with the goal of empowering them mentally and linguistically.

As a starting point, academic literacy[3] can be characterised by a number of adjectives or 'qualifiers':

---

distanced – decontextualised – dispassionate – exact – objective – complex – highly structured – complete – unambiguous – explicit – hedged and cautionary

---

These features are the basis for the epistemic capability to acquire and communicate meaning across time and distance, beyond face-to-face interaction, in a generalised, abstract way understood by both speaker/writer and the listener/reader (Mosher and Heritage, 2017).

This list already shows where the linguistic and mental challenges lie for the learner, especially for students who are not necessarily familiar with this kind of abstract thinking or reasoning and its linguistic embodiment. Yet every learner must be given the opportunity to become educated along these lines, to become empowered for learning with the tool of academic language 'proficiency' and as an endowment for life.

It is possible, of course, to let students first experiment with alternative ways of analysing a text and expressing their understanding and views in relation to a specific issue, before they are confronted with the specifics of genres and their more conventionalised forms of naming, describing, explaining, reasoning and so on. But the goal of such experimentation, and the discovery process that goes with it, is to discover and acknowledge better ways, or even the best way, of putting things into words.

As mentioned above, for migrant learners in particular, as well as for those from families of low socioeconomic status, the acquisition of this specific language register is a real challenge since they normally do not bring with them to school the basics for this type of language use. Thus, it is more difficult for them to develop the (cognitive-linguistic) basis for specialised communication. At the same time, it would be most important for them, not only to access what the school has to offer, but also to make use of it in their personal development and 'survival' at school, and beyond school.

In short, academic language use is the condition for acquiring *literacy* in different content areas (subject/disciplinary literacy, 'pluriliteracies'[4]) as well as good mastery (academic literacy) in the dominant language of society as a prerequisite for active citizenship.[5] Often students who are unpractised in the use of the language register that is prevalent in the context of formal education are seen as 'failures', 'academic illiterates' or 'inept in critical thinking'. Many practitioners may not realise that the lack of mastery of academic language might be the cause of students not acquiring skills and knowledge at a competence level which is age-adequate, as predefined in the curriculum. It is often wrongly taken for granted that this type of language use will be picked up by everyone, implicitly or automatically, as learning progresses, without a need for supportive teaching and awareness-raising from the teacher's side.

Basic Assumptions and Principles of Language Competence in Subject Teaching and Learning

For the implementation of a language-responsible pedagogical reform of teaching and learning at school, both the recommendations of the Committee of Ministers (Council of Europe, 2014) [CM/Rec (2014)5] (see Chapters 1 and 2) and the 'Handbook' (Beacco *et al.*, 2016) assign pedagogical priority to a discovering, experimenting and awareness-raising approach to patterns of educational language use that is closely tied to the authentic content and goals of the respective subject lessons.[6] This rejects the idea that educational language competences can be taught and learned in a mechanistic way, e.g. by teaching lexico-grammatical inventories, so to speak, in addition to content, detached from it, and have it in stock or reserve when needed. The students' attention has to be drawn to linguistic usage patterns in the subject lessons while simultaneously raising awareness of the meaning and function of text and the context of usage.

For teachers of subject lessons, the position represented in the 'Handbook' (Beacco *et al.*, 2016) means, on the one hand, that they are not expected to have specialised linguistic knowledge, which is not usually included in their training. On the other hand, the focus-on-form approach does require subject teachers to direct the learners' attention to typical patterns of language use and their function for the production of subject-related intentions and meanings, and to provide learning opportunities for experimenting with and applying such patterns of language use. In doing so, meta-linguistic reflection and communication with the learners are not bound to correctness in the use of lexico-grammatical terminology, but can be based on intuitively functional categories (such as the distinction between describing and evaluating, the establishment of content and linguistic connections, intra-textual references, strategies of reader guidance, etc.).

What Approach is Needed for Language-sensitive Teaching and Learning?

Academic literacy cannot be taught systematically, independent of disciplinary content. School subjects and their teachers have their own specific discourse conventions, not only with respect to technical language, but also on the macro- and mezzo-levels (see below): e.g. use of basic language functions, genres, syntactic patterns, established figures of speech, textual conventions.

An integrated language and content approach for teaching/learning per subject and across all disciplines is needed. School as a relatively formal or fixed discourse community focusing on the mediation and acquisition of knowledge, uses language in such a way that meaning is exchanged between individuals and groups across time and space, with little or ideally no loss of information. However, in doing so, a number of pedagogically relevant facts have been underestimated in the past by many practitioners and also by educational authorities. We will summarise the main points:

- The language of formal teaching and learning is basically in written mode, consisting of strategies and linguistic means which are commonly found in written texts.

- Educational discourse communities expect that these patterns should also be used in oral communication for the identification, acquisition, exchange and extension of knowledge and thus to support and facilitate cognition at the same time.
- Language use in discourse is inextricably connected with thinking processes and cognitive development (in terms of basic functional operations such as describing, explaining, arguing, evaluating, hypothesising etc.; see also below).
- The trajectory of acquiring strategies and linguistic means of written language does not follow a universal age-dependent course, so that students at a certain point in their school career are all more or less familiar with specific modalities of writing and speaking. As already indicated above, the degree of students' mastery depends largely on the scope and intensity of how they were exposed to written language use in their families, among their friends and through further contacts with books and written media, all of which happens outside school.
- Within school, however, there have to be explicit ways of checking the development and degree of *academic language proficiency* of a student. In secondary education, teaching and learning are largely organised in subjects, taught by disciplinary specialists. Traditionally, this segmentation and the division of pedagogical labour among specialised subject teachers have often led to mistaken attitudes among staff that the language development of students is the exclusive responsibility of language-focused subjects, primarily of the principal language of schooling as a subject (English in England, Russian in Russia, Polish in Poland etc.). This assumption implies that so-called non-language subjects are not obliged to systematically contribute to students' language development apart from familiarising them with the special terminology of the discipline. This is a wrong perception, as the chapter on language in 'other' subjects demonstrates (Chapter 6).
- What students have learnt about the nature and means of academic literacy in one subject cannot easily be used in other subjects, although this would actually be desirable. So far there is not enough of a common transversal system of reference for identifying relevant textual and linguistic features of academic literacy across subjects and across other languages (so-called foreign, heritage, and other languages in the environment), which would enhance synergetic effects and allow for transfer of awareness, of language skills and knowledge. The whole issue of transfer, as central as it is, requires much further empirical study.
- Unlike acquiring language skills for engaging in informal everyday interaction (outside of school, in 'normal' life), learning how to handle the academic language of schooling becomes increasingly demanding with the complexity of the content, and with the complexity of the curriculum as a whole. Therefore, the need to support the

development of academic literacy is not restricted to the initial stages of education, but continues and is even more crucial in upper grades of schooling, not least with final examinations and certification in mind.

Examples of Practical Approaches[7]

In the following section, we would like to address some of the more practical aspects involved in trying to make the language dimension in all subjects and learning situations transparent and in supporting learners to deal with them in a reflective and productive way. The central concept to be introduced here will be that of 'scaffolding', which means constructing or building temporary support systems, for as long as learners need them. Since the handling of subject-related academic language cannot be taught satisfactorily in independent courses, learners must be able to acquire specific language and textual strategies themselves. For this purpose, students need suitable learning opportunities in the shape of models (spoken, written texts), instructions, suggestions, feedback, and provision of languages resources. However, only as much support should be offered as the learner absolutely needs in order to successfully deal with the learning task in question. To the extent that learners are able to cope with a learning task, the 'scaffold' of support is gradually dismantled. *Scaffolding* has become the umbrella term for teaching strategies and techniques that are compatible with (social) constructivist learning concepts, in so far as they support self-determined learning.

The linguistic turn in pedagogy (Schleppegrell, 2004) focusing on academic language together with the concept of scaffolding and self-determined learning allow a change of paradigm with respect to students 'at risk': from compensatory repair strategies such as increased learning times, differentiation in special groups, lowering of curricular standards, simplified language in textbooks etc. to positive strategies for the inclusion of such target groups in mainstream classes by offering targeted academic language support for mastering complex cognitive operations across all age-levels and across all disciplines. What then can be done in practical and effective terms?

Raise and support language awareness

Many teachers of so-called non-language subjects are not aware that whenever they deal with subject-specific content they automatically use a language variety that is characteristic of their profession as a discourse community. Furthermore, when working with texts, e.g. in History or Social Sciences, where students run into difficulties understanding complex concepts and logical connections, teachers tend to attribute learning difficulties to a lack of intelligence, ability or motivation. When dealing with basic concepts of their discipline they might direct students' attention to technical terms, but fail to see that students are confronted with a multitude of grammatical terms, complex nominal phrases, paraphrases, passive formulations, backward and forward references etc., which many students are not familiar with when talking to family members, peers or using social media on the internet. This means that, before being able to raise students' awareness of academic language phenomena, teachers themselves have to become aware of different domains of discourse for regulatory, social and cognitive processes and their specific patterns of language use. Teachers can get together as critical friends in small groups for mutual classroom observation. Using criteria for analysing language-sensitive teaching, they can support each other by exchanging feedback.

Thürmann and Vollmer (2012) have developed and evaluated an observation instrument with 48 criteria for the following six observation areas:[8]

- Transparency of language requirements.
- Teacher's use of language.
- Classroom interaction and students' opportunities for language action.
- Subject-specific language patterns, strategies and genres.
- Appropriateness of teaching and learning materials.
- Linguistic aspects of diagnosis and assessment.

Make expected language performance transparent and give feedback

Learning tasks are among the most important instruments in the design of teaching and learning processes. Before students start working on a task, they want to know what is expected of them, what they should pay attention to and which steps could lead to a successful completion. It follows that the aspects in Table 4.1 should be explicitly mentioned by the teacher when setting the task.

Table 4.1 Language aspects when setting tasks

Operators: specify type of language action	e.g. analyse, explain, list …
Field: subject-specific content	e.g. Agriculture of Central Valley, California
Type of text to be analysed	e.g. geographic map, textbook chapter
Type of target text to be produced	e.g. list of keywords, short oral summary
Conditions for the development of the target text	e.g. 20 minutes time for work in small groups, check choice of words, make it understandable for 10 year olds who have not participated in our lessons
Process steps	e.g. how further work on the topic should proceed

Table 4.2 Linking content and language objectives

At the end of the teaching unit (lesson) 'No life without water' we will have learnt:

Content	Language skills
what properties are attributed to water	how to combine several descriptive statements to form a short coherent text (e.g. for a children's encyclopedia)
how water is distributed around the globe	how to represent quantities in absolute and relative terms (e.g. 68.7% of water occurs in the form of snow or ice); how to summarise what diagrams can tell us

As an introduction to a lesson or new teaching unit, objectives should be presented and discussed with students. Especially in so-called non-language subjects such *advance organising* often only informs students about cognitive operations and subject-specific content. However, at the beginning of a teaching unit or lesson, learners should be able to see what academic language skills are to be acquired and how linguistic and content aspects are linked, as the example in Table 4.2 shows.

Obviously, it makes sense to check at the end of a lesson/teaching unit whether both the subject-based content objectives and the linguistic-textual goals have been reached. This does not necessarily have to be done in the form of tests. So-called 'exit slips' are also suitable which contain prompts and questions such as:

I didn't understand...
Write one question you have about today's lesson...
Please explain more about...
Name one issue that you have difficulty in understanding...

The dual focus of advance organisers and the evaluation of tests or exit slips allows teachers to plan and organise further scaffolding activities.

Provide linguistic means to support learning

In order to fulfil the psycholinguistic conditions attached to scaffolding processes, the provision of linguistic resources should be closely linked to student-activating processes that serve to reflect, anchor, expand and restructure available knowledge stocks of the mental lexicon. Probably the most widespread technique for providing linguistic resources for the purpose of mastering learning tasks is the area of vocabulary, especially concerning technical terms and typical subject-related expressions. The provision of suitable word lists for mastering learning tasks, for example in alphabetical order or chronological order of occurrence in a text to be worked on, is not very effective in terms of long-term availability.

Instead of handing out lists of words for a learning task, working with word-fields and word-families is one of the proven techniques of scaffolding lexical knowledge. At the beginning of a teaching unit on the concept of monarchy in late medieval times, a history teacher may ask students to recall from their memory words that will go with 'king' and 'queen', then she might hand out a short factual text as a 'quarry' for new word material. Up to this stage, students will come up with a colourful mix of words. Now this lexical material can be systematised according to lexico-grammatical criteria or specific topics or fields of meaning, and then for the rest of the teaching unit continue to be fed into a 'word store' (on a sheet of paper on a wall, on index cards, in a computer file).

castle, rich, protect, powerful, prince, crown, nobility, landed property, kingdom, serve, rule, throne, army, palace, sceptre, monarchy, conquer ...

Establishing concepts and adequate handling of key terminology can also be arranged following the Frayer model (first proposed by Frayer *et al.*, 1969) as in Figure 4.3.

The connection of concepts and associated terminology can also be worked out with graphic scaffolds, as in Figure 4.4 where the learners link the terms and descriptions.

Classroom observation of lexical scaffolding shows that in most instances it is focused on nouns and noun phrases, because such 'brick words' (Zwiers, 2008) facilitate the teacher's approach to subject-specific cognitive concepts. However, to construct complex statements, most students lack adequate linguistic resources to arrange nominal elements in a logical order within and across sentences, to clarify spatial and temporal relations, help the reader navigate through (parts of) a text and to indicate modality and the stance of the speaker/writer. These words and phrases or 'mortar words' (Zwiers, 2008) rarely occur in spoken colloquial language, but are used in academic language across all subjects and

Definition (in your own words):	Features:
one person or one group rules a country alone	Government consists of one person or one person appoints members of the government – no or only little political say – no or only little individual freedom for citizens
Examples:	
Hitler-Germany	**Examples to show the opposite:**
Democratic People's Republic of Korea (DPRK) Russia under Stalin	Germany today – France – Switzerland – Republic of Korea (ROK)

Dictatorship

Figure 4.3 Concepts and key terminology

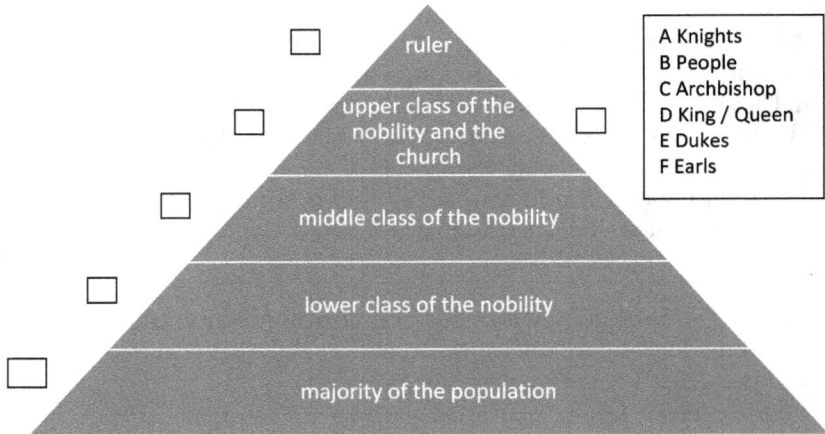

Figure 4.4 Connecting concepts and terminology

contribute significantly to the character of academic language use. They should be a major object of lexical scaffolding.

A very effective form of lexical scaffolding focuses the attention of learners on fixed expressions, sentence building blocks and useful phrases. Systematic language support can be organised in a topic-based way, for instance when dealing with different forms of diagrams, e.g. in Geography when dealing with climate zones:

> The subject of the pie chart is ... the bar chart shows ... this graph contains statistical information about ... gives an overview of ... enables the comparison of ... the course of the curve has increased ... the columns indicate that the proportion of ... has increased by 5% in three months ...

Scaffolding can also be organised in terms of interior textual moves which serve a specific function, e.g. modalising statements that emphasise, strengthen or weaken (boosters, hedges) as well as displaying degrees of certainty. These scaffolds can furnish answers to the question, 'Which expressions can I use when I want to do the following:

> identify the central object or the topic of my text
> capture characteristics, properties in a descriptive way
> compare/contrast objects, processes
> explain causes and effect
> clarify requirements, conditions
> draw conclusions
> convey opinions
> criticise a statement/opinion
> concede
> position myself
> announce or explain text-organising procedures ...?'.

How Can Schools Support Academic Language Use and Literacies across the Curriculum?

This section provides examples of how language can be supported in the context of three specific subjects. Here we provide in more general terms a list of priorities on which a content and language integrated approach should be based:

- Concern for language does not have a regulatory function, but rather a facilitating one. It helps students to tackle a learning task, e.g. when dealing with extreme climate conditions and analysing weather reports in a Geography lesson. Hence, which textual and/or linguistic phenomena are looked at depends on the kind of performance required by *learning tasks*. These should be designed in such a way that expected academic language performances are explicitly defined and thus become transparent for students as reference points for their own problem-solving attempts. Such reference points will help students to decide on suitable textual procedures and on language elements suitable for expected cognitive activities.
- Subject-specific *content* is the most important point of departure for focusing on cognitive activities, associated textual procedures and academic language activities. Learning tasks will indicate on which kind of knowledge the learning activities are focused:
  - Factual knowledge (e.g. terminologies, specific and basic elements within a specific subject area)
  - Conceptual knowledge (e.g. classification, generalisations, models and theories, models that constitute or explain a larger structure)
  - Procedural knowledge (e.g. techniques and methods, knowing how to do things)
  - Metacognitive knowledge (e.g. awareness of one's own learning disposition, social context, learning strategies and gaps, assessment of learning results and activities).
- The students' search for and decision on suitable, appropriate textual procedures and academic language elements also depend on which *field(s) of communicative classroom action* the learning task is focused upon:
  - Oral classroom interaction and negotiation of meaning and subject knowledge
  - Retrieval of relevant information from (mostly) factual texts, graphic (e.g. diagrams) or non-language forms (e.g. statistics, mathematical formulas) of representation
  - Critical evaluation and (re-)structuring of subject-specific concepts and procedural knowledge
  - Presentation, exchange and proof of learning outcomes through writing, oral monologues or media-supported presentation.
- Cognitive problem-solving procedures depend on longer stretches of coherent thought which coexist with longer stretches of coherent

language, whether spoken or written. Thus, directing students' attention to patterns of academic language use should always take into account how and in which function they are embedded in a paragraph or in a text as a whole. This includes awareness-raising of the respective *genre* and its subject-specific structure and features, e.g. History: recount, narrative, report, procedure, explanation, exposition (Martin, 2013).

- On a macro-level, linguistic and textual phenomena can be associated with general *academic language functions* (*cognitive discourse functions*, Dalton-Puffer, 2013) which are also called *epistemic* and which are common to all curricular subject areas.

  These macro functions indicate the specific purpose of language moves in a text and serve as umbrella terms for *textual procedures* at a mezzo-level, e.g.

NAMING/DEFINING – DESCRIBING/ILLUSTRATING – EXPLAINING/CLARIFYING – NARRATING/REPORTING – ASSUMING/HYPOTHESISING – POSITIONING/ARGUING – ASSESSING/EVALUATING

On a micro-level the concern for the dimension of academic language use will be directed at general lexico-grammatical building blocks and fixed conventional expressions. Thus, whenever integrated content and language methodologies deal with lexical and grammatical issues, they will make students aware of their functional contribution to textual procedures and epistemic-cognitive functions.[9]

- On the lowest level of this reference system for subject-based academic language teaching and learning, subject specialists will have to determine which language elements (words, technical terms, fixed expressions, function words, syntactic structures, etc.) are already at the students' disposal and serving the envisaged purpose – as delineated above – and which elements students should acquire additionally on the basis of a teacher's targeted support (cf. 'scaffolding' – see above).

Conclusion

This chapter has presented the case for recognising the importance of language in all subjects, and addressed the question of how education systems can support the literacy dimension of teaching and learning. However, it is not sufficient that teachers simply be told that they should address this language dimension. Guiding concepts and practical tools are needed in order to understand what this means in concrete terms. The Recommendation CM/Rec(2014)5 of the Committee of Ministers of the Council of Europe to Member States highlights the importance of high quality education based on a coherent approach to the language dimension of all school subjects, so that students have equal opportunities to acquire the necessary competences in the more 'academic' language essential for successful learning. Education authorities, schools, curriculum developers and teachers alike are encouraged to promote quality and equity in education by making these competences explicit for all learners and provide professional support. Experiences from local and regional initiatives show that quality, equity and inclusion in education can be significantly improved if the language dimension is taken into account in the following fields of the national and/or regional educational system:

- **Teacher education:** In many countries, pre-service training of educators who teach so-called non-language subjects focuses on factual knowledge, disciplinary concepts and methods, and their terminology. An additional mandatory module should also familiarise future teachers of Mathematics, Chemistry, Social Sciences etc. with subject-specific as well as transversal aspects of academic literacy and with practical scaffolding skills to overcome language induced learning difficulties. Corresponding offers should also be made for continuous education of this target group.
- **Curriculum development:** Comparative studies by an advisory group to the Council of Europe have shown that existing national/regional curricula in most cases do not define expected academic language skills and competences for teachers, schoolbook authors, teacher trainers and examination boards on a reliable basis. At least obligatory exit criteria at the end of primary and compulsory secondary education should be specified for all subjects in a way that schools can harmonise their own syllabi along shared references for e.g. genres, basic academic language functions, writing and oral presentation, adequateness and correctness, etc.
- **Academic literacy advisors:** Very often, schools that are ready for reform do not have the necessary expertise and experience to adapt their own practice of teaching and learning to the new challenges. This especially holds true for the dimension of general and subject-specific academic literacy. They would willingly accept help from the outside if the education system would offer specially trained and certified academic language advisors. Together with a school-based project group they are the ones who could provide the school's staff and stakeholders with necessary information on the linguistic dimension of teaching and learning and achieve quality improvements through peer teaching and criteria-based peer observation.
- **Local, regional school networks:** Education systems will hardly be able to implement necessary reform measures quickly and across the board, especially since many practical questions regarding the linguistic dimension of teaching and learning still need to be clarified

further through accompanying research. In the meantime, many schools already want to reform their own practices. This process can be facilitated by individual schools supporting each other on a local/regional basis and by jointly establishing curricula, discussing criteria for language-sensitive subject teaching and developing the right teaching and learning materials (or revising existing ones). Such networking should be supported by the education system through, among other things, the provision of academic literacy advisors and the allocation of time for developmental work (as part of the teaching load).

The approaches and practical measures outlined above can help to ensure quality and equity in education by bringing the language dimension more clearly into focus in teaching and learning processes.

Notes

(1) The documents used include, *inter alia*, Beacco, Fleming, Goullier, Thürmann and Vollmer (2016) *The Language Dimension in All Subjects: A Handbook for Curriculum Development and Teacher Training*. Strasbourg: Council of Europe (in the chapter also referred to as 'Handbook').
(2) The term 'academic' in this context does not mean university-related or formal, but rather relating to complex cognitive tasks and levels of demand or processing.
(3) We speak of *literacy*, of *subject or disciplinary literacy* and even of *pluriliteracies* when referring to the mastery of processing and analysing information or text competently and being able to write about such content accordingly, which requires the successful management of the language component. The nature of literacy is changing or rather widening because of the ongoing digitalisation and globalisation, including 'the ability to extract and use knowledge from an ever-growing number of online resources' (European Commission, 2014: 21; cf. Martin, 2013, Coyle and Meyer, 2021).
(4) This notion was coined by a group of researchers at the European Centre for Modern Languages in 2018 (cf. Coyle and Meyer, 2021).
(5) This comprises the mastery of what we call *Bildungssprache* in the German educational context.
(6) Educational language learning is conceptualised by the Handbook (Beacco *et al.*, 2016) in terms of the acquisition of form-meaning pairs (cf. Tomasello, 2003), as is also the case in modern foreign language didactics (cf. Long and Robinson, 1998).
(7) Some examples are based on or taken from Thürmann *et al.* (2017).
(8) The checklist can be found in English as an appendix of the Handbook (Beacco *et al.*, 2016) or in an extended German version in Thürmann and Vollmer (2012).
(9) Sets of basic academic language functions (also called cognitive discourse functions) which are relevant across the whole spectrum of school subjects, have also been presented and discussed for CLIL programmes, *inter alia*, by Dalton-Puffer, 2013; Vollmer, 2009, 2011; Zydatiß, 2005.

References

Beacco, J.-C., Fleming, M., Goullier, F., Thürmann, E. and Vollmer, H.J., with contributions by J. Sheils (2016) *The Language Dimension in All Subjects: A Handbook for Curriculum Development and Teacher Training*. Strasbourg: Council of Europe.

Council of Europe (2014) Recommendation CM/Rec(2014)5. *The Importance of Competences in the Language(s) of Schooling for Equity and Quality in Education and for Educational Success.* Strasbourg: Council of Europe. https://search.coe.int/cm/Pages/result_details.aspx?ObjectID=09000016805c6105.
Coyle, D. and Meyer, O. (2021) *Beyond CLIL: Pluriliteracies Teaching for Deeper Learning.* Cambridge: Cambridge University Press.
Dalton-Puffer, C. (2013) A construct of cognitive discourse functions for conceptualizing content-language integration in CLIL and multilingual education. *European Journal of Applied Linguistics* 1 (2), 216–253.
European Commission. Directorate General for Education and Culture (2014) *EU High Level Group of Experts on Literacy: Final Report, September 2012.* Brussels: Publications Office. https://data.europa.eu/doi/10.2766/34382
Frayer, D.A., Fredrick, W.C. and Klausmeier, H.J. (1969). A schema for testing the level of concept mastery. Report from the Project on Situational Variables and Efficiency of Concept Learning. Madison: Wisconsin Research and Development Center for Cognitive Learning.
Long, M. and Robinson, P. (1998) Focus on form: Theory, research and practice. In C. Doughty and J. Williams (eds) *Focus on Form in Classroom Second Language Acquisition* (pp. 15–41). Cambridge: Cambridge University Press.
Martin, J.R. (2013) Embedded literacy: Knowledge as meaning. *Linguistics and Education* 24 (1), 23–37.
Mosher, F. and Heritage, M. (2017) A hitchhiker's guide to thinking about literacy, learning progressions, and instruction. *CPRE Research Reports.* University of Pennsylvania. https://repository.upenn.edu/cpre_researchreports/97
OECD (2018) *Equity in Education: Breaking Down Barriers to Social Mobility.* Paris: OECD Publishing.
Schleppegrell, M.J. (2004) *The Language of Schooling: A Functional Linguistic Perspective.* Mahwah, NJ: Lawrence Erlbaum.
Thürmann, E. and Vollmer, H.J. (2012) Schulsprache und Sprachsensibler Fachunterricht: Eine Checkliste mit Erläuterungen. In Ch. Röhner and B. Hövelbrinks (eds) *Fachbezogene Sprachförderung in Deutsch als* Zweitsprache (pp. 212–233). Weinheim: Juventa.
Thürmann, E., Vollmer, H.J. and Pieper, I. (2010) *Languages of Schooling: Focusing on Vulnerable Learners.* Strasbourg: Council of Europe.
Thürmann, E., Krabbe, H., Platz, U. and Schumacher, M. (2017) *Sprachbildung als Aufgabe aller Fächer und Lernbereiche.* Münster: Waxmann.
Tomasello, M. (2003) *Constructing a Language: A Usage-based Theory of Language Acquisition.* Cambridge, MA: Harvard University Press.
Vollmer, H.J. (2009) Diskursfunktionen und fachliche Diskurskompetenz bei bilingualen und monolingualen Geographielernern. In S.-A. Ditze and A. Halbach (eds) *Bilingualer Sachfachunterricht (CLIL) im Kontext von Sprache, Kultur und Multiliteralität* (pp. 165–185). Frankfurt: Lang.
Vollmer, H.J. (2011) Schulsprachliche Kompetenzen: Zentrale Diskursfunktionen. Osnabrück: University of Osnabrück. Unpublished paper. https://www.home.uni-osnabrueck.de/hvollmer/VollmerDF-Kurzdefinitionen.pdf
Walsh, B. (2008) How to win the war on global warming. *TIME Magazine* 171 (17) (April 28); Cover Story. http://content.time.com/time/specials/2007/article/0,28804,1730759_1731383_1731363,00.html
Zwiers, J. (2008) *Building Academic Language: Essential Practices for Content Classrooms.* San Francisco: Jossey-Bass.
Zydatiß, W. (2005) Diskursfunktionen in einem analytischen curricularen Zugriff auf Textvarietäten und Aufgaben des bilingualen Sachfachunterrichts. In *Fremdsprachen Lehren und Lernen* 34, 156–173.

5 What Do I Need to Know about Language as a Tool for Learning-and-Teaching and Assessing When Teaching Competences for Democratic Culture and Intercultural Competences?

Florentina Sâmihăian and Diana-Maria Beldiman

Introduction

In this chapter, we address the use of language as a means for learning-and-teaching and assessing competences for democratic culture and intercultural competences in various school subjects. Drawing on the most influential conceptual models of these competences, the authors provide practical guidance by illustrating different ways of exploiting language in a variety of communicative activities, and also present two examples in the field of social studies subjects (history and civic education).

A Holistic Perspective on Language and Communication

The exponential development of knowledge in different fields, globalisation and the valuing of plurality[1] are contributing to a new vision of education. In recent decades, the change of focus from 'knowledge' to 'competences' related to the needs of learners has characterised a new way of understanding the role of education. Today, however, new challenges also require a holistic view of how different subjects and competences can and should complement each other in the process of learning. While intra-disciplinary learning is constantly demonstrating its limits, pluri-, inter-, cross- and transdisciplinary approaches are designed to open the minds of learners so that they connect their knowledge from different fields in order to develop critical and reflective thinking, with a focus on stimulating their metacognitive competence and their creativity. In the values-focused perspective promoted by the Council of Europe (CoE), language plays a key role not only in language as subject (language of schooling/mother tongue(s) or second/foreign languages), but also in all other learning experiences, including learning and teaching democratic competence. This perspective is set out in 'Recommendation CM/Rec(2022)1 of the Committee of Ministers to member States on the importance of plurilingual and intercultural education for democratic culture' (see Chapter 1).[2] This high-level CoE policy statement encourages implementation of the unified vision and integrated approach necessary for teaching and learning competences for democratic culture across the curriculum.

A holistic competence-based approach to language implies that all teachers need to know how to create opportunities for their students to use language in a meaningful way, so that they develop their knowledge and understanding of the world, society and themselves that will help them fulfil their potential.

The importance of language and communication in all subjects can be highlighted by addressing the implicit values involved as follows:

- At the social level, communication is a means of acquiring knowledge about 'others' and this materialises through different types of interactions. The attitudes that students can develop from this point of view are flexibility, tolerance, respect for the opinions of others, active listening, openness to otherness.
- At the cognitive level, communication is a means of acquiring knowledge of the world, by using language awareness and different strategies of learning, such as selecting and processing information, analysing, comparing facts and ideas, expressing an opinion, or building an argument. The attitudes that are associated with the cognitive value of communication are curiosity, desire for knowledge, and interest in enriching knowledge in various domains.
- At the individual level, communication with people and texts helps students to gain knowledge of themselves. Assuming responsibility for what they communicate and for how they use language has consequences for the self-image that each student creates, for the understanding of their own values and how they decide to act in relation to these values.

A coherent approach to dealing with language and communication across the curriculum is necessary and can be implemented by involving students in communicative activities, by encouraging them to express and justify their own points of view, exchange ideas, solve problems and analyse texts using their knowledge of language in an appropriate and adequate way.

It is worth recalling that the concept of 'competence' has been refined over time: since the 1970s the CoE has linked competences to learners' needs and to effective communication, and has promoted an action-oriented approach illustrated by 'can-do' statements as used in the level descriptors of the CEFR (Council of Europe, 2001). A more values-oriented dimension of competences was fostered in the *Reference Framework of Competences for Democratic Culture* (RFCDC) (Council of Europe, 2018), based on the cornerstones of core Council of Europe values: human rights, democracy, and the rule of law. The vision of plurilingualism and interculturality promoted by the CoE, especially after 2000, strongly influenced this new reference framework which we shall illustrate by relating 'competence for democratic culture' to the concept of 'intercultural competence'.

We discuss here specifically the role of language and communication in teaching democratic and intercultural competences, based on two models: the description of the 'butterfly' model of 20 competences in the RFCDC (Council of Europe, 2018: 38), and Byram's (2021) combined model of intercultural communicative competence and intercultural competence.

The competences for democratic culture listed in the *Reference Framework of Competences for Democratic Culture* (see Chapter 1) comprise four categories: values, attitudes, skills, knowledge and critical understanding. They include competences that are *explicitly* related to language: *linguistic, communicative and plurilingual skills*; *skills of listening*; *knowledge and critical understanding of language and communication*. They also include competences that are *implicitly* related to language and communication, i.e. values, attitudes and skills that can be perceived or expressed by the use of language: *valuing human dignity and human rights*; *valuing cultural diversity*; *valuing democracy, justice, fairness, equality and the rule of law*; *openness to cultural otherness and to other beliefs, world views and practices*; *respect*; *self-efficacy*; *tolerance of ambiguity*; *co-operation*; and *conflict-resolution*.

Byram's model of intercultural competences highlights the complementarity of two areas:

(a) *intercultural competence*, which includes knowledge (of self and of others), skills of interpreting and relating, critical cultural awareness (valuing others' values, beliefs and behaviours, and relativising one's self), and attitudes (curiosity and openness);
(b) *intercultural communicative competence*, which, under the heading 'communicative language competences', includes the three dimensions in the CEFR:[3] linguistic competence (referring to general linguistic

knowledge, vocabulary range and control, grammatical accuracy, phonological and orthographic control); sociolinguistic competence (referring to sociolinguistic appropriateness, such as linguistic markers of social relations, politeness conventions, register differences, dialect and accent); and discourse competence (referring to flexibility, turn-taking, thematic development, coherence and cohesion, propositional precision, and fluency).

A comparison between the two models of competences described above pinpoints the similarities: they both include knowledge, skills and attitudes (although the CDC also explicitly incorporates education for values); both refer to language and communication as a component of the two competences; both focus on a broader language-as-discourse perspective, on language functions and the ways language is used to create meaning in social contexts.[4] Understanding the key role language and communication play in developing democratic and intercultural competences provides some challenges for teachers who deal with these competences, either those teaching a specific subject (i.e. education for citizenship, history) or for those approaching these competences under the umbrella of cross-curricular topics. In either case, teachers need to have a holistic view of the role of language in learning and need to know how to create opportunities for students to acquire specific academic language (CALP – Cognitive Academic Language Proficiency) (Cummins, 2012), and to use language in the process of learning as a means of constructing their own knowledge. This requires teachers to have knowledge about language itself, and to know how to build meaningful communicative activities for their learners.

Aspects of Language and Communication that are Relevant for Learning-and-Teaching and Assessing Competences for Democratic Culture and Intercultural Competences

Knowledge and critical understanding of language

Language has two important dimensions: one is *instrumental*, as it helps us express observations, thoughts (conclusions and judgements based on observations or ideas), feelings and needs; the other is *relational*, based on the interaction among the participants in various communicative contexts. This emphasises the communicative power of language when it is both appropriate (according to rules and patterns that involve a good control of morphology, phonology, orthography, semantics and syntax) and adequate (related to context, meaning, purpose and deep understanding). By using language effectively in this manner, we can express our identity and better understand other people and the world around us. In developing the competences for democratic culture and intercultural competences, language is used both as a means of acquiring knowledge – by constructing meaning from what we read or listen to, or by what we express orally or in writing – and as a means of social interaction.

The most common challenge for teachers dealing with the two competences (democratic culture and intercultural competences) is to develop CALP, the academic language that is specific to the domain of CDC or to the domain of interculturality. Generally, teachers focus on explaining the technical vocabulary (the resort to etymology can be helpful in this respect), but it is also important to involve students in tasks that require complex, academic reading and writing. This means not only being able to understand and use the terminology, but also to become familiar with a different type of discourse, characterised by longer and more complex sentences, by impersonal statements and abstract terms, by the use of language functions such as describing, explaining, arguing etc., so that students can develop their critical, abstract thinking and their communicative skills. The process can be difficult for some students (who are not native speakers or who come from disadvantaged social groups), and therefore teachers may need to address CALP progressively and use differentiated learning approaches when tackling academic reading and writing (see also Chapter 4).

Teachers may expect students to be able to apply the reading and writing strategies they acquired in language as subject to new academic contexts. While some students may be able to do so, this is not the case with every student. The teacher can therefore make use of effective strategies

Table 5.1 Reading and writing strategies

Reading strategies	Writing strategies
• activating prior knowledge • scanning a text for specific information • skimming a text for the overall idea • paraphrasing parts of a text • making inferences • distinguishing between fact and opinion • distinguishing between main and secondary ideas • clustering the information in a text • deducing the meaning of unfamiliar lexical items • identify the author, the context and the purpose of the text • integrating the new knowledge in one's own system of reference	• prewriting (understanding the purpose and the audience, brainstorming the ideas related to the topic, documenting for the topic) • writing (organising the ideas according to the type of text to be written, using graphic organisers for this purpose) • responding (receiving feedback from peers or teacher, self-evaluating the first draft according to given criteria) • revising (clarifying, reorganising, refining ideas using precise language) • editing (checking the structure of sentences, the spelling and punctuation) • publishing/sharing (presenting the text to others)
By using appropriate reading strategies and sharing with others their understanding, students can construct meaning from what they read; they can evaluate the ideas of the text and make their own judgements, and decide how to use the text for their own study.	By using the writing strategies specific to each stage of the writing process, working individually, in pairs or in small groups, students can construct and share knowledge by using language in a meaningful way.

for developing students' proficiency in CALP. Those we present in Table 5.1 relate mainly to developing analytical and critical thinking skills, based on knowledge and critical understanding of language and communication (key CDC competences in the butterfly diagram), and to fostering discourse competence and the skills of interpreting/relating (from intercultural communicative competence).

A synoptic view of the strategies that might be used by the teacher is presented in Table 5.1.

Examples of communicative activities

While reading and writing are the dominant activities for developing students' proficiency in CALP, there are many other kinds of communicative activities that can also support the development of CDC or intercultural competences. A wide spectrum of purposeful language activities can stimulate students to:

- formulate their observations, perceptions, representations, existing knowledge, points of view;
- read a text;
- retrieve, process and interpret new information and express it in different modes;
- present, discuss and negotiate information;
- answer questions;
- check findings and arguments critically; express (non-)understanding, doubt, degrees of certainty, or reflect about their own procedures and evaluate them. (Vollmer & Beacco, 2010)

Active listening can be used in every lesson in order to receive relevant feedback on how students follow and understand a presentation given by the teacher or by their peers, or a classroom discussion around a certain topic. Teachers can detect students' level of attention, their openness or their empathy to others' ideas by observing, among other things:

- how they can paraphrase or summarise what they have listened to;
- whether they are able to request clarification, or ask open-ended questions or probing questions, avoiding prejudice;
- if they understand the purpose of communication and if they signal encouragement to the speaker.

The teacher could start by giving clear tasks to the class referring to the response that is expected (i.e. note down the main ideas/the new ideas or the new piece of information; ask questions to clarify understanding; identify who is speaking, who is being addressed, the purpose of communication; describe the nonverbal elements that emphasise or counter the message etc.). Active listening can also be used for audio or video materials; teachers can use VideoAnt (https://ant.umn.edu/), a digital application, which allows the material to be interrupted to add annotations, comments or questions for each sequence of a web-hosted video. Active listening can help teachers identify ideas, concepts or behaviours that are not clear to their students and they can build new activities to support effective learning.

Exploratory talk is 'a specific mode of social interaction in the class by which knowledge is made publicly accountable and reasoning is visible in the talk'.[5] Linguistic and communicative skills, as well as cooperation skills, are put to work to acquire new knowledge and a critical understanding of the world.

In exploratory talk the students discuss critically but constructively each other's ideas. Each student expresses their own point of view, trying to explain the reasoning behind it. The others can express a different perspective, giving counter-arguments, or can build on each other's ideas. The purpose is to find an agreement as a basis for common progress in reaching a broader understanding of a topic. Emphasising the constructivist nature of learning, Barnes argues that 'coming to terms with new knowledge requires *working on understanding* which can most readily be achieved through talk' (Barnes, 2008: 1). The role of talk in organising our understanding of the world was argued by Vygotsky (1962) who highlighted the idea that our ability to talk and think is in the first instance social and only later becomes individual. In exploratory talk, the teacher does not ignore the forms of words and sentences by which students express their ideas, but they focus more on 'the meanings and purposes they represent, and the social relationships in which they are embedded' (Barnes, 2008: 9).

From this perspective, a deeper understanding is based on the active involvement of the students in their own learning, and exploratory talk challenges students to build knowledge by relating new ideas and ways of thinking with existing understanding and expectations in order to modify them. The teacher can foster this kind of learning by encouraging students to listen actively, share relevant information, challenge others' ideas, give reasons for challenges, build on what has been said, contribute, treat with respect others' ideas and opinions, enjoy an atmosphere of trust, have a sense of shared purpose, seek agreement for joint decisions. Exploratory talk can be planned after a short explanation by the teacher, after watching a video or after reading a document or a literary text that refers to the topic of the lesson.

Reading and discussing various types of texts (i.e. documents, laws, articles, fiction) represents a common activity in different subjects that is associated with developing CDC and intercultural competences. A collaboration between the teachers of L1 (mother tongue or the principal language of study) and other teachers can help students to transfer and apply the reading strategies for a deep understanding of texts to new learning contexts. An example is offered in Vignette 1.

Vignette 1: Cultural diversity

Activity description: The main goal of this activity is to develop students' democratic and intercultural competences through self-reflection, collaborative learning and sociohistorical awareness while analysing texts from a graphic novel. For this purpose, we have chosen fragments of *Persepolis: The Story of a Childhood and The Story of a Return* by Marijane Satrapi (2008), an Iranian-born French graphic novelist. The fragments may also have an emotional value due to the fact that they highlight problems that teenage students face or have faced (e.g. coping with examinations for faculty admission; coming to terms with physical development and physical appearance reflected by Western and Eastern fashion). The approach could be used in History high school classes, with students of 17–18 years old.

The selected fragments target the following aspects:

- cultural differences between Eastern and Western cultures;
- restrictions faced by people living under a totalitarian regime;
- the condition of women in an Islamic society.

The source is analysed by using 'text-to-self' (connection with students' lives and experiences), 'text-to text' (connections between characters, events and settings from at least two given texts) and 'text-to-world' (connections to history and events) methods. See Figures 5.1, 5.2 and 5.3 below. These were chosen for the following reasons:

- they have a high potential for developing critical analysis of the text from multiple perspectives and for facilitating interdisciplinary transfer;
- self-reflection is assured while establishing for each student an individual dialogue with the text; in this stage, basic comprehension is assured through active reading strategies;
- the students have the chance to establish similarities and differences between the society in which they live and the one presented in the extracted fragments – thus, they can become aware of themselves and 'the other';
- while using 'text-to-text' analysis, the extracts can be placed in a comprehensive dialogue with other types of non-fiction narrative texts. For Romania, we have used famous women's memories related to their youth spent under the Communist regime (Popescu, 2008) or non-literary texts presenting social aspects of a totalitarian regime.

Components of intercultural competence and democratic citizenship may be demonstrated as follows:

- Students will interact in small groups in order to discover cultural differences while reading a text.

- Students will develop their skills of critical thinking while analysing facts mentioned in a graphic novel and individual recollections of persons who lived under another totalitarian regime (in this case, the Romanian Communist regime).
- Students will demonstrate knowledge and critical understanding of themselves, the world and will accept cultural diversity.
- Students will manifest interest in human rights and their respect for living in a democratic society.

TEXT-TO-SELF (INDIVIDUAL WORKSHEET)

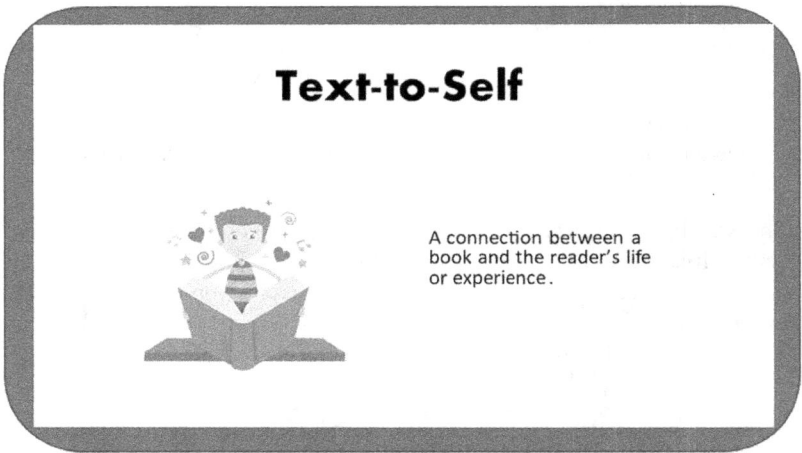

Figure 5.1 Text-to-self

Students are to read the extracts selected from the graphic novel *Persepolis* and to note in a table (like the one below) the connections they establish with their own experiences, with their lives or with the feelings they experienced while reading the text.

The following table presents in italics some responses to this activity provided by high school students:

1. This text reminds me of...	• *Women's activities for obtaining political rights.*
2. Setting of the scene makes me think of...	• *Present political regimes from some countries;* • *Society under a totalitarian regime;* • *Taking the exam for secondary school graduation and high school admission.*

3. I have understood what the main character feels because...	• *I am also a girl and there were situations in my life when I felt discriminated against, but these situations did not have a huge impact upon myself;* • *Even nowadays there are many women who face the restrictions imposed due to religious or political reasons.* • *There are many women who face societal pressure for various reasons.* • *I was also stressed about taking an exam;* • *Everything is clear because the author described the facts in detail.*
4. The narrated events are similar to my life because...	• *My grandmother lived in a period when women faced the restrictions of a totalitarian regime;* • *Romania had a Communist regime (even if the restrictions were not so severe);* • *I don't find any similarities with my life.*
5. The narrated events are different from my life because...	• *We live in a democratic society;* • *In our country there are not rules related to clothes compulsory to wear;* • *In our country, girls and boys take the exams together;* • *I do not live under a totalitarian regime or a dictatorship.*

TEXT – TO – TEXT

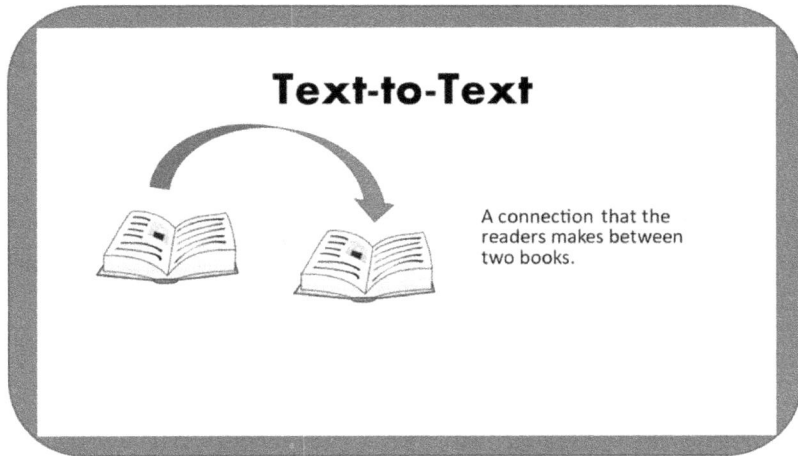

Figure 5.2 Text-to-text

Students are challenged to make connections between the excerpts in *Persepolis* and another text dealing with the same problem, but approached from another perspective. The table below presents some guiding questions for students and, in italics, some answers provided by high school students.

1. What is the main idea of text 1? What about text 2?	• *The first text presents some life aspects of a young woman living in Iran.* • *The second text deals with the memories of a Romanian author and her youth experiences in the early 80s (under the Romanian Communist regime).*
2. What similarities can be identified between the two texts?	• *Both texts are written from the perspectives of two young women;* • *Both women lived under a dictatorship;* • *Both of them present issues regarding education under a dictatorship;* • *Both of them present how the regime affects personal life (clothing).*
3. What are the differences that we may establish while reading the two texts?	• *In comparison with Iran where women had to wear certain type of clothes because of religious reasons, in Communist Romania women used to wear regular clothes. It was almost impossible for a young Romanian lady living under the Communist regime to find a pair of blue jeans (for example).* • *While the first text deals with restrictions imposed by religion, the second one does not take into account the religious aspects.* • *In Iran, the persecution was more severe if the religious norms were disobeyed.* • *In Iran there was a dictatorship based on political and religious reasons while in Romania there was a totalitarian regime.* • *While in Iran there were different tests for boys and girls at faculty admission, in Romania there were common tests which did not take into account any differences among the candidates.*
4. How does reading of these two texts together allow me to see or understand things that I might not if I had read them separately?	• *Due to the fact that we have worked in small groups, we had the chance to debate on various aspects (religion, politics, private life) taking into account various perspectives, experiences and histories from our own families.*
5. What are the questions that the texts raise for me? What about reactions?	• *Is there any possibility that women from traditional cultural communities have the same rights as those of us who live in democratic countries?* • *How would a woman from Iran have perceived a woman's life under the Communist regime from Romania?* • *Reactions: surprised because of the realities presented in Persepolis, cultural shock, we have already known about the restrictions from Romanian communism due to our families' recollections. Girls from our team consider that they couldn't obey the rules under a dictatorship.*

TEXT – TO – WORLD

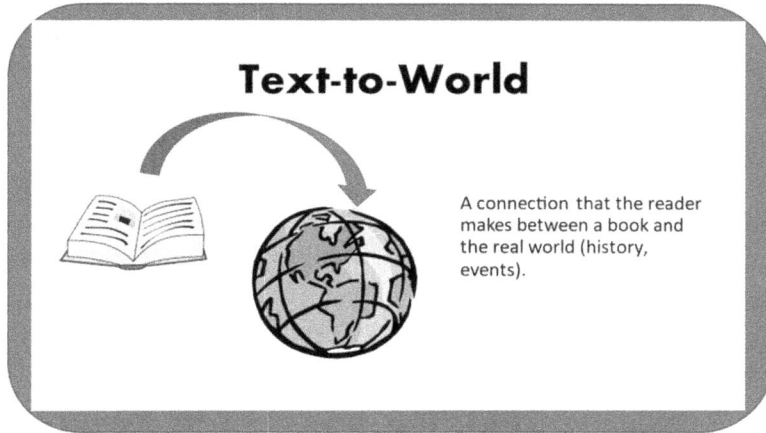

Text-to-World

A connection that the reader makes between a book and the real world (history, events).

Figure 5.3 Text-to-world

This is the moment to put in context (historical, geographical, cultural) the achievements of the previous stages. The following table presents questions/guidelines given to students and, in italics, some of their answers.

1. The events that can be historically documented are…	• *Dictatorships*
2. These events took place when…	• *Romania: 1948–1989* • *Iran: 1979–present*
3. The events presented in the text happened/are happening because…	• *The main characters do not agree with the political situation from their countries.*
4. What I have read is similar to something that I have seen in the news (mention)…	• *Some TV shows dealing with Romanian Communist regime;* • *News regarding the events that took place in 1989 in.Romania;*
5. About the theme of the texts, I have also read in…	• *I have never read.*
6. The theme of the texts is also presented in the movie…	• *I have never watched a movie with this subject.*
7. How do these books, movies, news help you to better understand the theme of the two texts?	• *These texts offer some patterns regarding personal experiences under dictatorships. After reading them, it is easier for us to understand what we have learned during our history classes related to democracy and totalitarianism during the 20th century.*

What have students learned from the previous activities about dictatorship, human rights and cultural diversity?

Knowledge and understanding: cultural, religious, political diversity; personal life under dictatorships; women's status; human rights (education, private life) under totalitarian regimes.

Skills: differentiating historical facts from opinions; critical thinking in analysing memories and graphical novels.

Values: valuing diversity, human rights and democratic means of leadership.

Attitudes: respect, tolerance, openness to knowing other spaces and cultures.

Assessment

At the end of the activity students' achievements can be assessed using various methods and instruments (observation, case study, self-reflection etc.).

In Table 5.2 a list of descriptors is given that could be used for assessment purposes or adapted, using the first person, as an instrument of self-reflection for students

Difficulties that teachers may face while applying this learning strategy

- Students' lack of knowledge related to the subject – this can be overcome by organising a lead-in activity that will provide the necessary content for the historical analysis;
- Teachers may have to provide sufficient training for students so they can differentiate facts from interpretations when analysing various types of sources;
- While teaching historical sensitive issues, teachers may have to deal with representations regarding the subject that students have received in informal environments – parents who lived under a totalitarian regime, for example, provide a subjective image of the period which may affect students' knowledge, values and attitudes towards the historical analyses carried out in schools;
- Analysing alternative sources that emphasise aspects related to social history can be challenging both for teachers and students due to its specificity. A step-by-step approach in discovering the historical meaning using graded questions, for example, is very important in developing students' multiliteracy and critical thinking skills.

Table 5.2 Descriptors for use in assessment or self-reflection

	Below requirements	Meets requirements	Beyond requirements
Analysis of historical, social or cultural facts	Identify the main ideas and key words of the text(s).	Identify the main and secondary ideas of the text(s) and relate them to personal experiences; highlight the wider context of the facts.	Identify the main and secondary ideas of the text(s), take into account the causes and the consequences of certain facts while relating them to personal experience or general context.
Formulating points of view and illustrating them with arguments and examples	Hesitantly formulate a point of view, without sustaining it with arguments and examples.	Formulate a simple point of view and sustain it with arguments and examples selected from text(s) or personal experiences.	Formulate an elaborated point of view and sustain it with arguments and examples selected from text(s), personal experiences or society in which the students live.
Respect for other points of view	Show respect when listening to other points of view, but without replying or contributing to group conversations.	Explore the alternatives offered by classmates in conversations while demonstrating knowledge, interest and respect towards intercultural learning and democratic values.	Explore the alternatives expressed in groups by classmates, but also search to expand the arguments through supplementary documentation.
Appropriate use of language and intercultural communication	Intervene in group work and in writing individual tasks but without meeting all the requirements. The grammar and vocabulary structures are not appropriate for meeting the requirements of the task(s).	Intervene in group work and in writing individual tasks meeting all the requirements. The grammar and vocabulary structures are appropriate for meeting the requirements of the tasks.	Intervene in group work and in writing individual tasks illustrating creativity and innovation. The specialised vocabulary, advanced grammar structures and appropriate register are used for meeting the requirements of the tasks.

Role play. Among the various drama activities, role play has a special part in challenging students to better understand the functions of language and to gain knowledge and critical understanding of the world in the field of politics, law, human rights, cultural diversity and so on. Learning is facilitated by playing a role in a given social or cultural context, which is relevant for the topic of the lesson and for developing democratic and intercultural competences. Two students can act out their roles to explore a particular scenario: e.g. a meeting between two teenagers from different cultures in a holiday/in a study tour/in their family; a conversation between a student-candidate for the school council and a voter in the context of an election meeting.

Teachers can stage a role play by following some steps. First, it is important to identify the situation, by introducing the problem to be discussed in order to stimulate students to start thinking about the problem before the role play begins. Next, a scenario with clear roles is presented, so that the participants in the role play understand what is expected of them to achieve by the end of the session. The roles may be allocated by the teacher, or the students can themselves choose the roles they want to play. The teacher needs to present and clarify the criteria for assessing the performance of each pair. Only after the students understand what they are expected to do, will they then be given time to prepare. They can discuss, in pairs, the main ideas they will tackle in their role play, and they can note down some of the features of the 'character' they have to play: what are their motivations, perspectives and feelings? Sometimes, they may need time for writing down their ideas if they have to assume a role they are not familiar with. After two or more pairs perform the role play, their peers and the teacher can evaluate the activity, based on some given criteria. A discussion about what students have learned from the experience of role play both in terms of understanding a new concept and in understanding how language and communication can be used effectively can end the activity.

The role play can also provide the opportunity for exercising different registers of language (according to the status of the enacted role), and different functions of language (to describe, explain, persuade etc.) and can allow students to 'experience autonomy in their speaking skills' (Thornbury, 2005: 106). Readers can find an illustration of how to use role play for developing civic engagement in the project presented in Vignette 2.

Debate is a challenging method, one that implies not only developing and refining the communicative competences, but that also has an impact on the axiological dimension of learning, on the student's set of values and attitudes. It is important that both teachers and students understand the difference between school/academic debate – which is a method of learning – and public debate. While in public debate, the result is what counts (as the winner who imposes his/her point of view takes all the credit), in the debate used in school, every participant is a winner in the end as the focus should be mostly on the process: how students are able to prepare in writing, how they can cooperate in a team by negotiating their ideas, how they can build a robust argument, how they can detect the weak points in their opponent's discourse, and can produce counterarguments, or how they can adopt appropriate communicative behaviour during the debate, showing flexibility, tolerance and fair-play. Appropriate and coherent use of language has an important role in the quality of argumentation, as well as the use of nonverbal and paraverbal means of communication which can add persuasive power to their speech.

The first stage of a debate consists in presenting or choosing a proposal from a number offered by the teacher and then listing on a board the arguments and counterarguments students come up with in a brainstorming activity. It is important that the proposal allows for both pros and cons. The students, guided by the teacher, group similar arguments and counterarguments, connect arguments with counterarguments, and delete the ones that are not relevant. The next stage focuses on building the cases. For this purpose, the students work in groups of three to five and develop, starting from the arguments on the board, two sets of arguments: one for the affirmative case (that defends the proposal) and another one for the negative case (that confutes the proposal). This activity stimulates students to accept both perspectives as possible and to find valid insights for both cases. It is only after this activity that they will find out if their team will have the task to defend or to refute the proposal. An ethical issue arises from the fact that the distribution of roles does not necessarily take into consideration the standpoint that is preferred by each student, so they may feel manipulated or encouraged to be hypocrites. But the point here is they are challenged to change perspectives, to place themselves in the shoes of their opponents, in order to get a wider perspective on a concept, a situation or an idea. At the end of this stage, they will receive and discuss the evaluation criteria that will be used by the adjudicator team.

Different formats of the debate are possible (from impromptu debates to the Karl Popper model), but the teacher needs to make sure, irrespective of the choice they make, that every student has a role either in the proposing or opposing team, or in the adjudicator team. The debate can unfold in one or more rounds.

The last stage is the analysis/evaluation of the debate, which will be an activity of reflection for all the participants. The conclusion should not be directed towards accepting a single point of view, but in valuing the quality of arguments and counterarguments of both teams. It is not easy for the teacher to manage an open-ended conclusion, but this is an effective way of giving all students the chance to feel that they have experienced a complex process of learning. They should understand that every proposal can be discussed using pros and cons, and sometimes a problem has more than one solution. This is why, at this stage, the members of the adjudicator team should present their observations, focusing on the performance of each debater against each criterion, and not on the total results of the two teams.

The criteria for evaluating a debate are grouped in three main categories (according to Karl Popper Debate Rules):

• content, referring to the quality of arguments and examples (the arguments' logical correctness, their relevance to the thesis, the relevance of the examples given for each argument, consistency of the arguments offered by all the members of a team, the validity of refutation);

- style, focusing on the way language is used and the persuasive power of the discourse (a. language use – rich vocabulary, ability to clearly formulate ideas; b. manner of speaking – diction and nonverbal communication; c. fluency and persuasiveness; d. attitudes – politeness, flexibility, fair-play, cooperation within the team);
- strategy, looking at the way speakers engage with the topic, respond to other people's arguments and structure what they are saying (the structure of the speech – introduction, body and conclusion, the logical sequence of arguments in the speech of each debater and in the whole line of argumentation developed by all the members of a team, ordering the arguments from the weakest to the most powerful ones, and the effective use of time).

The RFCDC portfolio may be useful for developing new ideas on assessing this type of activity (Council of Europe, 2021). The debate brings into the spotlight values related to language and communication: the social value (based on the interactions among a team and between teams), the cognitive value (acquiring new knowledge, new perspectives on a topic), the individual dimension (forming an image of oneself, of one's abilities as a communicator and reassessing one's own set of values).

Project is a method teachers can use in order to move beyond surface-level learning (Schwartz, 2016), by using a diverse, complex approach to language and communication. Research shows that when students are challenged to discover new concepts and to make meaning out of them on their own, they learn better than when teachers merely deliver the information to them. Starting with brainstorming their ideas on the project's topic through to sharing their work with others, their knowledge on language and communication is activated.

Vignette 2: Civic engagement

Simulation of civic engagement and institutional decision-making provides a good opportunity for teenagers to use specific language functions in order to identify a problem within their community and to establish a solution. This approach is appropriate for students of 7th–8th grades (13–14 years old) or for high school students (14–18 years old) because at these levels they study the way in which the three branches of power work within a democratic society and the way in which citizens can address the institutions in order to provide a solution for a specific need of their community.

They work in small groups to identify a problem that can be solved by authorities by adopting and implementing a law. Each group takes one of the following roles: citizens, representatives of legislative, executive and judicial branches.

Citizens identify a problem and take the necessary steps in order to include it on Parliament's agenda; in this respect, they describe the problem, find arguments and use persuasive writing in order to present the problem.

The representatives of Parliament analyse the citizens' proposal, simulate the decision-making process and write a draft of a law in order to solve the problem identified by the community. They debate in order to solve a problem, carry out research to find solutions for the problem, and write a draft in which they use vocabulary, grammar and register specific to a law.

The Government and local authorities put the law into practice. In this respect, the steps necessary to implement the law are taken into account. They may establish a list with necessary measures to be taken at central and local level or to assign various tasks. The language functions involved in this group activity include researching the ways in which the law can be put in practice, identifying the authorities that are in charge of certain aspects of the identified problem, describing and providing information to local authorities on the subject.

Justice representatives analyse the law and put it in accordance with the constitution of the state. For younger students, they could identify a list of activities that are illegal according to the law and to establish punishments that could be applied in this respect. Students document on the internet ways in which the law can be put in accordance with the constitution. They also write a list of activities that may be regarded as violations of law and write a list of punishments that are to be applied.

Components of intercultural competence and democratic citizenship may be demonstrated as follows:

- Students will interact in small groups in order to simulate/discover the mechanisms of political decisions and citizens' involvement in decision making.
- Students will collaborate to put in place the mechanisms necessary for adopting a law and putting it into practice.
- Students will demonstrate openness to other colleagues' systems of beliefs.
- Students will value democracy and rule of law.

What have students learned from the previous activities about democracy and rule of law?

Knowledge and understanding: separation of power principle, institutions at central and local level.

Skills: critical thinking, self and group reflection, creativity.

Values: valuing diversity, human rights and democratic means of leadership.

Attitudes: respect, tolerance, civic-mindedness.

Assessment

At the end of the activity students' achievements can be assessed using various methods and instruments (observation, case study, self-reflection etc.).

A project-based activity which enables students to do some research, to assume roles and to take decisions in order to solve a community problem produces learning about the ways in which democratic institutions work, the way in which political power is divided in three branches and what are their specific attributes.

Difficulties that teachers may face while applying this learning strategy

- Students' misunderstandings related to institutions and the principle of separation of powers can be overcome by organising some previous lessons in which the subject is explored in some depth while watching movies, analysing fragments of a constitution where the principle is presented etc.;
- Students who are reluctant to participate in group work are assigned to a working group in which they have classmates willing to support them, who are good at sharing tasks and monitoring the outcomes;
- Using relevant sources of information is also a challenge while asking students to do some research. In this respect, teachers should provide some sources of information and should organise an intermediary activity where they can check students' research, materials to be used and give them feedback.

Online forums give students the opportunity to connect with each other virtually and to make their voices heard. The ability to responsibly engage in online discussions is a necessary skill for students living in the 21st century. Teachers can diversify the communicative activities by using digital apps. Before starting to teach a new concept or at the end of a lesson, teachers can post one or more questions on an online forum in order to get an understanding of the knowledge and experience students can bring into the learning process or to obtain feedback on the level of understanding students have gained by the end of the lesson. The forum can also be used for exploring a new topic based on students' different opinions or the different solutions they identify in response to a problem, or to share ideas on current issues. Some advantages of using this form of communication include the following: for the more intro-vert students, online discussions can be less intimidating than speaking in front of the class; the students tend to be more critical about their ideas and how to express them in writing as compared to spelling them out orally; students can better understand and analyse others' ideas or arguments presented in a written form as compared to listening to an oral presentation; students can compare different opinions that are posted on a forum. After writing their answers on the forum, students are usually much more willing to share and comment on their ideas with the whole class.

Conclusion

Teachers who teach CDC and intercultural competences need to understand the role of language and communication in developing these competences across the curriculum and to diversify the communicative activities that develop language awareness (face-to-face or online interac-tions, oral presentations, written responses/essays). In this way, they can give students the opportunity to experience different communicative roles (active listeners, speakers, observers/evaluators of different kinds of dis-course) and challenge them with tasks that require the use of different language functions. In this context, cooperation with L1 teachers in using a common repertoire of strategies for active listening, oral presentation, interaction, reading and writing is beneficial.

Notes

(1) 'The Language Education Perspective: Complexities and Orientations', paper pre-sented at the Prague Conference. Council of Europe, 2007.
(2) https://calec.org/wp-content/uploads/2022/02/Resolution.pdf
(3) CEFR (2001), Chap. 5, 'The CEFR Illustrative Descriptor Scales: Communicative Language Competences'.
(4) 'The mistake is to see language as system as the only way of considering knowledge about language, instead of recognising that it needs to be viewed within a broader language-as-discourse perspective' (Council of Europe, 2020: 11).
(5) https://www.igi-global.com/dictionary/exploratory-talk/51478

References

Barnes, D. (2008) Exploratory talk for learning. In N. Mercer and S. Hodgkinson (eds) *Exploring Talk in School: Inspired by the Work of Douglas Barnes* (pp. 1–16). London: SAGE.

Byram, M. (2021) *Teaching and Assessing Intercultural Communicative Competence: Revisited* (2nd edn). Bristol: Multilingual Matters.

Council of Europe (2001) *Common European Framework of Reference for Languages: Learning, Teaching, Assessment*. Strasbourg: Council of Europe.

Council of Europe (2018) *Reference Framework of Competences for Democratic Culture, Volume 1: Context, Concepts and Model*. Strasbourg: Council of Europe.

Council of Europe (2020) *Reference Framework of Competences for Democratic Culture: Competences for Democratic Culture and the Importance of Language.* Strasbourg: Council of Europe.

Council of Europe (2021) *A Portfolio of Competences for Democratic Culture: Standard Version.* Strasbourg: Council of Europe. https://www.coe.int/en/web/reference-framework-of-competences-for-democratic-culture/portfolios

Cummins, J. (2012) BICS and CALP. In M. Byram and A. Hu (eds) *Routledge Encyclopedia of Language Teaching and Learning* (pp. 83–86). London: Routledge.

Popescu, S. (2008) *HoRor! Cool!* In R. Gheo and D. Lungu (eds) *Tovarăşe de drum* (pp. 191–216). Iaşi: Polirom Publishing House.

Satrapi, M. (2008) *Persepolis: The Story of a Childhood and The Story of a Return.* London: Vintage Publishing.

Schwartz, K. (2016) Five ways to ensure real learning happens in maker-enhanced projects. *KQED Inform. Inspire. Involve.* 30 August 2016. https://www.kqed.org/mindshift/46221/five-ways-to-ensure-real-learning-happens-in-maker-enhanced-projects

Thornbury, S. (2005) *How to Teach Speaking.* London: Pearson Education.

Vollmer, H. and Beacco, J.-C. (2010) *Procedures for Describing Linguistic Competences in 'Non-Language' School Subjects.* Council of Europe Intergovernmental Policy Forum, Geneva, 2–4 November. Strasbourg: Council of Europe.

Vygotsky, L.S. (1962) *Thought and Language.* Cambridge, MA: MIT Press.

6 What Do I Need to Know and Do to Ensure that My Own Subject Contributes to Learners' Plurilingual, Intercultural and Democratic Competences?

Helmut Linneweber-Lammerskitten, Silvia Minardi and Irene Pieper

Introduction

As explained in Chapter 4, language is an important dimension in all subjects and learning situations. In this chapter, the writers focus on the importance of language in three different subjects: Helmut Linneweber-Lammerskitten on mathematics, Silvia Minardi on physics and Irene Pieper on literature. They highlight themes of equity and quality in the context of plurilingual and intercultural education. The three accounts illustrate that, despite commonalities, each subject raises issues specific to the discipline that need to be considered and addressed. In a final section, the three authors bring together their perspectives and take up the leading question of the chapter informed by each other's approach.

The Language Dimension in Mathematics Education

(Helmut Linneweber-Lammerskitten)

Linguistic and communicative competences as constitutive and thus integrated parts of mathematical competences

Though it is widely accepted among mathematicians that mathematics itself can be seen as a universal language for all sciences, awareness of natural language is often missing among mathematicians at universities and mathematics teachers at school. There is still a widespread prejudice that natural language and linguistic competences are less important, if not irrelevant, for the understanding and practice of mathematics. It is further assumed that language or even linguistic competence should not form part of a curriculum for the subject mathematics at school. The Council of Europe document *Items for a Description Of Linguistic Competence in the Language of Schooling Necessary for Learning/Teaching Mathematics (in Secondary Education): An Approach with Reference Points* (Linneweber-Lammerskitten, 2012) challenges this view. It states that linguistic and communicative competences are not only preconditions for participating in mathematics classroom talk and thus preconditions for having mathematical experiences and learning mathematics, but are also constitutive parts of educational standards in mathematics and the OECD/PISA concept of mathematical literacy. The further development of linguistic and communicative competences in mathematics classrooms is a precondition for mastering the numerous communicative situations in learners' future lives, where mathematics plays a role, and thus for their participation in different domains as 'thoughtful, engaged, and reflective citizens in the 21st century' (OECD, 2018: 3). Though the primary intention of the Council of Europe document is to help in creating curricula for the teaching and learning of mathematics which explicitly take into account the discursive and linguistic dimensions of this subject area, it can also help mathematics teachers to recognise the significance of linguistic and communicative competences in teaching and learning mathematics. The text tries to demonstrate that such competences are inherent in the educational values targeted by mathematics education, that they are needed in numerous personal, educational, occupational, public and scientific situations and that they are integrated parts of national educational standards. On this basis, examples and checklists have been developed to help teachers become aware of and foster such competences in mathematics classrooms.

That language competences form preconditions for participating in classroom talk and therefore also in mathematics is generally acknowledged, but the extent to which such competences are needed in mathematics lessons is, as compared to other subjects, often underestimated. The prejudice that communication in mathematics classrooms can and should be restricted to teachers posing a problem in the simplest language (or even better: *without* any normal language, e.g., as $2x^2 - 8x + 6 = 0$) and students answering just by naming a number (or a set of numbers) embedded in a stereotypical phrase '$x_1 = \ldots$ and $x_2 = \ldots$' is still alive. Some parents still complain that the mathematics textbooks and lessons of their children are too 'text-heavy' and if their children were asked in the 'right' way, they would certainly give the right answer. Of course, there should not be any language barrier in the long run in mathematics classrooms, but the goal should be to help students to participate and not to lower the level of language generally over time by adapting and thus discarding the values and objectives of today's standards for mathematical education. The eventual aim should be to remove language barriers in mathematics classrooms, but the goal should be to help students to participate, not to lower the level of language by simplifying and thus discarding the values and objectives of today's standards for mathematical education.

Whether linguistic and communicative competences are constitutive and thus integrated parts[1] of mathematical competences or not, and if they are, to what extent, is dependent on the educational values and objectives of mathematical education, which may differ between countries and may change over time. On an abstract level today's educational values and objectives of mathematical education in western democracies are outlined by the OECD/PISA concept of mathematical literacy, which had and still has much influence on different national educational standards and curricula. It is however important to realise that there is no once-and-for-all-time definition of mathematical literacy, since the concept takes into account that the requirements for learners to be able to participate adequately in the future world are subject to change. For that reason, the definition of mathematical literacy has been slightly modified for different studies (cf. OECD, 2018: 7). For the purposes of the PISA-Studies 2022 mathematical literacy is defined as follows:

> Mathematical literacy is an individual's capacity to reason mathematically and to formulate, employ, and interpret mathematics to solve problems in a variety of real-world contexts. It includes concepts, procedures, facts and tools to describe, explain and predict phenomena. It assists individuals to know the role that mathematics plays in the world and to make the well-founded judgments and decisions needed by constructive, engaged and reflective 21st century citizens. (OECD, 2018: 7)

This and earlier definitions of mathematical literacy make clear that mathematical literacy means much more than low-level knowledge and skills (OECD, 2018: 6). It culminates in the vision of a constructive, engaged and reflective 21st century citizen, who is able (and in fact is dependent on being able) to make well-founded judgements and decisions. Competences in mathematics that encompass linguistic and communicative competences help to make this vision a reality. The verbal constructions used to describe the capacities inherent in mathematical literacy – 'to reason', 'to describe', 'to explain', 'to predict', 'to know the role that mathematics plays in the world' and 'to make the well-founded judgements and decisions' – merge cognitive and linguistic aspects of doing mathematics. In principle mathematics, in contrast to other subjects, can be done in isolation without any social contact and any contact with the world outside, but mathematical literacy as conceived here focuses on citizenship and on participation in different domains and thus includes communicative competences. The change in understanding mathematical competence (with consequences for mathematics education and teaching and learning mathematics) is well expressed in the following passage

> Each country has a vision of mathematical competence and organises their schooling to achieve it as an expected outcome. Mathematical competence historically encompassed performing basic arithmetic skills or operations, including adding, subtracting, multiplying, and dividing whole numbers, decimals, and fractions; computing percentages; and computing the area and volume of simple geometric shapes. In recent times, the digitisation of many aspects of life, the ubiquity of data for making personal decisions involving initially education and career planning, and, later in life, health and investments, as well as major societal challenges to address areas such as climate change, governmental debt, population growth, spread of pandemic diseases and the globalising economy, have reshaped what it means to be mathematically competent and to be well equipped to participate as a thoughtful, engaged, and reflective citizen in the 21st century. (OECD, 2018: 3)

Among typical communication activities in contemporary mathematics classrooms we can find the following (for these and more examples cf. Linneweber-Lammerskitten (2012: 19ff.). The coding is based on the CEFR: R = reception; P = production; I = interaction; M = mediation; O = oral; W = written):

- Learners presenting the results of their homework using visual aids (OWP), comparing the results (OR, WR), asking and answering questions using visual aids (OWI);
- Learners explaining a mathematical conception, an assertion, a rule, a procedure, a proof etc., to others (OWI);
- Learners interact with fellow pupils in group work (WR, WP, OI, OWI) solving a problem or working together in a learning environment.

Since mathematics education should prepare students to use mathematics in real future situations in the personal, educational, occupational, public and scientific domain (cf. Council of Europe, 2001: 45ff.; OECD, 2003: 32) and since the mastering of these situations in most cases presupposes linguistic and communicative competences, mathematics education could and should contribute to developing these competences. This could be done by a problem-based mathematics instruction, which focuses on real problems, discussed in the media (internet, newspaper, TV) like the ones mentioned in the OECD quotation above: 'climate change, governmental debt, population growth, spread of pandemic diseases and the globalising economy …' (OECD, 2018: 3). It is clear that for a satisfactory understanding of these problems and, furthermore, for the discussion of possible solutions, mathematical competences are needed that comprise linguistic and communicative competences. This of course does not mean that conventional mathematics instruction should be totally replaced by problem-based instruction nor that addressing these problems is restricted to mathematics classrooms.

Beside contexts dedicated to big problems, there are a lot of other communicative situations in the personal, educational/occupational, public and scientific domain, where mathematics plays a role and thus presuppose linguistic and communicative competences as integrated parts of mathematical competences (cf. Linneweber-Lammerskitten, 2012: 13ff.).

The need for equity, quality and fairness principles in mathematics education

The overall objectives and values of education, and hence of mathematics teaching and learning too, concern the personal welfare of the individual and the public welfare of society, as well as rights and responsibilities on both sides. Learners are entitled to acquire certain competences, skills, knowledge and experiences as prerequisites for a successful future life. Society in turn places requirements on learners: they are expected to use the opportunities for learning offered to them and to make efforts to acquire the necessary competences for their future, especially for their future role as democratic citizens. Principles of equity, quality and fairness as stated in Chapter 1 are central elements of democratic citizenship and human rights education fostered by the Council of Europe. What is the potential of these ideas with respect to mathematics education and how can we bring the development of mathematical competence and democratic and intercultural competences closer together?

It is noteworthy that one, indeed the first, of the six principles in the *Principles and Standards for School Mathematics* published by the National Council of Teachers of Mathematics [NCTM] (2000)[2] is concerned with equity, quality and support. The book starts with a 'Vision for School Mathematics' which is quite in the spirit of the Council of Europe:

> Imagine a classroom, a school, or a school district where all students have access to high-quality, engaging mathematics instruction. There are ambitious expectations for all, with accommodation for those who need it. Knowledgeable teachers have adequate resources to support their work and are continually growing as professionals. The curriculum is mathematically rich, offering students opportunities to learn important mathematical concepts and procedures with understanding. [...] Teachers help students make, refine, and explore conjectures on the basis of evidence and use a variety of reasoning and proof techniques to confirm or disprove those conjectures. Students are flexible and resourceful problem solvers. Alone or in groups and with access to technology, they work productively and reflectively, with the skilled guidance of their teachers.

Orally and in writing, students communicate their ideas and results effectively. They value mathematics and engage actively in learning it. (NCTM, 2000: 3)

The *principles* the book deals with are derived from this vision in the sense that they answer the question 'which principles are needed to make this vision a reality?'. The *standards* formulate the corresponding set of competences as goals for all students from pre-kindergarten through grade 12 and thus make the vision more concrete. The first principle, which is simply called 'The equity principle', captures the first part of the vision. It states: 'Excellence in mathematics education requires equity – high expectations and strong support for all students' (NCTM, 2000: 12). The primary intention of this principle is to 'challenge a pervasive societal belief [...] that only some students are capable of learning mathematics' (NCTM, 2000: 12). Contrary to this belief, the authors affirm that 'mathematics can and must be learnt by all students', that this is expected of every student by teachers, that these expectations are high and, perhaps the most important point, that 'high expectations for mathematics learning be communicated in words and deeds to all students'. Thus, the equal right to have access to high-quality mathematics instruction is complemented by a kind of promise and a 'weak obligation': that each and every student can and is expected to learn mathematics.

In addition to this normative aspect, the equity principle here has also a psychological and motivational component: each and every student should get the feeling that their teacher trusts them to learn mathematics and this in turn will be a stimulus to apply themselves to do so. In fact, to have low expectations concerning one's own capability in learning and practising still seems to be a greater issue among students in mathematics than in other subjects.

The assertion that 'mathematics can and must be learnt by all students' immediately raises the question to which level mathematics can and must be learnt by all students. The vision, the principles and especially the standards of the NCTM make clear that the expected mathematical knowledge, skills, understanding and competences shared by all students are not confined to a trivial level, but concern high-quality mathematics, i.e. important mathematical concepts and procedures, the making, refining and exploring of conjectures, as well as their confirming or disproving on the basis of evidence, to name just a few. This of course implies and presupposes high-quality mathematics instruction, including support and accommodation for weaker students:

Students with disabilities may need increased time to complete assignments, or they may benefit from the use of oral rather than written assessments. Students who have difficulty in mathematics may need additional resources, such as after-school programs, peer mentoring, or cross-age tutoring. (NCTM, 2000: 13)

Thus far, the equity principle expresses and underpins the vision that all students can and will learn high-quality mathematics due to the fact that they are supported by their teachers, their peers or older students. In addition, the principle entails that everyone is aware of, values and assists this principle.

On the other hand, the principle does not restrict the extent of what should be learnt in mathematics to what can and should be learnt by all students. Furthermore, support and accommodation are not restricted to weaker students:

> Likewise, students with special interests or exceptional talent in mathematics may need enrichment programs or additional resources to challenge and engage them. The talent and interest of these students must be nurtured and supported so that they have the opportunity and guidance to excel. Schools and school systems must take care to accommodate the special needs of some students without inhibiting the learning of others. (NCTM, 2000: 13)

This passage highlights another and possibly conflicting aspect of equity (cf. Chapter 1 of this book), since it seems to postulate equity in consideration of talents and interests and thus to demand an equal amount of support time for all students. If so, this postulate could easily conflict with the vision that all students can and should learn mathematics: if each student gets the same amount of support (measured in time), the weaker students will probably not get enough support to learn the mathematics they are expected to learn. In fact, the passage above does *not* postulate such an equity. Nevertheless, mathematics teachers should be aware that equity in the context of mathematics education is sometimes misunderstood in this way by parents, who complain that the talents of their children are not sufficiently fostered.

The principle of equity as conceptualised in the NCTM, i.e. that high-quality mathematics can and must be learned by all students, can only be realised if every student feels responsible not only for his or her own learning, but also for the learning of his or her peers; moreover if each student values and accepts the equity principle and his or her responsibility for its realisation. Here mathematics education can contribute to the development of education for democratic citizenship and human rights education. Democratic competence in the sense of the *Reference Framework of Competences for Democratic Culture* (Council of Europe, 2018a) (cf. Chapter 1, Figure 1.1 of this book) encompasses *values* (e.g. to value fairness), *attitudes* (e.g. respect and responsibility), *skills* (e.g. empathy; flexibility and adaptability; linguistic, communicative and plurilingual skills; co-operation skills; conflict-resolution skills) and *knowledge* (e.g. knowledge and critical understanding of language and communication). To accept that weaker students need more support is a matter of valuing fairness: to respect these needs and to feel responsible for the learning of others are consequences of valuing fairness, but must nevertheless be learned and further developed, as well as the necessary skills and knowledge.

Conclusion

Mathematics as a school subject is defined by a long and honourable history of mathematics and mathematics education, but may also be influenced by visions for future development. Some of these visions are already manifest: the OECD/PISA concept of mathematical literacy combines mathematical skills/competences in a narrow sense with linguistic and communicative competences. To be mathematically competent in this sense means the ability to think and communicate mathematically in one's own language of thought as well as in the academic language of mathematics.

The vision on the other hand that every student in a mathematics classroom feels responsible not only for their own learning, but also for the learning of their peers, is still far from being realised. But if a certain degree of mathematical competence is a precondition for satisfactory participation in the world of tomorrow, it is a matter of fairness and thus of democratic competence to share this vision.

The Language Dimension in Physics Education

(Silvia Minardi)

'The question is,'
as Alice says to Humpty Dumpty,
'whether you can make words mean so many different things.'
(*Alice in Wonderland*, 1865)

All learning is language learning and 'whatever the subject, all knowledge building in the school context involves working with language' (Beacco *et al.*, 2010: 5). In all subjects, language is the key to understanding and presenting content as well as managing activities (Schleppegrell, 2004; Martin *et al.*, 1987). And yet when it comes to the language used in subject teaching and learning, 'the question of "why" language is used in the way that [it] is often seems less significant than a more immediate focus on "what" is being said' (Cross, 2016: 2).

Based on the assumption that all disciplines are first and foremost discourse communities, we will here present a four-move framework to be used by teachers who want to enact disciplinary literacy teaching practices when teaching their disciplines. Some examples drawn from physics lessons will be used to illustrate how to use the framework.

'Lo so. Ma è difficile da dire!' – The role of language in content learning

What follows is an exchange between a Physics teacher in an Italian high school class and a student during a lesson about magnetic fields.[3]

The slide used by the teacher shows that the magnetic North Pole of the Earth does not coincide with the geographic North Pole, also called the True North, as the magnetic North Pole is located in the Southern Hemisphere. The needle of the compass that indicates the North has a positive polarity and is attracted by the magnetic South Pole, which is instead negative and is located in the north of our planet: therefore, the magnetic South Pole to which the compass refers is conventionally called the Magnetic North.

> T: [reads the slide] 'The magnetic North Pole which is near the True North is a South Pole'. The Magnetic North Pole of the Earth is actually a magnetic south pole.
> St1: The needle of the compass has the North Pole and the South Pole of the needle.
> St2: Okay.
> St3: The North Pole is attracted to the South Pole because opposite poles attract. So the Magnetic South Pole means... I understand that, but it's difficult to explain!

When St3 says 'I understand that, but it's difficult to explain!' she admits her lack of *disciplinary literacy*, i.e. the ability to appropriately participate in the highly specialised communicative practices and discourse of a discipline. Mastering content relies on mastering the communicative practices with which disciplinary knowledge is interpreted and generated (Council of Europe, 2016). Disciplines, as they are referred to in the *Handbook*, are:

(a) domains or cultures, i.e. highly specialised human constructions in which certain kinds of text are read and written for certain purposes and thus require specific kinds of literacy practice.
(b) discourse communities with their own communicative practices and 'just as one has to learn the conventions and practices of a new culture, so does one have to learn the conventions and practices of a discipline' (Moje, 2015: 258).

As regards physics, disciplinary literacy generally includes (a) writing and speaking the language of physics; (b) graphically depicting phenomena; (c) creating and conducting experiments representing phenomena; and (d) translating phenomena into mathematical representations (Hurley & Henry, 2015). The example above and this list of components of physics disciplinary literacy show that in physics, literacy is *multimodal*. It involves not only language as it extends 'to the multiliteracies inherent in science schooling – where language, mathematics, images, specialised symbolic formulae, animations and demonstration apparatus all need to be read as one and reorganised where necessary in assignments and exams' (Doran, 2021: 162). This means that being able to read and write using the language of physics may not be enough.

Teaching disciplinary multiliteracies; examples from physics lessons

St3 in.the example seems unable to organise the meanings she is learning in an appropriate manner as disciplinary learning does not only help the acquisition of knowledge but also produces it. Constructing knowledge requires skills that go much deeper than learning the technical words used in the discipline or memorising a text. From a content teacher's perspective this implies a shift from transmitting information to showing students how to use knowledge in meaningful and relevant ways, thus engaging them in the multiliteracies that make up the discipline.

Developed from Moje's 4E heuristic (2015) (engaging, engineering, examining and evaluating), we suggest a model to embed disciplinary multiliteracy strategies in content teaching practices. It involves four moves:

- engaging learners in disciplinary and literacy practices (*engaging*);
- scaffolding learners' access to those practices (*eliciting*);
- supporting learners as they examine the language dimensions of the discipline (*examining*);
- evaluate 'ways with words' and other forms of representation, and make decisions about their own literacy practice across domains (*evaluating*).

This model can be applied at classroom level when planning and teaching. In the following sections it will be exemplified for physics.

Engaging

This first move refers to the epistemological processes of the discipline. In it, learners are faced with questions about a problem that would be recognisable to members of the discipline. In this move questions are real questions asked in everyday life, questions that stimulate interest and spark curiosity.

In physics, answers to life's fundamental questions come from observation and experimentation. Figure 6.1 is part of a page from a Physics textbook used in Italian high schools. The chapter on Newton's Laws of Motion starts with a question embedded in a problem from daily life, e.g. 'an engineer has to build a ramp for books to be returned in a library...'. The step-by-step procedure suggested by the book to answer the question is the one normally used by physicists and starts with observation.

From a disciplinary literacy point of view this move includes the content practices and literacy strategies shown in Table 6.1.

Eliciting

The second move implies teaching the cognitive strategies useful for text processing. Students are not members of the discipline. Therefore, we

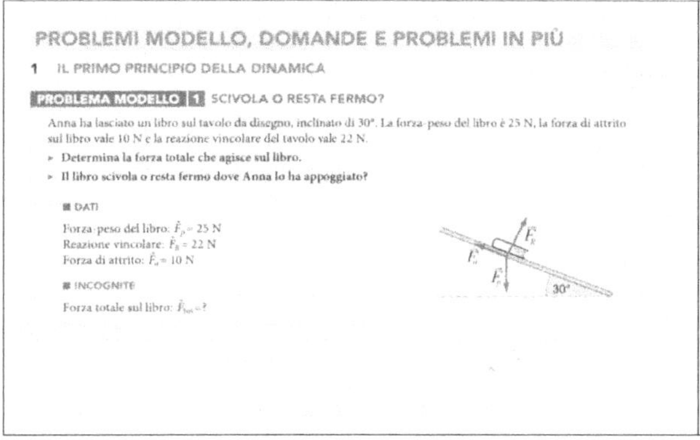
PROBLEMI MODELLO, DOMANDE E PROBLEMI IN PIÙ

1 IL PRIMO PRINCIPIO DELLA DINAMICA

PROBLEMA MODELLO 1 SCIVOLA O RESTA FERMO?

Anna ha lasciato un libro sul tavolo da disegno, inclinato di 30°. La forza-peso del libro è 25 N, la forza di attrito sul libro vale 10 N e la reazione vincolare del tavolo vale 22 N.

- Determina la forza totale che agisce sul libro.
- Il libro scivola o resta fermo dove Anna lo ha appoggiato?

DATI

Forza-peso del libro: $\vec{F}_p = 25$ N
Reazione vincolare: $\vec{F}_R = 22$ N
Forza di attrito: $\vec{F}_a = 10$ N

INCOGNITE

Forza totale sul libro: $\vec{F}_{tot} = ?$

Problem to be solved: *does the book slide down the table or not?*

A step-by-step procedure with data and suggestions to solve the problem. It starts with an observation phase during which data are gathered.

Figure 6.1 Extract from a physics textbook (Amaldi, 2017)

Table 6.1 Engage: content practices and literacy strategies

ENGAGE: problematising a concept or a topic

Content practices	**Disciplinary multiliteracy strategies**
framing a disciplinary problem	* describing the problem students will work on
posing a question	* asking specific questions to guide learners' inquiry
using (written/oral/multimodal) texts to	* reading and writing texts for
– generate questions	– note-taking
– pursue disciplinary questions	– data analysis
– communicate findings	– findings synthesis
returning to questions and disciplinary concepts under study	
reframing the disciplinary problem	

cannot expect them to have the knowledge or the reading, writing and language skills that members of the discipline possess. Teachers should teach – *elicit* – the necessary knowledge, skills and practices for students to make meaning as they engage in the discipline.

From a disciplinary literacy point of view the content practices and literacy strategies shown in Table 6.2 are typical of this move.

Questioning is an important practice in Move 2. The following exchange takes place during a Physics lesson in an Italian high school (Minardi, 2020: 138–139). The teacher wants to introduce the characteristics of the magnetic field and asks a series of questions that help learners to build on what they already know about the electric field.

Table 6.2 Elicit: content practices and literacy strategies

ELICIT: facilitating students' access to and use of texts

Content practices	Disciplinary multiliteracy strategies
activating students' knowledge demonstrating literacy practices and processes	* activating prior knowledge (warm-up activities, introducing key vocabulary, activities to connect students' experiences with new concepts, free-writing/speaking about a topic…)
supporting students' use of literacy practices and processes providing students with an approach for meaning making with multimodal texts	* using a specific literacy practice or process – reminding students of specific literacy strategies when dealing with a text (e.g. using a graphic organiser to organise and remember information) – modelling reading and writing strategies or routines
encouraging metacognitive discussion	* naming norms, assumptions, purposes, tools used by disciplinary experts when processing texts
	* using sentence starters, writing frames for academic discourse
	* naming literacy learning objectives and discussing learning accomplishments

T: [new slide] So let's start the magnetic field. Well. The magnetic field, first of all, is indicated with the letter B. So… What do you see here? [points to the slide], B with an arrow. And what does that mean?	**Il campo magnetico** · Le forze agenti tra magneti si descrivono introducendo il *campo magnetico*, *B*, che *ogni magnete genera* nello spazio circostante. Il vettore $\overline{B}$, **campo magnetico** o **induzione magnetica**, ha: - un modulo - una direzione - un verso
St: That it is a vector quantity.	The 'magnetic field' from a slide used by the teacher
T: That it's a vector quantity. Right. It's indicated by letter B. Next, let's consider the characteristics of this magnetic field. Now, let's try to understand how, let's say, it works. If we have a magnet, this magnet generates… Like when we have a charge, right? What does a charge generate? What does it do around the…	
St: It changes the space.	
T: Right, it changes the characteristics of the space around it. So, changing the characteristics of the surrounding space means that there is a modification. So, in some way, it changes, you understand. Okay. And so, what do we need to understand this field?	
St: A testing area.	

T: A testing area to understand the characteristics, to have people explore what the characteristics of this field are. All right. And so we're talking about electric force. Right? Very well. Similarly, here. We have a magnet. This magnet somehow modifies the surrounding space and this surrounding space is what we call a magnetic field. Right?

The slide contains the following sentence: 'The forces acting between magnets are described by introducing the magnetic field, B, that each magnet generates in its surrounding space'. It is a sentence with characteristics of academic discourse (see section 'Examining' below).

The teacher's first question is used to verbalise a graphic symbol, the horizontal arrow placed above letter B on the slide ('What does it mean?'). The second question ('What does a charge generate? / What does it do around the…?') is used to establish an analogy between a magnet and a charge: it is intended to help students recall a notion they already have. The third question ('What do we need to understand this field?') is used to introduce the next step: a testing area is needed if we want to prove the existence of a magnetic field. In the teacher's discourse, questions come with conjunctions and adverbs all indicating the logical steps of the teacher's speech: 'first of all'; 'so… what do you see?'; 'and what does that mean?'; 'next, let's consider…'; 'now, let's try to understand how…'. From a cognitive point of view, the teacher starts with designation, then she proceeds to explanation and ends with a hypothesis: questioning leads toward more cognitively complex operations.

Examining

This move implies dealing with the linguistic processes of the discipline. Research studies[4] in the discourse of the disciplines have highlighted that academic language is different from everyday language on account of:

(a) the density of information presented;
(b) the level of abstraction of concepts;
(c) the technical nature of concept presentation;
(d) the use of multiple semiotic systems, for example resources of mathematical symbolism, images and language;
(e) the type of voice that dominates.

As regards the language of science we have learnt from Systemic Functional Linguistics that its key features[5] are:

• *Interlocking definitions*: in a definition where words are mutually defining, they are all used to define each other through the intermediacy of two other terms which are assumed to be already known.

- *Lexical density*: this is the measure of the density of information in any passage of text, according to how tightly the lexical items (content words) have been packed into the grammatical structure.
- *Grammatical metaphor*: this is like a metaphor in the usual sense except that, instead of being a substitution of one word for another [...] it is the substitution of one grammatical class, or one grammatical structure, by another; for example, 'his departure' instead of 'he departed'.
- *Technical taxonomies:* in which technicality is elaborated through classification or composition.
- *Grammatical intricacy*: it can be derived from dividing the total number of clauses by the total number of sentences. The higher the index, the more grammatically intricate the text.[6]
- *Nominalisation:* a pervasive feature of academic and particularly scientific texts [...] enables a lot of information to be packed into a nominal element. Students have to process more ideas per clause when they read academic texts and are expected to incorporate more information into the nominal elements of the texts they write. Students who are unfamiliar with this grammatical resource may have difficulty understanding the meanings being constructed.[7]

In Move 3 students learn to look closely at how language is used to represent concepts (Schleppegrell, 2004) in the disciplinary area under study. From a disciplinary literacy point of view content practices and literacy strategies shown in Table 6.3 can be used in Move 3.

In the disciplinary discourse of physics, as in science in general, the use of metaphors plays a major role in bringing about cognitive change during explanations of scientific phenomena (Beger & Jäkel, 2015).

Table 6.3 Examine: content practices and literacy strategies

EXAMINE: analysing the discourse of a discipline

Content practices	Disciplinary multiliteracy strategies
examining – discipline-specific language features: linguistic choices, genre features and conventions – functions of language – implicit messages in an author's way with words	* working with language features, conventions, genres, text types or representations (e.g. graphs) * looking up words in a dictionary * analysing the use of nominalisation; unpacking and repacking nominalisation * recognising sources of ambiguity in a text * comparing and contrasting how language is used in different registers * discussing different ways of expressing the same thing or idea * reading sample paragraphs and identifying features of a specific use of a genre in the discipline

What follows is another exchange in an Italian high school between a Physics teacher and a student on the concept of 'magnetic field' (Minardi, 2020: 242–243). The teacher, with questions referring to the everyday use of a cell phone that students are familiar with, defines the concept of 'field' in academic language. The exchange is based on the word 'campo'/field which, in Italian, is used in the sentence 'non ho campo'. When using a cell phone the sentence 'non ho campo' means 'I don't have a signal'.

(1) T: The key word here is 'campo', 'non c'è campo' means that my cell phone is not connected, but what does the word 'campo' refer to? That is, what is the 'campo' that I don't have? What is the object? Huh? A magnetic field? I've heard of it. Maybe the magnetic field is the Earth's magnetic field, the one that follows the lines, delimits the compass, etc, etc. So, there is an idea of magnetic field, but is it just a magnetic field?

(2) St: It is the net.

(3) T: The net. [nods] But the net is represented by what? I mean how do I have a network that allows my phone to receive the information?

(4) St: The radiations.

(5) T: Radiation, but what kind of radiation are we talking about?

(6) St: Magnetic?

(7) T: Electromagnetic. Right? We talked about that earlier this year when we talked about electromagnetic waves. But then what is the difference between electromagnetic waves and field?

(8) St: The field is constituted by electromagnetic waves.

(9) T: So, the field consists of electromagnetic waves. Better yet, the field is propagated by an electromagnetic wave. 'Non avere campo' [trans: not having a signal] means not receiving the electromagnetic waves that are emitted by an antenna.

What we see here is the teacher comparing and contrasting the use of the same word (campo) in two different registers and as the discourse evolves the language become increasingly academic. The teacher deliberately uses a metaphor as a tool to mediate scientific knowledge and to support the students' understanding of the scientific concept of 'magnetic field'. In the example given the metaphor of the 'field' allows the teacher and the student to negotiate complex information in the explanation of an abstract concept.

Evaluating

This move focuses on the link between everyday and academic discourse to encourage students to *evaluate* 'why, when, and how

Table 6.4 Evaluate: content practices and literary strategies

EVALUATE how, when, and why to use particular discourse features

Content practices	Disciplinary multiliteracy strategies

evaluating
– analogies and differences in ways with words within a discipline
– relationships between texts and the contexts in which they are produced
	* analysing specific discourse features, rhetorical strategies or genres to see if they are effective to reach a specific objective
	
	* comparing and contrasting how texts are constructed and produced across disciplines
	
	* considering how and why physicists use
	  – mathematics
	  – tables, charts and graphs to display data

disciplinary discourses are useful and why, when, and how they are not useful' (Moje, 2015: 268). This move implies teaching how to linguistically navigate within a disciplinary field and its own conventions for communicating and representing knowledge and ideas.

The move includes the content practices and literacy strategies shown in Table 6.4.

Onward and outward

In this section I have illustrated a four-move framework for embedding multiliteracies in everyday content teaching practices. The framework can be used to plan learning units by content teachers. As a tool to guide them in the process here is a list of questions to go through while planning and teaching:[8]

(a) What are the concepts you want to teach?
(b) How might you frame a problem for learners to study?
(c) What texts would be useful for helping them investigate the problem?
(d) Considering the texts you have chosen in (c), what would your students need to know and be able to do in order to understand the big ideas and apply them to the problem under study?

As an experiment, take a piece of text from your content area and analyse the necessary language skills, content knowledge and thinking skills needed to build deep meaning from the text.

Once the text analysis is complete, build a learning unit around the problem you have chosen and then use the text(s) you have analysed. Try building in some of the teaching practices and strategies illustrated in this chapter.

This suggestion may appear ineffective to content teachers who do not see the language dimensions as challenging in content learning. And this is often the case for disciplines where there is universally agreed terminology across languages and contexts, e.g., Physics and other Natural Sciences, as research on content and language integrated learning (CLIL) (Airey, 2012; Lo, 2017; Minardi, 2020) has shown. A first step could be to design tailor-made programmes for teachers in different school contexts, at different stages of their career, teaching different subjects and under the aegis of a school-based approach to teacher education with collaboration between language and content subject teachers in the same school, together with support and mentoring from academic researchers or teacher educators in the field of language education.

Conclusion

Disciplinary literacies in Physics, as in any other subject, imply being able to take an active part in the discourse community of Physics. Students learn Physics through a particular language while learning the language of Physics, which they need if they are to become literate in the discipline. With the aim of helping Physics teachers to develop literacies while teaching their subject a four-move framework has been illustrated. The perspective is to encourage Physics teachers, as teachers of all subjects, to see the language not as a barrier but as a resource in learning any content matter.

The Language Dimension in Literature Education

(Irene Pieper)

Why it makes sense to consider literature when asking about the languages of schooling and language across the curriculum

It may come as a surprise that we deal with literature in a section on the notion of language across the curriculum. In many, perhaps even in most, school systems literature does not form a subject of its own, but is part of 'language as subject' from primary to secondary education.

Of course, a subject like Danish in Denmark or French in France deals with texts in a broad sense and covers literature and other media as part of its core areas. However, there are good reasons to consider literature separately, and the potential of literature education can best be elaborated upon where literature is considered independently in curricular reflection.

The line of argument in this chapter draws on and extends the thinking in the paper *Items for a Description of Linguistic Competence in the Language of Schooling Necessary for Learning/Teaching Literature* (Pieper, 2011).[9]

Two aspects seem central within our framework of plurilingual and intercultural education. Firstly, literature is a rich source not only for encounters with the most varied, enriching and often surprising use of language that allows learners to gain awareness of the potential of language in a broad sense not only as a means of communication, but also for moving beyond the actual and offering insights into how the world can be conceived through art. Since literature will both be culturally bound and transform cultural boundaries these insights are of particular value for creating intercultural awareness. Besides, in recent years more and more plurilingual authors increasingly transcend linguistic boundaries and reflect experiences of being at home in more than one language.

Secondly, the notion of literature does not only apply to printed or other media in the material sense but also to a cultural praxis that is both individual and social. Reading literature may often be a private praxis – with a huge potential for strengthening personal resources. It may also be a social praxis where readers exchange their views on a piece of literature, recommend books, visit book clubs or attend events such as readings by authors. Furthermore, the performative arts (theatre, film, opera ...) are strongly linked to social practices. It is particularly the entitlement to engage in cultural practices of both kinds that education should grant.

The link between literature and literary praxis is key to grasping the core role of literature as contributing to personal development and identity formation. Students should thus be granted the resources to take part in the various communicative situations where literature plays a role. Hence, it is essential that the curriculum pays attention to the linguistic repertoire students need to have at their disposal.

It should also be noted that the curricular concept of literature has developed over time. In the 19th century with the formation of a general education in mother tongue up to upper secondary the notion of literature was generally linked to the notion of literary canon and cultural heritage. It had a key role particularly in higher education where it was expected to support nation building. Nowadays, given the radical changes in societies and their educational systems as well as the evolution of the media, literature is understood in a far broader way. Highly valued literary works still form part of this more heuristic notion, but so too do other media, including multimodal printed and digital texts. Furthermore, literature addressing young readers has found its place in the literature classroom, too. Besides, 'literature' may be used not only for products and practices around pieces of art, but also for pragmatic texts, although the connotation of literature as art works showing literary characteristics remains strong and even the rather elitist connotation of the 19th century may sometimes show.

This development of the notion of literature is very important when considering the larger educational context. Aiming at equity and quality in education, it is essential that rich learning opportunities are provided for all students and that all students are entitled to enriching encounters with literature in a broad sense. Sometimes it may, at first sight, seem more appropriate to insist on literacy education in a narrower sense particularly with students who struggle with the acquisition of basic competences. Thus, the curriculum may stress reading comprehension and reading strategies and mainly deal with pragmatic or factual texts, be they in print or digital. However, though a sound basis in literacies is crucial for learning in all subjects and of course for learning far beyond schooling, it would be wrong if a narrow form of literacy education dominated at the expense of literature. Encounters with literature as art – including those works that are highly valued and/or used to belong to the canon – allow for participation in cultural memory and offer opportunities to engage in key questions of humanity and culture.

An example from a Berlin classroom: Lessing's 'Nathan the Wise'

The following case goes back to the author's visit to a 9th grade classroom (with students 14 to 17 years old) in a comprehensive school in Berlin.

A student was teaching the 9th graders as part of her Master's studies for a degree in teaching. As her university supervisor I had received an extended lesson plan the day before my visit and was impressed by the choice of text. The student who I call Farah here was teaching Gotthold Ephraim Lessing's play *Nathan the Wise* (1779), a piece that some teachers might consider demanding even in upper secondary. The piece is translated into some 40 languages and can certainly be considered a German contribution to world literature. Reading the 18th-century play with students in grade 9 seemed quite a challenge, since students would probably experience difficulties with the unfamiliar language. Besides, the reflective dimension is demanding, since it addresses the issue of religious tolerance as a central theme.

The story is situated in 12th-century Jerusalem during the Third Crusade and links a rather dramatic family plot around Nathan the Wise and his foster-daughter Recha to reflections on truth and morality which appear to be at risk because of the prejudiced and unreasonable behaviour of some powerful protagonists. These protagonists also represent the monotheistic religions Judaism, Christianity and Islam. In the play it is through Nathan the Wise, a respected and wealthy Jew, that the conflicts are resolved and an enlightened encounter with religion in a spirit of tolerance becomes a reality at least on stage.

The lesson I visited dealt with the Ring Parable. Here, the issue of religious tolerance is dealt with in the format of a tale: The Sultan Saladin asks Nathan which religion is true. Nathan answers via a story about a father and three sons. Over generations fathers of the family had passed on a magical ring to the son they loved most. The magic power of the ring consists in making the person who wears it pleasing in the eyes of God and humankind. The current father has a problem of allocating the ring to one of his three sons, as he loves them equally. To solve his problem he has replicas made and hands them over separately to each of them. When the sons work out that they have all received a ring they are desperate to know which one is the original. They go to a judge for help, who explains to them that the issue cannot be solved by comparing the rings since they cannot be distinguished from each other anymore. Hence, the main task for each son would be to behave in a way which makes him pleasing in the eyes of God and humankind.

For the lesson, Farah focused on the question about which religion was the right one. The 9th graders were to grasp the allegorical character of the parable and then work out that it would be impossible to declare one religion more true than another, just as it was impossible for the sons to distinguish between the rings. They had been asked to read the relevant part of the play as homework but to stop before the sons met the judge so that they could compare their solutions to the judgement Lessing provided. Watching the students working with the text I was not surprised that it took a little while until a common understanding of the basic storyline had been achieved – despite using an edition which provides linguistic help and even textual changes for readability. However, once students had grasped the plot, they engaged in their task and were committed to solving the judge's problem or rather to reflect upon the key question the teacher had put to them. There was a remarkable seriousness in the room strongly supported by Farah's attitude towards both theme and task.

When reflecting on the lesson with her later, Farah explained that she had deliberately chosen Lessing's work because she thought it relevant for dealing with the question of religious truth in a multicultural and multi-religious environment. It was very clear to her that Lessing's play addresses an urgent issue of today's societies, including the class she was currently teaching, and that it does so in a meaningful way. It was impressive that the question whether the text would initially be demanding and not immediately inviting or engaging for the students did not hinder her at all. The commitment I had witnessed from both teacher and students proved her right. I also learnt that Farah's family had immigrated from Palestine and that Farah, who is Muslim, looks back to an important encounter with Lessing's 'Nathan the Wise' at school when she was a student herself.

In the context of the present book and our concern with values, quality and equity in education, it would be most interesting to come back to *Nathan the Wise* and read it with regard to intercultural relationships: the plea for tolerance is relevant not only to religions, but more generally with regard to the value-basis today's diverse societies might need. With respect to the specific issue of language and learning, it is evident – and was made evident to the 9th graders – that it is important to engage with the linguistic formulation of ideas, here by the need for them to understand the language of another epoch.

How to root literature in a curriculum to support plurilingual, intercultural and democratic education

In order to specify the potential of literature in education, four relationships should be considered: the relationship between literature and reading, the question how literature relates to key questions of humankind, the link between literature in its various forms and the associated practices, and the link between literature, media and mediality.

Reading literacy in various situations of reading and assessing the textual demands

As mentioned above, literature today is seen as a broad concept. Within the curriculum of language as a subject, literature in the sense of printed texts plays an important role. Particularly since the PISA surveys, considerable attention has been paid to reading literacy. Teaching and learning with literature can benefit from the associated research and development in at least four respects:

(1) It has become increasingly obvious that constructing meaning from text is a demanding process. Thus, comprehension is not achieved more or less automatically even with secondary students. Rather, the process of creating sense will often need careful guidance through specific tasks and the use of strategies in sensitive ways. In Farah's classroom, time was allocated to making sure students could develop meaning from the text. Teachers need to support the process of constructing meaning by prompts or other tasks relating to all levels of the text, to sentences, paragraphs, line of argument, not just to the meaning of single words. Textual meaning is not achieved via isolated information on vocabulary.

(2) While the above holds true for reading irrespective of the genre, literary texts in a narrower sense in particular offer rich opportunities for developing reading competences: literariness is often linked to ambiguities and gaps when it comes to textual information (e.g. is the message of this story, poem, play, altogether clear?) and to experiences of alienation and surprise with respect to the way language is used and a plot is developed (think of the murderer in crime fiction, to give one obvious example). Moreover, a literary text might require the construction of further meaning beyond the textual world that is presented, as allegoric or parabolic texts like the 'Ring Parable' show. Of course, there will be clues in and around the text that help.

Hence, reading literary texts offers specific opportunities to gain insights into what we do when we read and to follow our own reading processes, thus developing metacognitive awareness when reading. At the same time, well-chosen stories will attract student-readers and help them to become curious about what will be told, thus potentially feeding motivation for reading and supporting the development of a

habitual practice of reading. As the latest PISA study has demonstrated again, educational institutions should pay attention to supporting such developments particularly since habitual reading among
students is declining. In this context, it is noteworthy that in a recent
study on literature education in both Switzerland and Germany we
found that students of grade 8 would opt for reading books with a
strong story line that keeps readers engaged in the text (Siebenhüner
et al., 2019). Given the value of literature as an important resource for
personal development it is important that education constantly opens
paths into reading and pays attention to potential and actual interests
of the students.

(3) The way reading processes are analysed helps with understanding
those processes that are integral to digital rather than printed texts.
These reading processes have become more or less habitual in learners
who spend a lot of time reading on the web. Where texts are not only
arranged in a linear fashion on the page, but are multimodal and
hyperlinked, processes of meaning-making are characterised by inferences between text, images and other forms of information to a larger
extent than before.

These processes are also characterised by navigation since readers
develop their own pathways rather than following the sequence of
lines and pages. They need to evaluate the textual information on the
spot: Does this text offer what I am looking for? Should I rather move
on, e.g. via a hyperlink? Reading many texts at the same time – poly-
textual reading – has become a new challenge.

Furthermore, texts published on the web may draw readers into
interactive encounters with authors and other readers. For example,
the more recent genre of InstaPoetry asks not only for likes, but also
for other comments – and may inspire students to connect reading and
writing. Some platforms offer possibilities to comment on reading
experiences and exchange them with others, getting suggestions for
other reads and developing one's own perception of texts. The processes linked to reading (and writing) in digital contexts need to be
addressed in the classroom; the options social reading platforms offer
should be taken into account.

(4) Not only the different processes of reading need attention, but also the
textual demands of different kinds of texts. These demands need to be
analysed: What is the major theme of the text? Can it be grasped
easily? Does the text contain a large amount of hidden information?
What inferences will students need to make in order to achieve text
comprehension? How demanding is this text for the students of this
grade and the anticipated competences? What are the specifics of the
text that need attention, e.g. complex syntactical structures because
of verse and metre plus a vocabulary that is partly unfamiliar because
of the historical distance (as in *Nathan the Wise*)?

Table 6.5 Aspects of text complexity © Council of Europe

Vocabulary: specific and unfamiliar/outdated or common and current
Syntax: length of sentences and complexity
Text length (in prose), density (in poetry)
Text genre: meeting or varying the familiar/the pattern
Arrangement of plot and storyline: action/suspense easy conceivable or not; several lines or straightforward arrangements; number of characters; chronology and its explicitness
Perspectives: clear and few, unclear and many
Aesthetic structures/tropes: indirectness, imagery (metaphor/symbolic language), irony
Layers of meaning
Demands on prior knowledge and interests

These questions of form need to be focused upon along with the question of the meaningfulness and relevance that a piece of work can have for students at a particular stage of development. The aspects of text complexity have been identified as shown in Table 6.5 (Pieper, 2011: 14).

With multimodal literary texts such as graphic novels, illustrated works or audio- and audio-visual texts (film and theatre), the relationship between the different modes should be considered. How does pictural or auditive information relate to textual information, how does multimodality help to develop meaning or even challenge it, e.g. if pictural information contradicts textual information?

Particularly when choosing books, the various aspects of the text should be considered in light of the competences students may show as readers. A helpful instrument has been proposed by a group of international teacher educators and researchers who developed the Literary Framework for Teachers in Secondary Education, LiFT-2.[10] Here, profiles of learners of different grades are distinguished and the instrument helps to reflect on the notion of meaningfulness for learners. For each level the students may achieve, different books seem appropriate, and a guideline is provided which helps to assess complexity with longer narratives and link the assessment to students' profiles, the so-called bookscan. This instrument also proves to be inspiring where teachers discuss the choice of texts with colleagues and compare books along different criteria.[11]

Literature as a source for engaging in key questions of personal, social and cultural life

One potential of literature (in the sense of literary texts) is that the rich and artistic use of language, the ways formal traditions are dealt with and fictional worlds are set up through language are strongly linked to meaningfulness. Key questions of humankind are taken up and readers are invited to engage in societal and personal issues in various ways.

Particularly through literature, students can grasp the strong link between personal existence and the societal and political context. In *Nathan the Wise* audience and readers will suffer with the protagonists and be able to grasp how the dramatic family history is linked to the question of truth. Very often, canonical texts are strong in addressing moral values, also in a critical perspective, e.g. towards the question of leadership and responsibility as is the case with many plays by Shakespeare. But this is not exclusive to classic literature that is highly valued. Current youth novels also offer opportunities. They may allow for insights into societal structures of discrimination, and engage students in critical considerations of the link between individual lives and society in a given context. For example, the novel *The Hate U Give* (2017) by American author Angie Thomas starts with the death of a young black man who is shot by the police. It presents a case of racism that seems immediately relevant to many adolescent readers within a very engaging plot. The book has been very well received both as a private read and in classrooms, not least because it allows for identification with the female main character, Starr. Since readers often develop a certain closeness to the literary protagonists, they get insights into psychological phenomena which might otherwise be beyond their own reach. As a consequence, the way literature addresses key questions of humankind is particularly strong because readers follow the plot with the eyes and emotions of the protagonists. As the example of *Nathan the Wise* has shown, literature may also invite explicit reflection. Of course, the classroom is a privileged place to make room for engaged and critical encounters with the questions raised.

Following this line of argument, the *Reference Framework of Competences for Democratic Culture* (RFCDC) suggests that texts are selected that have a potential for students to engage in social and political issues (Council of Europe, 2018b: 39). Considering the contribution of education to educating students for democratic citizenship, it is evident that literature education can play a significant role when attention is paid to the ethical, societal and political dimension of literature.

Literature, interaction and praxis

It has already been mentioned that dealing with literature often takes place in a communicative frame. On a more fundamental level, it has been argued that processes of learning and of reaching meaningfulness depend on co-constructive situations. As Lev Vygotsky (1978) has shown, learners interact with competent others and thus may develop within the zone of proximal development. For literature, the notion of co-construction and interaction is not only rooted in this concept of learning but also in the fact that literature forms part of cultural practices: meaningfulness is often established in social settings.

The classroom is an important place for experiencing the social roots of constructing meaning. Discussing an attractive and/or thought-provoking film, a short story or a novel is often appreciated by students since it offers options for exchanging views and developing one's own perceptions, reconsidering opinions and more. Farah's classroom also showed that these discussions often move beyond the actual experiences of the students, who can thus develop new insights into what might have been unfamiliar, and perhaps link it to their own experiences. The classroom is also a place where critical encounters with literature and other media have their place.

A major concern nowadays is to enable students to critically assess content reliability on the web and avoid being manipulated, e.g. by so-called 'Fake News'. Appreciation of experiences as well as a critical assessment of what is offered in the media can be supported through appropriate communicative settings. This holds true both for media which are experienced as familiar and rather easily processed, and for demanding pieces of work which will seldom form part of students' leisure reading. It should be considered a core aim of literature education to grant students options for connecting communications based on media in various forms consciously and in purposeful ways. Given the evolution of social media it seems appropriate to reconsider this potential of literature education not only with regard to media reception, whether of written texts, films or theatre, but also with regard to other forms of practices mediated through digital media, not least to enhance critical awareness for participating in the respective practices.

Enhance reflections on media and mediality

The language subjects, whether the language of schooling or foreign languages, are the subjects where language as a medium is at the centre: a medium students learn to master and, particularly with first or standard language education, a medium students reflect upon. One potential of literature education is to enhance reflections on a variety of media, whether traditional printed or auditive and audio-visual media or the more recent digital space which is blurring the borders between production and reception to a large extent.

As argued above, the notion of literature should be considered as highly inclusive with regard to other media. It is thus with literature education that the dynamics of change and development with media can be addressed particularly well. Hence, literature education in the 21st century also aims at enabling students to participate in a thoughtful and enriching use of various media and develop a critical awareness of their potentials and risks. Thus, literature education reaches out towards the general demands of media literacy as a core competence for the 21st century.

Conclusion

I have argued that literature should be considered in a broad way so as to make sure that a wide variety of media can be addressed, their complexities and potentials assessed, and their emancipative and enriching use granted. However, we should also be aware of the huge potential of literature in the more traditional sense of the literary referring to aesthetic texts: both on a personal and a social level, with regard to both cultural heritages and to intercultural relationships, the potential of the literary in education is huge, as can be said of the arts in general. This potential should be open to all students whatever their linguistic and social backgrounds so as to support a participative education where all students are entitled to the richness of the arts as a way of conceiving, shaping and even changing the world.

The Core Question Revisited: What Do I Need to Know and Do to Ensure That My Own Subject Contributes to Learners' Plurilingual, Intercultural and Democratic Competences?

First and foremost, it is important to acknowledge the key role of language in subject learning. The language dimension of domain-specific learning processes is still underestimated. In order to ensure that students of various language backgrounds and linguistic abilities are entitled to rich learning opportunities it is essential that teachers perceive the content of their teaching in the light of its linguistic aspects: content may not only be language-based like in literature; approaching any subject matter means to deal with it via language. If the language base of learning is not acknowledged this will be particularly hard for students who are not yet well equipped linguistically and/or need specific support. Thus, the issue of language in subject matter is essential to an education that provides equal opportunities for all.

The three sections of this chapter highlight different facets of the core question from the point of view of three different content subjects, but what has been said with respect to any one of these can help as a guideline for the other two and for other content subjects.

Ambiguities as mentioned in the section on physics are also an issue in mathematics notation and a possible barrier for students. For example, if $4a = 4\frac{1}{2}$, then a is not equal to $\frac{1}{2}$, but to $\frac{9}{8}$, or even worse, if $34569 = 3456b$, then b is not equal to 9, but to $\frac{3841}{384}$; in geometry a, b and c are often used as names for the sides of a triangle and at the same time for the length of these sides, but an equation like $a^2 + b^2 = c^2$ does not make sense in the first case. Examples like these can be used to reflect on ambiguities in notation, on conventions, or more generally on the language dimension of mathematics. An adapted version of the 4e-method seems to be helpful as a guideline.

The notion of mathematical literature should not be restricted to contemporary texts and exercise books as media to teach and learn mathematics. It should include all sorts of texts, e.g. newspaper and journal articles, where mathematics is used or applied and mathematical understanding is needed. It should also include mathematical texts reflecting cultural heritage or intercultural relationship, e.g. Euclid's *Elements* or Plato's *Meno*.

For language to really become a tool of equity and democracy it is important to provide all students with rich learning opportunities. These are missed whenever language is seen as a barrier or an obstacle and the temptation to give simplified versions of a notion (see the section on mathematics) or to avoid complex literary texts full of ambiguities and subtle meanings (see the section on literature) becomes strong.

Reconsidering the section on literature in the light of the section on mathematics and the section on physics, it seems particularly important that equity in literature education is linked to offering the richness of literary texts to the students as well as to offering support for all students in coming to terms with literature and to benefit from its potential for their personal development. This is essential for an inclusive approach.

Literature often appeals to experiences and emotions but responding to it may be demanding in many ways. Taking up the key features of academic language as spelt out in the chapter on physics it seems noteworthy that learners will have to learn to respond to literature in different modes. One mode is close to the language of experience and everyday life, the other is shaped by abstraction and aspects of academic language. Both need to be dealt with in education.

In short, teachers need to apply a differentiated view to the language dimension of subject matter teaching and learning. Cross-disciplinary exchanges among colleagues that should of course extend beyond the three subjects addressed above will be beneficial in creating an inclusive curriculum which supports all learners to develop plurilingual, intercultural and democratic competences.

Notes

(1) By 'integrated parts' I mean that linguistic and communicative competences are not just preconditions or nice-to-have by-products of learning mathematics, but constitutive parts of the concept of mathematical competence.
(2) The National Council of Teachers of Mathematics (NCTM) is the world's largest mathematics education organization. *The Principles and Standards for School Mathematics* had – as well as the PISA-concept of mathematical literacy – a great influence on the development of educational standards for mathematics in Western Europe.
(3) The lesson was in Italian, the language of schooling. The translation into English is here provided by the author to help the reader understand the situation.
(4) See Veel, 1997, 2006; Schleppegrell, 2004; Coffin, 2006; Fang and Schleppegrell, 2008; Vollmer, 2010; Beacco *et al.*, 2010; Linneweber-Lammerskitten, 2012; Polias, 2016.
(5) The list has been drawn from Halliday and Martin (1993) and Fang (2016).
(6) Fang (2016: 196).
(7) Fang *et al.* (2006: 254).
(8) The questions have been adapted from Moje and Speyer (2014).

(9) See also *Text, Literature and 'Bildung'* (Pieper ed. 2007).
(10) http://www.literaryframework.eu
(11) See here for more information and the book-scan: http://www.literaryframework.eu/

References

Airey, J. (2012) I don't teach language. The linguistic attitudes of physics lecturers in Sweden. *AILA Review* 25, 64–79.
Amaldi, U. (2017) *L'Amaldi per i licei scientifici. Blu. Idee per insegnare.* Bologna: Zanichelli. https://online.scuola.zanichelli.it/amaldiscientificiblu2ed-files/PaginePDF/Cap02_PaginePDF_AmaldiBlu.pdf
Beacco, J.-C., Coste, D., van de Ven, P.-H. and Vollmer, H. (2010) *Language and School Subjects: Linguistic Dimensions of Knowledge Building in School Curricula.* Strasbourg: Council of Europe.
Beger, A. and Jäkel, O. (2015) The cognitive role of metaphor in teaching science: Examples from physics, chemistry, biology, psychology and philosophy. *Philosophical Inquiries* 3 (1), 89–112.
Coffin, C. (2006) *Historical Discourse: The Language of Time, Cause and Evaluation.* London: Continuum.
Council of Europe (2001) *Common European Framework of Reference for Languages: Learning, Teaching, Assessment* (CEFR). Strasbourg: Council of Europe. www.coe.int/t/dg4/linguistic/source/framework
Council of Europe (2016) Mathematics and its characteristic contribution to language education. In *A Handbook for Curriculum Development and Teacher Training: The Language Dimension in All Subjects* (pp. 70–73). https://rm.coe.int/a-handbook-for-curriculum-development-and-teacher-training-the-languag/16806af387
Council of Europe (2018a) *Reference Framework of Competences for Democratic Culture.* Vol. 1. Strasbourg: Council of Europe. https://rm.coe.int/prems-008318-gbr-2508-reference-framework-of-competences-vol-1-8573-co/16807bc66c
Council of Europe (2018b) *Reference Framework of Competences for Democratic Culture.* Vol. 3. Strasbourg: Council of Europe.
Cross, R. (2016) Language and content 'integration': The affordances of additional languages as a tool within a single curriculum space. *Journal of Curriculum Studies* 48 (3), 1–21.
Doran, Y.J. (2021) Multimodal knowledge: Using language, mathematics and images in physics. In K. Maton, J.R. Martin and Y.J. Doran (eds) *Teaching Science: Knowledge, Language, Pedagogy* (pp. 162–184). Abingdon: Routledge.
Fang, Z. (2016) Academic language. In J. Liontas (ed.) *TESOL Encyclopedia of English Language Teaching.* New York: Wiley. https://onlinelibrary.wiley.com/browse/book/10.1002/9781118784235/toc
Fang, Z. and Schleppegrell, M.J. (2008) *Reading in Secondary Content Areas: A Language-based Pedagogy.* Ann Arbor, MI: University of Michigan Press.
Fang, Z., Schleppegrell, M.J. and Cox, B. (2006) Understanding the language demands of schooling: Nouns in academic registers. *Journal of Literacy Research* 38 (3), 247–273.
Halliday, M.A.K. and Martin, J. (1993) *Writing Science: Literacy and Discursive Power.* London: Falmer.
Hurley, B.P. and Henry, M.P. (2015) Using a disciplinary literacy framework to teach high school physics: An action research study. *i.e.: Inquiry in Education* 7 (1), Article 3.
Linneweber-Lammerskitten, H. (2012) *Items for a Description of Linguistic Competence in the Language of Schooling Necessary for Teaching/Learning Mathematics (in Secondary Education). An Approach with Reference Points.* Strasbourg: Council of Europe. https://rm.coe.int/16806adb7e&usg=AOvVaw3PP3FbK6XfrKh-e1lRbJs_

Lo, Yuen Yi (2017) Development of the beliefs and language awareness of content subject teachers in CLIL: Does professional development help? *International Journal of Bilingual Education and Bilingualism* 22 (7), 818–832.

Martin, J.R., Christie, F. and Rothery, J. (1987) Social processes in education. In I. Reid (ed.) *The Place of Genre in Learning* (pp. 58–82). Geelong: Centre for Studies in Literary Education, Deakin University Typereader Publications.

Minardi, S. (2020) *Lingua, Apprendimento e Discipline. La fisica in lingua di scolarizzazione e in CLIL/AIDEL*. Pisa: Pacini Editore.

Moje, E.B. and Speyer, J. (2014) Reading challenging texts in high school: How teachers can scaffold and build close reading for real purposes in the subject areas. In K. Hinchman and H. Thomas (eds) *Best Practices in Adolescent Literacy Instruction* (2nd edn, pp. 207–231). New York: Guilford.

Moje, E.B. (2015) Doing and teaching disciplinary literacy with adolescent learners: A social and cultural enterprise. *Harvard Educational Review* 85 (2), 254–278.

National Council of Teachers of Mathematics (NCTM) (2000) *Principles and Standards for School Mathematics*. Reston, VA: National Council of Teachers of Mathematics.

OECD (2003) *PISA 2003 Assessment Framework: Mathematics, Reading, Science and Problem Solving Knowledge and Skills*. Paris: OECD Publications. https://www.oecd.org/education/school/programmeforinternationalstudentassessmentpisa/pisa2003assessmentframeworkmathematicsreadingscienceandproblemsolvingknowledgeandskills-publications2003.htm

OECD (2018) *PISA 2021 Mathematics Framework (Draft). November.* https://www.oecd.org/pisa/pisaproducts/pisa-2021-mathematics-framework-draft.pdf

Pieper, I. (2011) *Items for a Description of Linguistic Competence in the Language of Schooling Necessary for Learning/Teaching Literature (at the end of compulsory education). An Approach with Reference Points*. Strasbourg: Council of Europe. http://www.coe.int/t/dg4/linguistic/langeduc/BoxD2-OtherSub_en.asp#s4

Pieper, I. (ed.), Aase, L., Fleming, M. and Sâmihăian, F. (2007) *Text, Literature and 'Bildung'*. Strasbourg: Council of Europe.

Polias, J. (2016) *Apprenticing Students into Science: Doing, Talking, Writing and Drawing Scientifically*. Stockholm: Hallgren and Fallgren.

Schleppegrell, M.J. (2004) *The Language of Schooling: A Functional Linguistics Perspective*. Mahwah, NJ: Erlbaum.

Siebenhüner, S., Depner, S., Fässler, D., Kernen, N., Bertschi-Kaufmann, A., Böhme, K. and Pieper, I. (2019) Unterrichtstextauswahl und schülerseitige Leseinteressen in der Sekundarstufe I: Ergebnisse aus der binationalen Studie *TAMoLi*. *Didaktik Deutsch* 47, 44–64. urn:nbn:de:0111-pedocs-210158.

Veel, R. (1997) Learning how to mean – scientifically speaking: Apprenticeship into scientific discourse in the secondary school. In F. Christie and J.R. Martin (eds) *Genre and Institutions: Social Processes in the Workplace and School* (pp. 161–195). London: Continuum.

Veel, R. (2006) The 'Write it Right' project. In R. Whittaker, M. O'Donnell and A. McCabe (eds) *Language and Literacy: Functional Approaches* (pp. 66–92). London: Continuum.

Vollmer, H.J. (2010) *Items for a Description of Linguistic Competence in the Language of Schooling Necessary for Learning/Teaching Sciences (at the end of compulsory education). An Approach with Reference Points*. Strasbourg: Council of Europe,

Vygotsky, L.S. (1978) *Mind in Society*. Cambridge, MA: MIT Press.

7 What Do I Need to Know about Quality and Equity in the Assessment of Plurilingual, Intercultural and Democratic Competences and the Use of Portfolios?

Claudia Borghetti and Martyn Barrett

Introduction

Assessment plays a major role in education. At the very least, it is essential for understanding whether instructional practices have resulted in the achievement of the intended learning outcomes. In addition, assessment is important for identifying learning outcomes that have not been achieved, and obstacles or difficulties that learners may be encountering. This in turn helps teachers to monitor and improve their methods and practices, as well as learners to become aware of their own learning difficulties and strategies. Assessment is also a key tool for educational systems and societies at large, as it provides evidence that their values and principles are being passed on to younger generations.

Assessment can also impact seriously on equity in access to quality education. In some educational systems, results in tests or exams are used in streaming practices, which separate learners into different classes based on their abilities and achievements. In cases where the streaming is accompanied by a different curriculum, the consequence can be the introduction of significant educational inequities.[1] In addition, poor results in assessment are one of the principal reasons why many learners drop out of education. Assessment, being an interface between school and society, thus potentially represents a major social barrier for many learners.

While in many of these cases assessment is possibly more a visible manifestation than a cause of inequalities in education, it can itself also be a further source of educational discrimination when it fails to recognise (and encourage) learners' distinctive personalities, social needs and learning diversities. This may happen for example when assessment tasks presume a specific background knowledge that only majority-group learners have, or when the difficulties of taking a test in a second language are ignored. In this sense, we argue, pursuing equity in assessment is a vital way to ensure both equity and quality in education more generally.

Based on the considerations above, this chapter focuses on how developing plurilingual, intercultural and democratic competences in schools, colleges or universities, when viewed from the perspective of quality and equity in education, requires the use of responsible and ethical ways to assess such competences. In this respect, it will be argued that portfolios represent a highly suitable method for assessing plurilingual, intercultural and democratic competences, because they can help to ensure that assessment practices are not only accurate, but also mindful of the consequences of assessment, respectful of learners' differences, and attentive to the value of everyone's background, learning, and personal and social needs. Portfolios owe most of these features to their being ideal methods to use for formative assessment. Even though they can potentially be employed for summative purposes (when 'assessment *of* learning' finally prevails over 'assessment *for* learning'), their optimal use is formative, as their main scope is providing learners 'with the opportunity to reflect on their competences, to collect data and documents which support and stimulate their reflections, and to think about how they will further develop their competences in the future' (Council of Europe, 2021a: 5). In other words, portfolios link assessment to learning, by focusing on learners' awareness, critical reflection and self-evaluation.

This chapter starts by outlining some key features of assessment that, in education at large, can foster or inhibit quality and equity. It then shifts the focus to the specific cases of plurilingual, intercultural and democratic competences, whose specificities cannot be ignored and require a competent use of portfolios as a primary assessment tool. The following section is dedicated to the description of two portfolios, developed by the Council of Europe, which can be used to assess these competences. The final section draws some general conclusions.

Quality and Equity in Assessment

Regardless of the specific learning outcomes being assessed – whether these are related to language skills, disciplinary knowledge, or indeed plurilingual, intercultural or democratic competences – assessment is a complex activity. This is for at least two reasons. First, the basis of any form of assessment consists of gathering enough evidence of learning (in terms of quantity and variety of data) to make sound inferences about the learners' actual competences (Pellegrino *et al.*, 2001; Wiliam, 2020). However, while it is important to ensure that any collection of evidence is conducted accurately, there is always a certain amount of approximation in the conclusions one can draw from it in terms of what the learner's *real* competence is. Second, the inference processes are themselves challenged by a number of constraints, linked to the nature of the competence to be assessed, the assessment method, and the interpretation procedures. For example, what does mastering a topic in geography mean? What specific items of knowledge or abilities are essential versus secondary? What method of collecting evidence is the most suitable for detecting them? And how can we make sure that our inferences about geographic competences are not influenced by other factors, such as the learners' communication style or (lack of) background knowledge?

These inherent properties of assessment can affect the *quality of assessment*. For this reason, a series of principles can be used as parameters to limit the intrinsic drawbacks of assessment. The Council of Europe uses six principles which are most relevant in thinking about quality: validity, reliability, transparency, practicality, equity and respectfulness (Council of Europe, 2018c, 2021c; see also OECD, 2013 and Siarova *et al.*, 2017). These principles will be briefly described here, because applying them – and thus pursuing quality in assessment – is a crucial way to strive for quality in education *tout court*, given the prominent educational and social role occupied by assessment within the overall schooling system.

Validity is the extent to which an assessment actually assesses what it has been designed to assess (e.g. an attitude, a set of skills, a body of knowledge) instead of some other unintended characteristics of the learner. For example, if writing processes are under investigation, one needs to ensure that the key writing components are being assessed (e.g. generating ideas, planning, transcribing or reviewing texts) rather than external factors (e.g. degree of familiarity with the topic, level of motivation to write); if learners know little about the topic they have to write about, they may have problems in both generating ideas and planning their texts. In other words, in an assessment that has a high level of validity, the inferences that are drawn from the assessment evidence are influenced only by the capacities that are of interest and not by incidental characteristics of the learner.

Reliability pertains to the consistency of assessment outcomes. Since the main purpose of assessment is making sound inferences about the learners' competences at a given time, ideally conclusions drawn from evidence of learning should be the same regardless of the person in charge of interpreting the results or the precise set of circumstances (e.g. time of day, location) under which the assessment takes place. Thus, efforts need to be made to minimise the risk that random factors (e.g. an inexpert assessor, or some loose scoring/interpretation criteria) affect the outcome of the assessment process. Among the actions that can be taken to enhance reliability is to use rubrics, which provide explicit descriptions of the expected outcomes as well as of different levels of achievement, so that different assessors can make similar – ideally identical – judgements on the basis of the descriptions.

Rubrics can also make a difference in terms of *transparency*. This third quality principle refers to the need to make learners aware of the assessment modes: What will be assessed? How? According to what criteria? Moreover, a transparent procedure is one where learners fully understand the purposes and uses of the assessment. For example, they are informed in advance whether the results will be used to sustain their learning further and improve teaching (formative aims) or to verify their level of achievement after a period of time (summative aims). They also know what is at stake, that is, whether the assessment results will have no or minimal impact on their educational and professional future (low-stakes assessment), or the opposite, whether their levels of performance in the test/task may affect their lives in the future, for example allowing or preventing access to better educational and employment paths (high-stakes assessment). Overall, within a schooling system, transparency can be guaranteed by involving the learners themselves in assessment practices as much as possible. For instance, they can be invited to read the rubrics in advance, comment on the scoring system, and share their queries about the overall process. Ideally, the learners could even help the teacher develop the assessment tools or, as happens with self- and peer-assessment, use the rubrics themselves – which is also a way to promote their learning further.

Sometimes, transparency may collide with the principle of *practicality*, which concerns the feasibility of the assessment in terms of the amount of time and the (human and material) resources needed to carry out the assessment. While involving the learners in the assessment processes is a highly valuable practice in terms of transparency, this same practice can increase the teachers' workload, slow down the curricular pace, and even be difficult to manage for the learners, thereby compromising practicality. Therefore, a good balance between these two quality principles is crucial to guarantee that the assessment processes are both comprehensible for the learners and feasible for all actors involved (the learners, the teacher, and the institution). Likewise, there may sometimes be a tension between practicality on the one hand and validity and reliability on the other. Once again, in these situations, some compromise might be necessary in order to ensure that the assessment is not only accurate (i.e. has an acceptable level of validity and reliability) but is also practically feasible.

Crucially, *equity* is a major criterion for quality in assessment. According to this principle, a fair assessment practice is one that does not favour some learners or groups of learners and penalise others. In other words, when approaching a test or a task, everyone should have equal opportunities to fully manifest the relevant competences and to have these recognised, regardless of personal and social factors such as low proficiency in the language of schooling, special learning needs, scarcity of material resources (e.g. technological equipment), family support (for socioeconomic or education-related reasons), or lack of background knowledge. In the case of the latter, for example, some learners may have cultural knowledge which differs substantially from that of learners who are members of the majority cultural group (e.g. knowledge of national historical facts or popular TV programmes). This means that, if an assessment explicitly or implicitly relies upon the majority cultural reference system, it breaks the criterion of equity by discriminating against learners who are members of minority cultural groups. Given its gateway role in education and society, assessment can then lead to the educational and social exclusion of minority group learners. Interestingly, transparency can be important for equity. Without transparency, learners will have to guess what is required in an assessment and some may make better guesses than others; this will in turn introduce inequities into the assessment outcomes.

In addition to being fostered by transparency, equity is also closely linked to *respectfulness*, which refers to the need for assessments to respect learners' dignity and human rights. Thus, learners should be allowed the freedom to express their own ideas and values (e.g. about ethical or sociopolitical issues) even when such opinions conflict with or differ from the expected ones; this principle also encompasses learners' rights to privacy. Furthermore, *respectfulness* includes the right of learners to be encouraged in their learning path through motivating feedback, regardless of their actual performance in assessment. Feedback should focus on learners' achievements, not solely on their deficiencies, so that the assessment experience is a positive rather than a negative experience overall, with any deficiencies instead being treated as learning opportunities. Poor performance in assessment should never lead to learners being dismissed as unworthy of further attention.

Generally speaking, assuring respectfulness implies being aware that assessment always has some impact on learners and thus making efforts to monitor its repercussions. First, the outcomes of assessment have consequences on individuals' learning, for example poor results may have demotivating and frustrating effects as much as good results may foster further development and autonomy. Second, especially in the case of high-stakes assessments, as noted earlier, the results may have a considerable influence on learners' future lives. A respectful and ethical assessment cannot overlook these effects. Interestingly, the impact that assessment has on teaching also raises issues of respectfulness and ethical responsibility. For example, there is much evidence that assessment produces a 'washback effect' on teaching, as teachers tend to prioritise those curriculum contents and competences that are subjected to summative assessment over others, especially when the assessment is high stakes. While this tendency can contribute to the promotion of dimensions of learning that might otherwise risk being neglected in curricula (and underestimated by the learners themselves), it may also lead teachers towards forms of 'teaching to the test' and thus prevent them from focusing on objectives and contents which, despite being excluded from assessment, would better serve their pupils' needs. When this happens, assessment is neither respectful nor fair, since it does not meet, value and cultivate the learners' own developmental, personal and social needs – which in the end is another way to discriminate against diversity.

The brief review above helps to highlight that the six principles which are advocated to guarantee quality in assessment also ensure *equity in assessment* (and, again, in education at large). First, as we have seen, equity is specifically one of the assessment principles. Second, equity is also implied in both transparency and respectfulness, which overall emphasise the need to recognise and safeguard learners' diversities against any risk of discrimination that may be implicitly introduced by assessment tasks, modes or inferential processes. Third, equity in assessment is ensured when all the other five principles are met, since it is only when the assessment procedures are suitable at every level (e.g. in terms of their validity, reliability etc.) that the risks of introducing biases against learners' diversities are reduced. In other words, one can say that *equity in assessment* is guaranteed by *quality in assessment*.

The Case of Plurilingual, Intercultural and Democratic Competence

Meeting the quality and equity principles of assessment presents specific challenges in the cases of plurilingual, intercultural and democratic competences, due to the type of learning they require. For example, while each of these competences requires items of knowledge (e.g. the grammatical structures of the languages in one's plurilingual repertoires), they are also characterised by the development of metacognitive abilities. This is because strategic reflection plays a major role in all three of these competences (e.g. in the case of plurilingualism, the ability to anticipate 'as to when and to what extent the use of several languages is useful and appropriate'; Council of Europe, 2020: 127). Moreover, all of these competences encompass an affective dimension which pertains to the learners' attitudes, as well as to their values in the case of intercultural and democratic competence. Thus, as highlighted by Borghetti (2017) in relation to intercultural competence, assessing these kinds of learning also necessarily leads to the assessment of the learners' personal traits and identity-related characteristics.

Despite these and other challenges, it is nevertheless possible to assess plurilingual, intercultural and democratic competences in such a way that quality and equity are maximised according to the principles summarised

Table 7.1 The two portfolios and their respective theoretical frameworks

Competence	Portfolio	Theoretical framework
Plurilingual and intercultural	*European Language Portfolio*, ELP (Council of Europe, 2001b)	*Common European Framework of Reference for Languages*, CEFR (Council of Europe, 2001a) and the *Companion Volume*, CV (Council of Europe, 2020)[2]
Democratic and intercultural	*A Portfolio of Competences for Democratic Culture*, PCDC (Council of Europe, 2021a, 2021b)	*Reference Framework of Competences for Democratic Culture*, RFCDC (Council of Europe, 2018a, 2018b)

above. As anticipated in the Introduction, we argue that portfolios can make the difference in this sense, especially when they are employed to serve low-stakes formative assessment purposes and provide ample space for both self-assessment and class collaboration.

Two portfolios have been developed by the Council of Europe which are specifically dedicated to supporting the development of, and assessing, learners' plurilingual, intercultural and democratic competences. Each of these portfolios is linked to a particular theoretical framework of the competences that are being supported and assessed by the portfolio (Table 7.1).

The theoretical frameworks on which the *European Language Portfolio* (ELP; Council of Europe, 2001b) and the *Portfolio of Competences for Democratic Culture* (PCDC; Council of Europe, 2021a) are based are better than other alternative frameworks that are available in terms of their comprehensiveness, level of detail and conceptual clarity. They each offer detailed specifications of the core learning components (e.g. attitudes, knowledge, etc.) which need to be assessed. This specification in turn can be used to maximise the *validity* of the method of assessment, by ensuring that it assesses only clearly specified components, rather than other incidental characteristics of the learner.

Meeting the principle of *reliability* in assessing plurilingual, intercultural and democratic competences is more challenging, because evidence of learning in these cases is dependent on contextual variables. For example, flexibility and adaptability are critical for all three competences, because these are the skills needed to adapt one's thoughts, feelings or (language and other) behaviours to a given interlocutor or situation. However, what is effective and appropriate depends on the context (e.g. in the case of a language performance assessment, the communication task, the other speakers' moves), and the likelihood that different situations will activate the same attitudes, knowledge and skills is low. This challenges reliability in the strict sense, which ideally requires that 'the same outcome would be obtained if the same assessment procedure were to be administered again to the same learner under the same conditions but at a different time and in a different place and with a different assessor' (Council of Europe, 2021c: 51). A portfolio offers a solution here, because it contains a purposeful selection of samples of a learner's work, collected over time and by means of different tasks. Its use therefore necessarily accepts that external factors influence performance and, thus, that conclusions about the learner's competence differ across assessment situations. Its reliability is instead guaranteed by the fact that, taken altogether, the portfolio tells the story of the learner's progression and achievements in a comprehensive way. In addition, involving more than a single assessor and employing explicit assessment criteria and rubrics – which accurately describe the levels of performance on each competence or component – are other useful ways to pursue reliability using portfolios.

Assessing plurilingual, intercultural and democratic competences through portfolios is admittedly time-consuming compared to other methods (e.g. obtaining written answers to open-ended questions). This lack in *practicality* is, however, considerably reduced as teachers become increasingly familiar with the principles and uses of portfolios. For this reason, teachers require assistance and training in the use of portfolios for assessing plurilingual, intercultural and democratic competences.[3]

Equity, *respectfulness* and *transparency* are all quality and equity principles that can be challenging to achieve in the case of plurilingual, intercultural and democratic competences. For example, for the assessment of values and attitudes, it may be necessary to limit transparency to reduce the impact of 'social desirability', meaning that learners display the expected values and attitudes because they know that these are expected from them rather than because they really hold such values and attitudes. Moreover, these competences are sensitive to assess because attitudinal dimensions (such as openness and curiosity) and values (such as valuing cultural diversity) can easily raise issues of fairness towards learners' diversities in terms of their sociocultural background, personal characteristics, and beliefs. For example, a learner may be shy about engaging with a specific cultural group, or she/he may be uninterested because of her/his cultural and family background. This raises questions about whether it would be fair and respectful to assess her/him negatively compared to others or against a set of given standards (Borghetti, 2017).

The use of the ELP and the PCDC help to address these quality- and equity-related challenges in assessment. First, these portfolios are particularly suitable for low-stakes formative purposes, where learning, instruction and assessment are inseparable. The compilation and analysis of a portfolio at a given time is a way to check ongoing achievements, plan future instruction, develop learners' awareness of their development, and nurture their self-directed learning and autonomy. In general, portfolios are criterion-referenced, where a learner's outputs are judged only against specified levels of proficiency and compared with her/his own previous performance, rather than judged against the performance of other learners (norm-referenced assessment). In the case of the competences considered here, this is a crucial feature since learners complete their own portfolios over a period of time (the school year or even the whole school cycle) and, at every instance of compilation and analysis, compare their new understandings, attitudes and value-related reflections only with the expected standards of performance and their own previous dispositions and ideas. Crucially, since the main purpose of this type of assessment is reflection and further development, a learner may even keep her/his portfolio private and decide – as happens with diaries – whether and when she/he wants to give permission to teachers (and perhaps parents) to read (parts of) it. All these features help portfolios to satisfy the assessment principles of equity, respectfulness and transparency.

These principles are also satisfied by a second possibility provided by the ELP and the PCDC, which is that they can be profitably used (and adapted) collaboratively. In class, teachers and learners may, for example, adopt one or more of the following collaborative practices:

- developing assessment tasks, commenting on the core abilities to be elicited;
- designing the rubrics, agreeing on the procedures to be adopted to conduct teacher-, peer- or self-assessments;
- reflecting together on the conclusions that the relevant 'assessor' (the teacher, a classmate, or the learner themselves) has drawn from reading the portfolio and applying the relevant rubrics.

Among the numerous advantages offered by these shared procedures, there is the contextualisation of the assessment of plurilingual, intercultural and democratic competences within the class environment, where a certain degree of familiarity and mutual trust among all the actors involved can further help pursue equity and respectfulness.

The ELP and the PCDC

There are evident and necessary overlaps among plurilingual, intercultural and democratic competences. To mention just a few of them, the *Companion Volume* notes that 'CEFR [is] a vehicle for promoting quality in second/foreign language teaching and learning as well as in plurilingual and intercultural education' (Council of Europe, 2020: 21), while the *Reference Framework of Competences for Democratic Culture* expressly conceives 'intercultural competence as being an integral component of democratic competence' (Council of Europe, 2018a: 32). This is expressed in a way that links all three competences:

> The development of *plurilingual competence* thus favours participation in *democratic processes* and leads to a better understanding of the plurilingual repertoires of other individuals as well as a respect for language rights. It allows citizens' discourses to be heard beyond their national frontiers, at a European level. The development of plurilingual competence should go hand in hand with the development of *intercultural competence* since the latter promotes appropriate knowledge, understanding

and attitudes for interaction with people of other cultures and social groups. (Council of Europe, 2009: 18; emphases added)

Given these connections, it is not surprising that the respective portfolios often mention and cover the same or similar learning phenomena. However, these tools also present significant differences, which are worth commenting on in more detail, with the aim of indicating how both can be used to ensure quality and equity in the assessment of plurilingual, intercultural and democratic competences.

The assessment of plurilingual and intercultural competence

The *European Language Portfolio*(ELP) is an editable document which can be used to assess both plurilingual and intercultural competence. It is organised in three sections:

- Within the *Language Passport* section, the learner can record up to six languages – other than their first language(s) – which they know at any level of achievement, irrespective of whether the languages have been learned formally (e.g. at school or in private language courses) or informally (e.g. by living abroad). The portfolio owner is invited to complete the passport periodically and, at every completion, to self-assess her or his progress in terms of five skills (listening, reading, spoken interaction, spoken production, and writing), proficiency levels for which (A1 to C2) are defined by the CEFR 2001 scales and descriptors.
- The *Language Biography* provides a series of prompts (e.g. 'Outside language classes, I use/have used the languages which I am learning or already know in the following situations:', 'I would like to be able to do the following with the languages which I am learning:'). These prompts encourage the learner to record her or his intercultural and language learning experiences, and to reflect on these experiences and on her or his ongoing achievements and future objectives.
- The *Dossier* is used to collect materials which document and illustrate achievements and experiences that have been recorded in the Passport or Biography (e.g. short essays, video presentations, language certifications).

Consistent with the CEFR, the ELP encourages the learning of a range of languages. However, while plurilingual competence is expressly mentioned within the CEFR, the CEFR itself tends to conceptualise the assessment of proficiency in each language separately from the others. This contrasts with the more recent application of the concept of a plurilingual repertoire, which is the overall set of resources which an individual learner acquires in *all the languages* they know or have learned, irrespective of whether these are languages of schooling, regional/minority and migration languages, modern or classical languages (Council of Europe, 2016). Thus, in developing the early conceptualisation presented in the CEFR, the later *Companion Volume* (CV) introduces several innovations, including the encouragement – in relation to assessment based on descriptors – of a vision of learners as social agents who draw on their plurilingual repertoire (including first languages and partial proficiency in one or more additional languages) to understand texts in other languages and to communicate effectively in multilingual contexts. These new inputs, which echo recent approaches to plurilingualism such as those of translanguaging (García, 2009) and intercomprehension (Doyé, 2005), represent a major innovation of the CV compared with the CEFR previous version. Three new scales have been introduced in the *Companion Volume*: 'Building on pluricultural repertoire', 'Plurilingual comprehension' and 'Building on plurilingual repertoire'. Overall, they present a view of an individual's languages and cultures as being interrelated and interconnected, as well as being valuable resources which all contribute to an individual's communicative competence, regardless of the level of proficiency in one particular language or familiarity with a particular culture. For example, these scales encourage learners to develop skills such as being able to participate effectively in conversations in two or more languages in their plurilingual repertoire, adjusting to the changes of language, and catering to the needs and linguistic skills of their interlocutors.

The ELP can be easily adapted to this updated perspective. For example, within the *Language Biography*, learners are asked to keep a record of the ways in which they have engaged with the language. Here, it can be made explicit that the task does not exclude but instead actually encourages recording episodes where they switched between or combined different languages, used automatic translations to comprehend a text, or negotiated the language of interaction with their interlocutors. Similar adaptations can be easily made to reinforce the intercultural dimension of the ELP (see also Little & Simpson, 2003). For example, while engaged in recording and reflecting on their plurilingual experiences, learners can be invited to recall and think about how they and the other speakers reacted to the encounter: Did someone feel confused or annoyed? Was something in the conversation surprising or challenging to deal with? What action (if any) led to a remedy of the impasse? Moreover, if they now think back to the episode, how do they make sense of what happened? Do they have a better awareness of cultural differences and of the adjustments that are needed to prevent and/or repair misunderstandings and cultural incidents? Generally speaking, learners and teachers should feel free to modify and expand the contents of the ELP appropriately in order to accommodate their plurilingual and intercultural needs.[4] An example of a possible adaptation for learners in secondary education is presented in Vignette 1.

Vignette 1

This vignette reports on a possible use of the ELP to foster learners' plurilingual and intercultural competences. It is intended for use by learners in secondary education, but some of the suggested tasks may also be employed with younger learners. In all cases, the individual teacher will need to adapt the teaching materials and procedures to their own specific educational context and learners.

Target group

Learners in secondary school (most suitable subjects: language education and foreign language classes).

Main learning objectives (adapted from *Companion Volume*, p. 124)

- Willingness to value all of one's own and others' developing language resources.
- Ability to exploit one's linguistic repertoire by purposefully blending, embedding and alternating languages at the levels of utterance and discourse.
- Capacity to deal with 'otherness' to identify similarities and differences, to build on known and unknown cultural features.
- Awareness of one's own plurilingual and intercultural learning.

Languages used

Regardless of the tasks (personal use of the ELP, peer-to-peer feedback, class discussion, text reading, etc.), learners are encouraged to flexibly use any language in their plurilingual repertoire. When needed, the teacher and the learners can translate for the benefit of those who do not understand specific words or utterances. Moreover, each learner is invited to use (online) dictionaries.

Resources needed

- A projector.
- Connection to the internet (if online dictionaries are needed in addition to hardcopy ones).
- Computers (to be used in pairs).

Teacher preparatory work

- Before Activity 1: Make sufficient copies of the ELP portfolio and of the *Companion Volume* scales and descriptors for 'Building on pluricultural repertoire', 'Plurilingual comprehension' and 'Building on plurilingual repertoire' (see pp. 125–128 of the *Companion Volume*). If the teacher judges that the three full scales would make excessive demands of their learners, they may decide to only use one or two scales, or indeed to not use all six levels of descriptors within each of the three scales.

- Before Activity 2: Select extracts from the learners' portfolios and design a document to be projected, and design some opening questions to stimulate class discussion.
- Before Activity 3: Make enough copies of the CV 'Building on pluricultural repertoire', 'Plurilingual comprehension' and 'Building on plurilingual repertoire' scales and descriptors.
- Before Activity 4: Design a form that learners can easily use to compare the stories and reflections they have annotated in their portfolio at three different moments. Two example items are:

	Moment 1 (date: ...)	Moment 2 (date: ...)	Moment 3 (date: ...)
How did I feel when I didn't understand what others said? What resources and/or strategies did I employ to overcome my difficulties?			
Comparing my accounts and reflections at Moments 1–3, what do I learn about my communicative practices and about my learning?			

Estimated time
- Two or three classes (approximately 1 hour each) are needed to complete each activity.
- Approximately one month should pass between one use of the portfolio and the following (e.g. between Activity 2 and Activity 3), to boost the chances that the learners can envisage changes or progress in their attitudes and behaviours.

Procedures
Activity 1: Designing the class portfolio
(1) The learners read the descriptors of the scales 'Building on pluricultural repertoire', 'Plurilingual comprehension' and 'Building on plurilingual repertoire'. The teacher provides explanations when needed (e.g. they define what a repertoire is and clarify what is meant by 'pluricultural' and 'plurilingual'), while the learners list the languages they know, and recall/imagine in what circumstances they employ or have employed more than one language in their lives.

(2) The teacher introduces the existing version of the ELP using a projector for the learners to get a concrete idea of its features. They explain that the ELP is a tool to develop self-awareness, monitor and support learning, and set future aims in relation to intercultural and plurilingual competences.

(3) In pairs, using an editable file and a computer, the learners adapt the existing version of the ELP to their plurilingual and intercultural experiences and make it relevant for themselves.

(4) The teacher guides a class debriefing, during which each pair introduces their revisions and the entire class progressively reaches an agreement on the core features of what will, at the end, become the class portfolio (e.g. what inputs are to be provided in the *Language Biography*: travel abroad, out-of-school language courses, films viewed in the original version, etc.).

(5) The teacher (or a group of learners) edits the document and shares the final version with the class.

(6) Individually, each learner completes the portfolio before the next meeting.

Activity 2: Experimenting with the portfolio

(1) [Before the class]. The teacher asks each learner for permission to read their entire portfolio and to share anonymised extracts with the class.

(2) [Before the class]. The teacher selects some extracts according to a given topic (e.g. episodes and reflections related to internet plurilingual experiences, to family plurilingualism, or to intercultural face-to-face encounters) and shows them through a projector.

(3) A class discussion is stimulated about the extracts. Some questions could be: What cultural similarities and differences are reported in the extracts? What cultural assumptions, preconceptions, stereotypes and prejudices (if any) emerge from the learners' stories? How has switching between or combining languages fostered or limited mutual understanding? What (language) behaviours would have helped? During the discussion, learners are invited to write down the core ideas in their notes.

(4) In pairs, learners write a report where all the main ideas and positions are commented upon. Texts are then read aloud in a plenary session.

Activity 3: Using the portfolio for peer-to-peer assessment

(1) [Before the class]. After approximately one month, the learners use the portfolio again.

(2) [Before the class]. The teacher asks each learner whether one classmate can read their portfolio, comment on it, and share selected extracts with the teacher and the class.

(3) The learners divide into pairs. Each member uses the three sets of descriptors about pluricultural and plurilingual competences to explore and make sense of their classmate's portfolio: they read it carefully, try to match the reported skills and manifested attitudes with the scales, and formulate recommendations.

(4) Each learner shares their considerations with the portfolio's owner, and together they prepare a brief oral/written report to be presented to the class in which they comment on each other's actual level of competence and support their assessments with extracts from the two portfolios.

Activity 4: Using the portfolio for self-assessment

(1) [Before class]. After approximately one month, the learners use the portfolio again.

(2) [Before class]. The teacher designs a form, which allows the learners to compare their own accounts and reflections across the three compilation moments (Activities 2–4). Some possible questions that may be included in the form are the following: Have you changed your mind about the practices that can better foster your communicative effectiveness? What has changed (if anything) in your language learning targets? Re-read the early plurilingual and intercultural episodes you reported in the portfolio and reflect on what you think now of your past behaviours; what would you do differently and how?

(3) Each learner re-reads their own portfolio and fills in the form.

(4) Each member uses the three sets of descriptors about pluricultural and plurilingual competences to explore and make sense of their own learning trajectory: they read their three portfolio entries and try to match each of them with the scales.

(5) Each learner writes a page of diary to describe and comment on their learning path.

Activity 5: Debriefing

• In a plenary session, the teacher guides a class discussion on the experience and stimulates reflections on how to better use the ELP to foster plurilingualism and interculturality.

As illustrated by the example in Vignette 1, once the ELP is clearly linked to plurilingualism via the descriptor scales provided by the *Companion Volume*, it can be used for assessing both plurilingual and intercultural competence through self- and peer-assessment (and through teacher assessment as well, if required). The use of these validated scales and explicit criteria helps to ensure the *validity* of the assessments that are made. *Reliability* in assessment is also supported because all assessors use the same explicit criteria for drawing their inferences about the learner's performance. Furthermore, as long as teachers provide sufficiently clear guidance to learners in advance and allow learners to draw upon any evidence of their proficiency in the use of the specified competences which they themselves choose to provide, *transparency, equity and respectfulness* are also assured. Finally, the practicality of using the ELP is enhanced by having step-by-step procedures like the ones provided in Vignette 1. In short, the ELP satisfies all of the key quality and equity principles, not least because it is focused on the learners themselves rather than on the teacher: the ELP enables learners to record their own experiences, to keep track of their own plurilingual and intercultural learning, and to make responsible choices about their further development.

The assessment of democratic and intercultural competence

As noted earlier, the RFCDC conceptualises intercultural competence as an integral component of democratic competence. This is because acting as a democratic citizen in a culturally diverse society requires the capacity to interact and communicate with one's fellow citizens who often have different cultural affiliations from oneself. For this reason, the RFCDC proposes that all of the competences shown in Figure 7.1 are required by citizens within culturally diverse societies; these include all of the

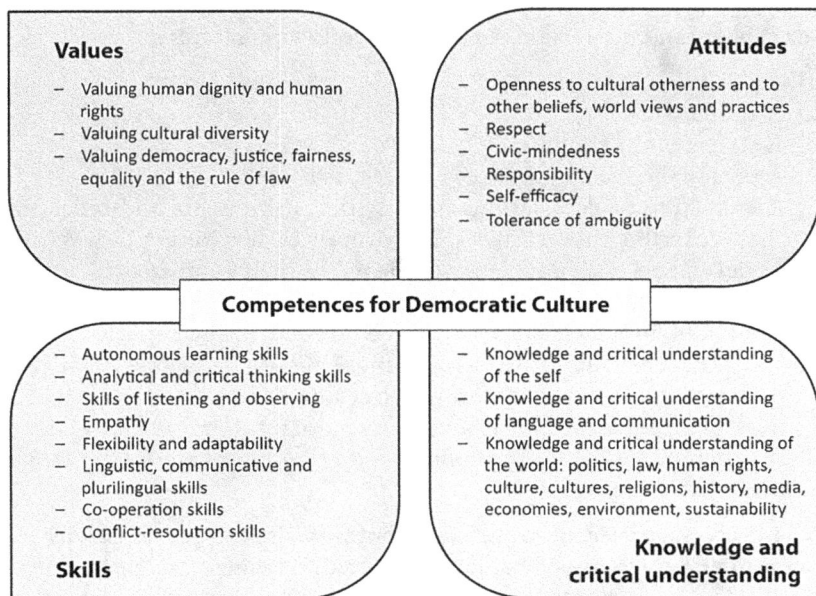

Values
- Valuing human dignity and human rights
- Valuing cultural diversity
- Valuing democracy, justice, fairness, equality and the rule of law

Attitudes
- Openness to cultural otherness and to other beliefs, world views and practices
- Respect
- Civic-mindedness
- Responsibility
- Self-efficacy
- Tolerance of ambiguity

Competences for Democratic Culture

Skills
- Autonomous learning skills
- Analytical and critical thinking skills
- Skills of listening and observing
- Empathy
- Flexibility and adaptability
- Linguistic, communicative and plurilingual skills
- Co-operation skills
- Conflict-resolution skills

Knowledge and critical understanding
- Knowledge and critical understanding of the self
- Knowledge and critical understanding of language and communication
- Knowledge and critical understanding of the world: politics, law, human rights, culture, cultures, religions, history, media, economies, environment, sustainability

Figure 7.1 The 20 competences required for democratic culture proposed by the RFCDC. Figure adapted from Council of Europe (2018a), © Council of Europe

components of both democratic and intercultural competence. All 20 of these competences are described in detail in volume 1 of the RFCDC (Council of Europe, 2018a), while volume 2 of the RFCDC provides validated and scaled descriptors for all of the competences (Council of Europe, 2018b). These descriptors provide examples of the concrete observable behaviours which a person will display if they have achieved a certain level of proficiency in a given competence, and they can therefore be used for assessing the proficiency of learners in the use of the competences.

In order to support teachers in promoting the development of these 20 competences in learners, the *Portfolio of Competences for Democratic Culture* (PCDC) (Council of Europe, 2021a, 2021b) has been developed. The portfolio provides learners with a means through which to compile documents demonstrating their developing proficiency in the use of the 20 competences. It is also designed to help them reflect critically on their achievements and on how they can develop their competences further in the future. Because the contents of the PCDC provide evidence about how a learner's proficiency is developing, it can be used for both formative and summative assessment purposes.

Two versions of the PCDC have been developed: a standard version for learners from approximately 10–11 years of age upwards (Council of Europe, 2021a), and a younger learners' version for children aged up to approximately 10–11 years (Council of Europe, 2021b). Both versions are accompanied by a guide for teachers. The portfolios can be compiled in hard copy (e.g. using binders, folders or box files) or digitally as an e-portfolio. The standard version contains the following sections:

(1) A title page.
(2) A contents list.
(3) A statement of purpose.
(4) A personal statement.
(5) A collection of descriptions of activities, documents and reflections that describe the learner's performance, learning progressions, achievements and proficiency in the use of their competences across a wide range of situations, both within and beyond the classroom.
(6) A logbook in which learners can record some of their specific experiences that they may wish to think more about.
(7) A general reflections section, which reviews experiences and changes over a longer period, for example, a school term or a school year.
(8) A summarising list of the competences that have been demonstrated in the portfolio.

The younger learners' version contains similar sections with the exception of the logbook which is omitted. Teachers are free to adapt these suggested contents to make them more suitable for their own education context and learners. However, when they do so, two features of the PCDC always need to be retained because of the role they play in facilitating the development of learners' competences: learners should always provide documentation on their uses of competences, and they should always provide critical reflections on their uses of these competences.

Vignette 2 presents an example of how one group of teachers has successfully used the standard version of the portfolio for teaching, learning and assessment purposes.

Vignette 2

In this example, the standard version of the PCDC was used in a secondary school with a class of 18 learners who were aged 16–17 years old. The teacher who coordinated the portfolio work was a teacher of Geography, and she was assisted in implementing the portfolio by a teacher of Sociology and a teacher of Religious Education. Both the school management and the parents of the learners who were going to use the portfolio were informed in advance about how the portfolio was going to be used. The learners wrote and compiled the contents of their portfolios using computers. The activity proceeded through the following steps.

(1) The learners were first briefed about how to compile their portfolios. The learners, none of whom had previously compiled a portfolio, initially found some aspects of the process difficult to understand. However, with further explanations from the teachers, and additional support where necessary, they began to find the compilation process easier as time progressed.

(2) The learners began by producing a statement about the purpose of the portfolio as well as a personal statement about how they saw themselves, about the things they liked to do, what citizenship meant to them at the local, regional, national and international levels, and what other people thought about their citizenship values, attitudes, skills, knowledge and understanding.

(3) The learners then moved on to compiling descriptions of concrete situations in which they were actively using and applying their competences. The range of situations upon which they drew included classroom lessons in Geography, Sociology and Religious Education, and situations that had arisen in the wider school context, as well as situations in other contexts outside the school including online activities, sporting clubs, volunteer organisations, a children's city council, free time at home, and a foreign language school. Each situation that was described was numbered for referencing purposes. The learner had to describe her or his own behaviours within the situation, and then reflect on the

specific competences that they had used, whether they had been successful in achieving their goals in the situation, whether they had enjoyed the situation and if not, why not, and what they might do differently in the future if they encountered that same situation again. In doing so, they referred to and used the descriptors from volume 2 of the RFCDC to identify their levels of proficiency in the use of the competences. In addition, the learners compiled logbooks containing reflections on situations and competences which they felt they needed to think further about.

(4) This process of documenting and reflecting on the use of competences lasted for a period of approximately three months, at the end of which the learners wrote more general reflections about their portfolio as a whole, using the following questions as prompts:
What do I remember most?
What is most striking in 'My Activities and Reflections' and in 'My Logbook'?
What could I have done differently?
What got in the way of me doing something differently?
What made me change over time?
What have I learnt about myself? What describes me best where I am now?

(5) The learners also completed a table in which the 20 competences from the RFCDC were listed. They were asked to indicate the reference numbers of the activities in which each individual competence had been exhibited. Some of the learners also used this table to introduce some final reflective comments on their use of individual competences (e.g. 'I would like to know more about that', 'I love getting to know new cultures and interacting with people', 'Sometimes I am not happy with my success and I always want to make more progress'). At the very end of the process, the learners compiled a contents list for their portfolio and produced a title page.

The teachers commented afterwards that what they appreciated most about the portfolio was that it helped to inform the learners about their own citizenship behaviours and their competences. The portfolio had provided the learners with a valuable opportunity to consolidate information about what they had been doing over the previous three months. It had also given them the chance to reflect on the progress that they had been making and on what they still needed to develop in the future. In addition, the descriptors had enabled the teachers to assess and understand the learners' levels of proficiency in the use of the various competences, and to discover where each individual learner still required further development.

As in the case of the ELP, the availability of not only clear and detailed descriptions of all 20 competences but also validated and scaled descriptors helps to ensure the *validity* of the assessments that are made using the PCDC. In addition, because the assessors (whether these are learners themselves, peers or teachers) use explicit descriptors to draw their inferences about learners' proficiency, the *reliability* of these inferences is strengthened. Furthermore, because learners themselves are in control of the contents of their portfolios and have the right to withhold any materials they do not wish to disclose through their portfolios, the PCDC is high on *respectfulness*. Moreover, the process of compiling the PCDC is both *transparent and equitable* as long as the teacher provides sufficiently clear guidance to all learners right at the outset of the process, and as long as this guidance provides the scope for all learners to document the full range of their competences and proficiency in their portfolios through whatever examples and means they themselves wish to use. Finally, the *practicality* of using the PCDC has been confirmed through extensive piloting in multiple countries and educational contexts. For all of these reasons, the PCDC satisfies all of the key principles for quality and equity in education.

Conclusion

In this chapter, we have argued that, in order to ensure quality and equity in education, when assessments of learners are being made, those assessments need to satisfy six principles: validity, reliability, transparency, equity, respectfulness and practicality. We have also argued that portfolios offer the optimal means to satisfy these six principles, especially in relationship to assessing plurilingual, intercultural and democratic competences. Two examples of portfolios that may be used for assessing these competences have been described and illustrated: the ELP and the PCDC.

In addition, it should be noted that because portfolios are typically embedded in everyday classroom practices where learners and teachers may discuss and use them to promote further learning, and because the behaviours that are documented in portfolios may be drawn from any context – the classroom, the wider school environment, the home environment, the local community or indeed the wider world beyond – portfolios are arguably the most suitable tool to use for learning-oriented assessment because they contain descriptions of learners' behaviour that has occurred within real-world situations which are chosen by the learners themselves for their personal relevance and significance. For all of these reasons, we believe that portfolios offer a solution to many of the challenges that are associated with assessment in general and with assessing plurilingual, intercultural and democratic competences in particular.

Notes

(1) There is also good evidence that, despite the widespread use of streaming, this practice has negligible effects on educational outcomes (unlike setting, where learners are divided into separate groups *within* the classroom for a specific subject based on their abilities in that subject, which does have significant benefits for outcomes) (Steenbergen-Hu *et al.*, 2016).

(2) Despite being published twenty years after the *ELP*, the *Companion Volume* can be conceived as part of its conceptual framework, because a substantial portion of the latter is intended to complete the *Common European Framework of Reference for Languages* precisely in relationship to the concept of 'plurilingual competence'.

(3) Detailed guidance for teachers is also available from the Council of Europe on how to use the ELP (see https://www.coe.int/en/web/portfolio/templates-of-the-3-parts-of-a-pel and https://www.coe.int/en/web/portfolio/elp-related-publications) and the PCDC (see Council of Europe, 2021a, 2021b).

(4) The Council of Europe has developed an additional set of tools, the *Autobiography of Intercultural Encounters* (AIE), to support learners' critical reflections on intercultural encounters, reactions to cultural differences, and intercultural communications (see also Chapter 2). As such, the AIE may be used by learners for inclusion within the *Dossier* section of the ELP (or in the documents section of the PCDC). For further information about the AIE, see www.coe.int/autobiography.

References

Borghetti, C. (2017) Is there really a need for assessing intercultural competence? Some ethical issues. *Journal of Intercultural Communication* 44. https://cris.unibo.it/handle/11585/592902?mode=full.2777 (accessed 3 October 2022).

Council of Europe (2001a) *Common European Framework of Reference for Languages: Learning, Teaching, Assessment.* Strasbourg: Council of Europe. https://rm.coe.int/CoERMPublicCommonSearchServices/DisplayDCTMContent?documentId=0900001680459f97 (accessed 1 October 2021).

Council of Europe (2001b) *European Language Portfolio.* Strasbourg: Council of Europe. https://www.coe.int/en/web/portfolio (accessed 1 October 2021).

Council of Europe (2009) *Autobiography of Intercultural Encounters: Context, Concepts and Theories.* Strasbourg: Council of Europe. https://rm.coe.int/context-concepts-and-theories-autobiography-of-intercultural-encounter/168089eb76 (accessed 23 October 2021).

Council of Europe (2016) *Guide for the Development and Implementation of Curricula for Plurilingual and Intercultural Education.* Strasbourg: Council of Europe. https://www.coe.int/en/web/language-policy/guide-for-the-development-and-implementation-of-curricula-for-plurilingual-and-intercultural-education (accessed 13 October 2021).

Council of Europe (2018a) *Reference Framework of Competences for Democratic Culture, Volume 1: Context, Concepts and Model.* Strasbourg: Council of Europe. https://www.coe.int/en/web/reference-framework-of-competences-for-democratic-culture/rfcdc-volumes (accessed 22 October 2021).

Council of Europe (2018b) *Reference Framework of Competences for Democratic Culture, Volume 2: Descriptors of Competences for Democratic Culture.* Strasbourg: Council of Europe. https://www.coe.int/en/web/reference-framework-of-competences-for-democratic-culture/rfcdc-volumes (accessed 22 October 2021).

Council of Europe (2018c) *Reference Framework of Competences for Democratic Culture, Volume 3: Guidance for Implementation.* Strasbourg: Council of Europe. https://www.coe.int/en/web/reference-framework-of-competences-for-democratic-culture/rfcdc-volumes (accessed 22 October 2021).

Council of Europe (2020) *Common European Framework of Reference for Languages: Learning, Teaching, Assessment – Companion Volume.* Strasbourg: Council of Europe. https://rm.coe.int/common-european-framework-of-reference-for-languages-learning-teaching/16809ea0d4 (accessed 13 October 2021).

Council of Europe (2021a) *A Portfolio of Competences for Democratic Culture: Standard Version.* Strasbourg: Council of Europe. https://www.coe.int/en/web/reference-framework-of-competences-for-democratic-culture/portfolios (accessed 22 October 2021).

Council of Europe (2021b) *A Portfolio of Competences for Democratic Culture: Younger Learners Version.* Strasbourg: Council of Europe. https://www.coe.int/en/web/reference-framework-of-competences-for-democratic-culture/portfolios (accessed 22 October 2021).

Council of Europe (2021c) *Assessing Competences for Democratic Culture: Principles, Methods, Examples.* Strasbourg: Council of Europe. https://rm.coe.int/prems-005521-assessing-competences-for-democratic-culture/1680a3bd41 (accessed 22 October 2021).

Doyé, P. (2005) *Intercomprehension: Guide for the Development of Language Education Policies in Europe – From Linguistic Diversity to Plurilingual Education.* Strasbourg: Council of Europe.

García, O. (2009) Education, multilingualism and translanguaging in the 21st century. In T. Skutnabb-Kangas, R. Phillipson, A.K. Mohanty and M. Panda (eds) *Social Justice Through Multilingual Education* (pp. 140–158). Bristol: Multilingual Matters.

Little, D. and Simpson, B. (2003) *European Language Portfolio: The Intercultural Component and Learning How to Learn.* Strasbourg: Council of Europe. http://archive.ecml.at/mtp2/elp_tt/results/DM_layout/Reference%20Materials/English/Templates%20for%20the%20language%20biography.pdf (accessed 22 October 2021).

OECD (2013) *Synergies for Better Learning: An International Perspective on Evaluation and Assessment.* Paris: OECD. https://www.oecd.org/education/school/synergies-for-better-learning.htm (accessed 22 October 2021).

Pellegrino, J.W., Chudowsky, N. and Glaser, R. (eds) (2001) *Knowing what Students Know: The Science and Design of Educational Assessment.* Washington, DC: National Academy Press.

Siarova, H., Sternadel, D. and Mašidlauskaitė, R. (2017) *Assessment Practices for 21st Century Learning: Review of Evidence.* NESET II report. Luxembourg: Publications Office of the European Union. https://nesetweb.eu/wp-content/uploads/2019/06/AR1_20172.pdf (accessed 22 October 2021).

Steenbergen-Hu, S., Makel, M.C. and Olszewski-Kubilius, P. (2016) What one hundred years of research says about the effects of ability grouping and acceleration on K-12 students' academic achievement: Findings of two second-order meta-analyses. *Review of Educational Research* 86 (4), 849–899.

Wiliam, D. (2020) How to think about assessment. In S. Donarski and T. Bennett (eds) *The Research ED Guide to Assessment: An Evidence-Informed Guide for Teachers* (pp. 21–36). Woodbridge: John Catt Educational.

8 What is My Role and Responsibility as a Language Teacher in Developing Language (and Other) Skills for Learning Across the Curriculum?

Mirjam Egli Cuenat and Marisa Cavalli

Introduction

Traditionally, language teaching in Europe has been thought of in terms of school subjects: on the one hand, the language of schooling and, on the other, 'second' or 'foreign' languages and, in some school systems, 'ancient or classical languages' (Latin and Greek). The learning of each was seen as the compartmentalised addition of a new skill (Fleming, 2010; Coste *et al.*, 2009). Plurilingual and intercultural education, based on the values of the Council of Europe as presented in Chapter 1 of this book, proposes a global rethinking of language teaching, to include all the languages present in the school, as well as the linguistic dimension in all subjects. It invites a series of changes in perspective that will have a direct impact on the role and responsibilities of language teachers, whether they teach a language of schooling or a second or foreign language. In order to implement curriculum-based learning that benefits all students, language teachers need to open their teaching to such a view and collaborate with each other and with teachers of other subjects.

In this chapter, this approach is considered from three perspectives:

- a reflection on the role of languages and values for the overall development of students, the comprehensive approach to languages in schools as conceived by the Council of Europe, as well as the central idea of the repertoire of plurilingual resources encompassing all of learners' languages and including tools for coherent curricula;

- the specific role and responsibility of language teachers and teachers of other disciplines in the implementation of such an approach – as individual teachers and in interdisciplinary collaboration – with some concrete suggestions, while highlighting the importance of a common ethical stance;
- explanation and discussion of some innovative tools and methods to implement this approach.

Why and How to Address 'Language Skills for Learning Across the Curriculum'

General student development through languages and values and attitudes

All school-based language learning – whether in the context of first or second language instruction, one (or more) foreign languages, or classical languages – enriches students' communicative and expressive abilities, as well as their learning-to-learn skills and autonomy. It also provides the opportunity to think critically about otherness, about the relativity of worldviews, and about the many similarities that characterise human groups. The languages used in the other school disciplines are also formative and each discipline contributes in different ways to the processes of construction of the identities (Byram, 2006), and intellectual and (inter) cultural capacities of students (Beacco, 2013). However, in order for all subjects to fully exercise this formative function, it is important that their language dimensions be fully taught (Beacco *et al.*, 2016b). Taking into account and valuing the language and cultural repertoire of each student helps to build a confident identity that is ready to open up to other linguistic experiences offered by the school. Democratic participation is also strengthened by a good knowledge of the language of schooling, by knowledge of other languages and by a use of language inspired by the values of the Council of Europe and a culture of democracy (Council of Europe, 2018). Figure 8.1 can help us to think about the articulation of these dimensions.

The aim of language teaching is not only to assist the learner in becoming competent in linguistic communication, but also to educate social agents. Plurilingual and intercultural education should enable learners to decentre from their own languages and cultures, to develop (meta)linguistic awareness, to be aware of and to avoid cultural stereotyping, to know how to take into account other points of view without prejudice and in a critical way, to understand and accept diversity, to be able to assume attitudes of openness and empathy towards any other subject or group, to behave as responsible citizens and, above all, to engage actively and positively in democratic life. This approach implies that the values and attitudes that the school wants to transmit are first embodied by the teaching team and that they are exercised, experienced and concretely acquired by learners in the daily functioning of school life. Pedagogical activities,

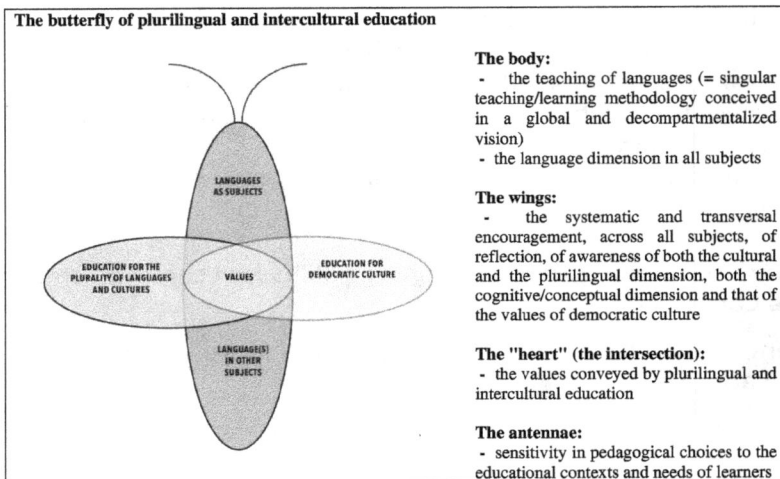

The butterfly of plurilingual and intercultural education

The body:
- the teaching of languages (= singular teaching/learning methodology conceived in a global and decompartmentalized vision)
- the language dimension in all subjects

The wings:
- the systematic and transversal encouragement, across all subjects, of reflection, of awareness of both the cultural and the plurilingual dimension, both the cognitive/conceptual dimension and that of the values of democratic culture

The "heart" (the intersection):
- the values conveyed by plurilingual and intercultural education

The antennae:
- sensitivity in pedagogical choices to the educational contexts and needs of learners

Figure 8.1 Representation of the relationships and integration of plurilingual and intercultural education. Graph created by the authors, with acknowledgement of Bernard Pottier's 'Semantic Butterfly' (Pottier, 1992: 19)

presented below, reinforce this education in living together, acted out in everyday life, through critical and 'meta' reflection (Jessner & Allgäuer-Hackl, 2020).

An integrated approach

An integrated approach starts from a plurilingual and pluricultural repertoire (see Chapter 1) that encompasses all the language and cultural resources of individuals, their needs for communication and/or interaction with others, and the necessity to develop this repertoire (see Figure 8.2).

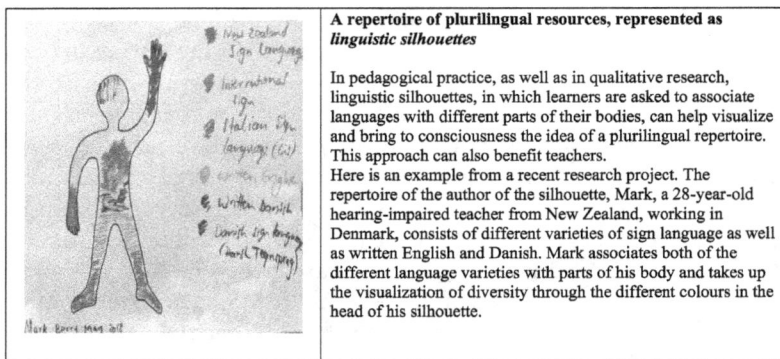

A repertoire of plurilingual resources, represented as *linguistic silhouettes*

In pedagogical practice, as well as in qualitative research, linguistic silhouettes, in which learners are asked to associate languages with different parts of their bodies, can help visualize and bring to consciousness the idea of a plurilingual repertoire. This approach can also benefit teachers.
Here is an example from a recent research project. The repertoire of the author of the silhouette, Mark, a 28-year-old hearing-impaired teacher from New Zealand, working in Denmark, consists of different varieties of sign language as well as written English and Danish. Mark associates both of the different language varieties with parts of his body and takes up the visualization of diversity through the different colours in the head of his silhouette.

Figure 8.2 Plurilingual repertoire and linguistic silhouette of a teacher (Kusters & De Meulder, 2019: 19)

In the plurilingual repertoires of individuals, resources are interconnected and interact dynamically. The pedagogical literature often refers to the double iceberg model of the Canadian researcher Jim Cummins to illustrate the idea of transversality: the surface structures of the different languages are like the tips of the same iceberg but emerging from a broad common base (Common Underlying Proficiency) which does not exclude the specificities of each one. In the context of a plurilingual approach, this metaphor can be extended to that of an iceberg with multiple points (see Figure 8.3).

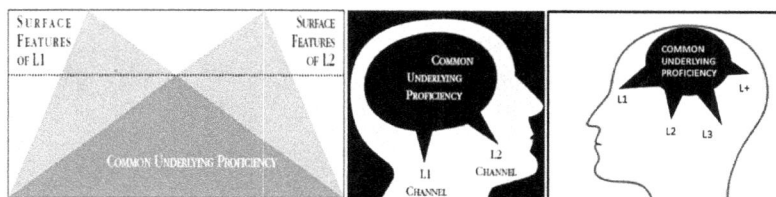

Figure 8.3 The double iceberg metaphor (Cummins, 2005) and the multiple iceberg metaphor (authors' representation)

A global and decompartmentalising approach to languages at school

The global approach focuses on the coherence and decompartmentalisation of school teaching and learning as proposed in the 'Languages in Education – Languages for Education' project of the Council of Europe, and illustrated by the representation in Figure 8.4.

The learners with their plurilingual repertoire are at the top of the diagram. They are the main actors, since the aim of Plurilingual and Intercultural Education is to contribute to the academic success of every individual – whether they become plurilingual through schooling or are plurilingual before entering school due to external circumstances or family origins. The language of schooling is shared by all students and because of its decisive role, is placed at the centre of the scheme. It is represented in its dual dimension of language as a subject and as a language used in the transmission and construction of knowledge in and through the other subjects. On the right of the diagram are other languages (foreign and classical), acquired mainly in the school environment, and on the left are regional, minority (including sign language) or migrant languages. Depending on the circumstances, all these languages can be taught in school as subjects or as languages of learning and teaching in subjects. This may involve bilingual or (partially) immersive teaching, plurilingual activities or CLIL (content and language integrated learning) activities, with each language assuming its own particular role in building plurilingual competence.

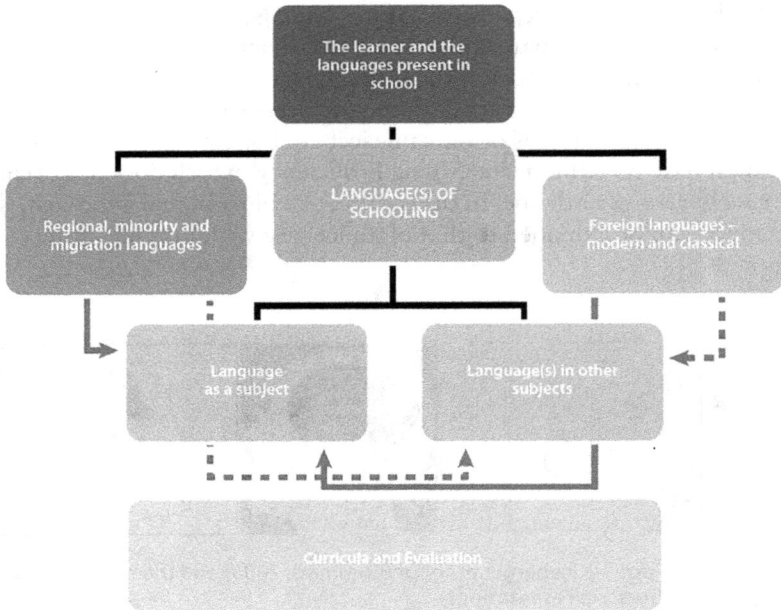

Figure 8.4 Comprehensive approach to languages in schools[1] © Council of Europe

Specific and cross-curricular competence objectives

In the context of school education, learning objectives can be defined in terms of both linguistic and cultural competences. This is the current approach in a growing number of school systems and is supported in particular by the *Common European Framework of Reference* (Council of Europe, 2001) as well as by its *Companion Volume* (Council of Europe, 2020), the *Framework of Reference for Plurilingual Approaches to Languages and Cultures* (Candelier *et al.*, 2012), the *Handbook for Curriculum Development and Teacher Training: The Language Dimension in All Subjects* (Beacco *et al.*, 2016b) and the *Reference Framework of Competences for Democratic Culture* (Council of Europe, 2018). In keeping with a global approach, a distinction can be made between objectives specific to the teaching of a language and cross-curricular objectives (see Table 8.1).

Within a comprehensive approach, both types of objectives can be formulated by teachers in pedagogical teams. The specific objectives concerning the competences built within the teaching of languages as subjects are traditionally well established. However, the transversal objectives between languages as subjects on the one hand and in the service of other school disciplines on the other are much less so and would be better and more easily established in co-operation among teachers (see below). The convergence of competences is also important in bilingual

Table 8.1 Specific and cross-curricular (transversal) objectives

Specific objectives for the teaching of each language or language variety concern

- the linguistic (grammar, vocabulary, phonology, orthography), sociolinguistic (formal/ academic vs. informal registers, linguistic markers of social relations) and pragmatic (discourse organisation, language use) knowledge (*savoir*), skills (*savoir-faire*) and attitudes (*savoir-être*) specific to each variety.

- the associated cultural dimensions, including intercultural communicative competence, i.e. the cultural knowledge, skills and attitudes of an 'intercultural speaker', i.e. someone able to relate to and critically understand other people's cultures and relate them to their own.

Cross-curricular (transversal) objectives for the teaching of all languages or varieties concern

- the objectives of plurilingual competence: knowledge, skills (including the ability to learn, *savoir-apprendre*) and attitudes related to the plurality of languages; to the construction of plurilingual repertoire resources; to strategies; to the patterns of genres of text; to the variability of norms as well as the composition of plurilingual and pluricultural repertoire resources; to reflexivity and (critical) awareness and to the simultaneous use of several languages.

- the objectives of intercultural competence and competences for a culture of democracy: knowledge, skills and attitudes related to explicit values, to intercultural dialogue, to a democratic culture, to an openness to otherness and cultural diversity, with a reflexive and critical return on one's own cultures.

and content and language integrated learning (CLIL) and teaching (for an illustration see the project *A Pluriliteracies Approach to Teaching for Learning*[2]).

A comprehensive approach to the curriculum

All these considerations require that coherence in learning be created through a global approach to the school curriculum, which can be defined as a tool for organising learning. Table 8.2, reproduced from the *Guide for the Development and Implementation of Curricula for Plurilingual and Intercultural Education* (Beacco *et al.*, 2016a) offers a structured approach to the components and decision-making levels which need to be brought together. The development and implementation of a curriculum involves many actors and a considerable number of actions at several levels of the education system (see Table 8.2, column 4). The aim of a concerted development of the different components of the curriculum (see columns 2 and 3) is to promote economy and coherence in teaching and learning. This depends on the different levels of decision-making and requires a precise analysis of the societal context and the status of the languages concerned.

Teachers and teacher teams work together at the level of the individual (NANO), the class (MICRO) and the school (MESO) (see Table 8.2, components 4 to 10), and the coherence of learning is facilitated by agreeing on the aims, objectives/competences and content.

Table 8.2 Components of curriculum planning (Beacco *et al.*, 2016a: 19)

		Components	Commonest level
1	General aims	What is/are the learner's/s'aim/s in learning?	MACRO (nation, state, region)
2	Specific aims/ competences	What aims are they pursuing/are assigned to them?	
3	Content	What are they required to learn?	
4	Approaches and activities	How are they required to learn?	MICRO (CLASS) and MESO (school)
5	Grouping and location	Where, and with whom, do they learn?	
6	Time	When do they learn? How much time do they have?	
7	Aids and resources	With what do they learn?	
8	Role of teachers	How do teachers promote, organise and facilitate learning processes?	
9	Co-operation	What types of co-operation, particularly between teachers, are needed to facilitate learning?	
10	Evaluation	How are progress and acquired competences evaluated?	From NANO (individual) to SUPRA (international)

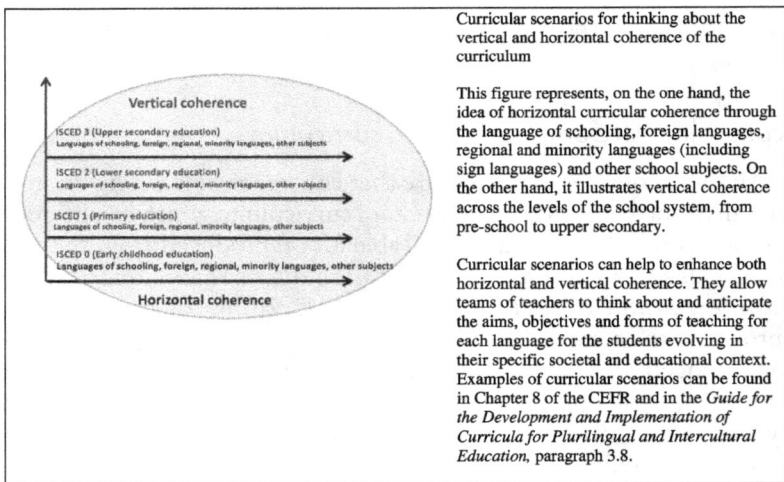

Curricular scenarios for thinking about the vertical and horizontal coherence of the curriculum

This figure represents, on the one hand, the idea of horizontal curricular coherence through the language of schooling, foreign languages, regional and minority languages (including sign languages) and other school subjects. On the other hand, it illustrates vertical coherence across the levels of the school system, from pre-school to upper secondary.

Curricular scenarios can help to enhance both horizontal and vertical coherence. They allow teams of teachers to think about and anticipate the aims, objectives and forms of teaching for each language for the students evolving in their specific societal and educational context. Examples of curricular scenarios can be found in Chapter 8 of the CEFR and in the *Guide for the Development and Implementation of Curricula for Plurilingual and Intercultural Education*, paragraph 3.8.

Figure 8.5 Horizontal and vertical coherence and curricular scenarios (adapted from Beacco *et al.*, 2016)

To contribute to the overall development and education of the learner, coherence in a decompartmentalised curriculum is necessary – both horizontally across languages and subjects, and vertically, across years and learning cycles. Curricular scenarios (see Figure 8.5) can help to improve these two forms of coherence.

The school curriculum is part of an experiential curriculum, which varies greatly from one individual to another, encompassing all the learning experiences that each person has, including but not limited to the school curriculum. These experiences allow individuals to develop their personality and identity as well as their linguistic and cultural repertoire. Addressing the individual learner's experiential curriculum is essential to ensure quality education.

Language teachers need to be aware of the importance of providing different types of learning experiences and of the different ways in which languages can be acquired. A variety of experiences to which learners are exposed must also be included in a school's curriculum in order to develop sound skills, exploit their potential and maintain motivation: see *Guide for the Development and Implementation of Curricula for Plurilingual and Intercultural Education* (Beacco *et al.*, 2016a: section 1.2.4).

Individual and shared responsibility of teachers

A global approach to languages implies changes to traditional teaching, carried out individually by each teacher. In a more holistic and integrated approach, teachers do not act solely as individuals, but are part of a team that works collectively at the heart of the school (see also Chapter 11). The various teaching teams usually contribute to the development of the school's language policy which represents the educational offer for the community and families it serves. This school language policy should address the particular needs of the school environment, policy guidelines (national, regional or local) and proven and innovative methodologies. Such a policy should guide and shape the individual choices of each teacher. They can adhere to it while making necessary adaptations to the needs of each class and student, thus making their own contribution. The individual teacher's professional action is therefore at the heart of a collective action, an action that is consistent with the choice of values, principles and educational goals that are common to the entire teaching body: see *Guide for the Development and Implementation of Curricula for Plurilingual and Intercultural Education* (Beacco *et al.*, 2016a); *Guide for the Development of Language Education Policies in Europe* (Beacco & Byram, 2007, Main version Part 3, Ch. 6: Organising Plurilingual Education, e.g. 6.4).

What is the Role of Language Teachers in Supporting the Development of Skills across Languages, Disciplines and Years?

The mediating role of every teacher

The Russian psychologist Lev S. Vygotsky (1997/1934) masterfully demonstrated the mediating role of language, both in the formulation of everyday concepts and in the construction of scientific concepts. Vygotsky's fundamental contribution was to highlight the centrality of language in its cognitive, heuristic and conceptual functions as well as in the formation of thought. He demonstrated the central role of the competent adult and their support in helping learners to progress more rapidly in the construction of knowledge when they are in their *zone of proximal development*. Furthermore, Vygotsky emphasised that learning a second or foreign language creates an increased awareness of (and distance from) the first language, and that the first language supports the new language.

A major function of any teacher – whether of languages or of other disciplines – is to mediate between the subject they teach and each student, in the zone of proximal development. Mediation in the broadest sense encompasses a wide range of procedures for supporting and collaborating in the construction of knowledge. Mediation in this broad sense is fundamental to pedagogical approaches that aim to expand individual and collective learner autonomy, create a democratic classroom culture, and make room in the classroom for the learner's voice (see Coste & Cavalli, 2015).

Embracing linguistic and cultural diversity as an asset for the whole class

Seeing the classroom as a learning space for all students implies that it is a place of emotional security where everyone feels accepted in their similarities with and differences from others – whether it is their plurilingual and pluricultural repertoire, their primary experiences, their personal talents or their desire to learn. Highlighting similarities is the basis, then, for valuing differences as opportunities for enrichment for the whole class. One major difference is the plurilingual repertoires of the students with their different varieties of the language of schooling but also (varieties of) other languages or dialects. Consequently, their repertoires manifest heterogeneous profiles of competence in their various languages and diversified cultural knowledge. Table 8.3 provides ideas and resources to assist in putting the linguistic and cultural diversity of the learners at the heart of learning and teaching, with a view to promoting equity, equality and inclusion.

Teamwork to achieve an integrated approach to languages education

The practical implementation of an integrated approach is based on collaboration and consultation between teachers, which can take place in a variety of ways depending on the degree of integration and personal commitment of the teachers (Cavalli, 2005: 205–206).

Informing each other, consulting and clarifying

The first, minimal level involves mutual information about teaching content, the development of a common language, and consultation on certain classroom management techniques. The latter imply, for instance,

Table 8.3 Council of Europe resources designed to promote equity, equality and inclusion

Questions relevant to equity, equality and inclusion in education	Some Council of Europe resources
(a) how to establish the starting point for each student in each of the second or foreign languages taught in school, and how to include plurilingual and intercultural competences for all languages in their repertoires?	The *Common European Framework of Reference (CEFR)* and *Companion Volume* can provide the means to determine the progress of each student in each second or foreign language, provided they are not used to establish an abstract, average level that everyone must achieve. The *Framework of Reference for Pluralistic Approaches to Languages and Cultures (FREPA)* with its descriptors of plurilingual and intercultural competences and accompanying resources opens ways to the development of transversal competences.
(b) how to assess, in order to take into account and to value the competences of pupils in the languages of their repertoire which are absent from the school curriculum?	*RECOLANG (Resources for assessing the home language competences of migrant pupils)* offers reflections, a set of devices for formative assessment and useful tests to include the languages that some students speak (but that the school does not teach) in order to value these languages and use them in the classroom.
(c) how can these skills be used as resources available to the child, and how can they be used in the classroom to support the child's learning of the language of instruction?	*MARILLE (Majority language in multilingual settings)* offers concrete examples of how the school language classroom can become a space for welcoming and reflecting on students' repertoires for better language acquisition. Classroom videos from the *Comparons nos langues* project (Auger, 2005) show, for example, these students questioning the functioning of articles in their languages that differ from that of French. Student become experts in their own languages and explain them to friends and to the teacher.
(d) how can we ensure that the family reinforces the skills in the family languages?	*Parents (Involving parents in plurilingual and intercultural education)* offers a variety of activities that can provide ideas, for example, concerning family language policies (e.g. which language to use in the home) or building constructive and collaborative relationships between school and family despite the differences in educational cultures.
(e) what explicit teaching should be provided for each student so that they are able to progress in acquiring the academic variety of the language of schooling?	The publication *The Language Dimension in All Subjects: A Handbook for Curriculum Development and Teacher Training* presents, describes and operationalises the work to be done on the language dimensions of subjects for quality and equity in education: the role of language in constructing knowledge, the forms of communication in

(Continued)

Table 8.3 (*Continued*)

	the classroom, the appropriation of scientific expression, convergences and specificity in academic language specific to school subjects, and teaching approaches. *Roadmap* (*A roadmap for schools to support the language(s) of schooling*) provides an IT tool for various school actors (head teachers, teachers, students and their parents, other staff) for an initial reflection on the language of schooling. The publication *Language skills for successful subject learning – CEFR-linked descriptors for mathematics and history/civics* is based on the project *Language descriptors*. This helps to determine the language needs of students with a migrant background by providing descriptors for the language of schooling in certain school subjects. The resource website *Language in subject* (*Developing language awareness in subject classes*) presents practical tools and material that help subject teachers to identify the linguistic needs of all students (particularly the vulnerable learners) and provides tailored support.
(f) what kind of specific support should be offered to students who have a gap in their language of schooling skills?	Paragraph 3.7 of the *Guide for the Development and Implementation of Curricula for Plurilingual and Intercultural Education* (pp. 95–99) describes different approaches according to target groups and situations; it outlines the attention to be paid to and some of the steps to be taken for this type of audience. Paragraph 5.3 of the publication *The Language Dimension in all Subjects* specifically describes the measures to be adopted for allophone students from a range of possible models of plurilingual education.

delicate and fundamental issues such as how to deal with errors or how to intervene in the case of students with difficulties. It is also essential that teachers make explicit (and, above all, agree on) the models of language description (conception of language, grammatical model, metalanguage to be used, type of metalinguistic and (inter)cultural reflection to be favoured...) that serve as a basis for their teaching. This first level represents a preparatory working method for an effective pedagogical integration and constitutes one of the essential requirements.

Planning together and agreeing on circumscribed areas

A second, intermediate level presupposes joint planning work that makes it possible to set objectives, content, methods, procedures and evaluation methods for specific areas of the curriculum.

Building and implementing an integrated curriculum

A third level, the most advanced and ambitious, is that of an integrated curriculum for the languages taught, within which teachers would:

- integrate objectives into common sequences (at least as far as basic strategies and fundamental textual typologies are concerned);
- aim for an economy of the curriculum by exploiting, whenever possible, the transfer of linguistic and pragmatic strategies and acquisitions from one language to another;
- agree, in a much more precise and global way than at the second level, on the modalities of assessment;
- plan, create and exploit occasions of use of several languages according to the communicative situations and goals of the communication, by valuing, in these situations, linguistic alternation (also called *translanguaging*, see below);
- systematically identify 'close' and 'distant' elements in the languages, in order to set up metalinguistic activities of comparison.

The emphasis on the term 'integration' should not obscure the need for 'concerted differentiation' as well. An integrated approach to teaching and learning is the exact opposite of linguistic homogenisation: it is effective when the right balance of fine-tuned reflection and concrete work is done on both the analogies and the differences between the languages involved. Concrete ideas for implementation can be found in the *Guide for the Development and Implementation of Curricula for Plurilingual and Intercultural Education* and are also provided below.

The support of school principals is essential for the implementation of these convergences: they can greatly support them by making resources available and by facilitating communication or arranging spaces (see Chapter 11).

Preparing and accompanying transitions and necessary breaks: The longitudinal dimension of learning

The need to create continuity in language learning over time can be in sharp contrast, or even contradiction, with the discontinuity induced by the structuring of the education system into levels or cycles. This is particularly striking in the teaching of foreign languages when the resources developed in the previous cycle are sometimes ignored and learners start from scratch (for example, during the transition from primary to secondary school) or when the learning of a language in the previous cycle is interrupted in the next. Research shows that this break is one of the main causes of the lack of success of foreign language teaching in primary school.

Teachers can play an active role in preventing disruptions, through communication and collaboration among colleagues, between cycles and across disciplines (e.g. by designing curriculum scenarios, see section *A Comprehensive Approach to the Curriculum*, above), but also individually, by looking at the objectives and materials of other cycles, by assessing learning in a learner-centred, coherent way and in line with the objectives of the previous cycle, and by looking at the learning pathways of individual students (e.g. the *PALINGUI* project – *Language learning pathways of young children*).

Integrate innovative approaches

What methods should be used to decompartmentalise language teaching and to encourage learners to use their full linguistic repertoire in the classroom – whether in languages or in other disciplines? How can plurilingual and intercultural awareness be developed? In the following, we present some ideas based on innovative approaches to plurilingual and intercultural education.

Teaching for transfer

Research suggests that reading and writing should be considered cross-curricular skills: strategies learned in one language can be used in another language. Transfer can be actively encouraged – from a strong language to a weaker language (e.g. from a language of schooling to a home language) and vice versa (e.g. from a foreign language to a language of schooling). Exchange and collaboration between teachers of different languages with the same students is a logical consequence. There are, for the moment, few ready-made materials for collaborative teaching for transfer, but teachers can, for example, compare existing syllabi, textbooks or other materials by asking themselves:

- What reading or writing strategies should be promoted across grades and disciplines?
- In which 'languages as subjects' have strategies already been addressed, when and how?
- How can interdisciplinary support be designed together?

It then becomes possible to reconnect students with what has been addressed in the other discipline. A common instrument (e.g. a notebook where students write down strategies and to which the teachers of different subjects refer) can be used as a vehicle for cross-curricular support.

> Forbes (2021) conducted an intervention study with 13–14-year-old learners in Year 9 in England, with German as a foreign language. The intervention consisted of training in writing strategies: planning (e.g. goal-setting, planning the content and the structure of one's text), monitoring (e.g. use a dictionary, refer to one's notes/textbook/plan, use another word if one gets stuck), evaluation (e.g. check spelling, punctuation and tense, peer checking).

This training was introduced in German, and then continued in English and German courses for eight months. Forbes initially observed a selective transfer of strategies from the foreign language to the language of schooling, without instruction on transfer. However, the strongest effect on the language of instruction was achieved by parallel instruction on transfer in both languages and explicitly linking the instruction of the two subjects. It was important that practice was planned by teachers jointly between the subjects, that the same terminology was used, and that students were systematically made aware of learning in the other subject. The book presents valuable information about how training in cross-language strategies affects different learners differently, as well as many suggestions for interdisciplinary cooperation.

Another example is provided by the SIMO project by German researchers Nicole Marx and Thorsten Steinhoff (http://www.simo.uni-bremen.de). The research involved Turkish-speaking children in the sixth grade (11/12 years old) attending school in Germany. The researchers showed how strategies for writing and revising texts could be taught in German, the language of schooling, and applied by the students in Turkish, which was minimally supervised by a weekly support class. The didactic sequence targets the description of fictional super-heroic characters (see Figure 8.6).[3]

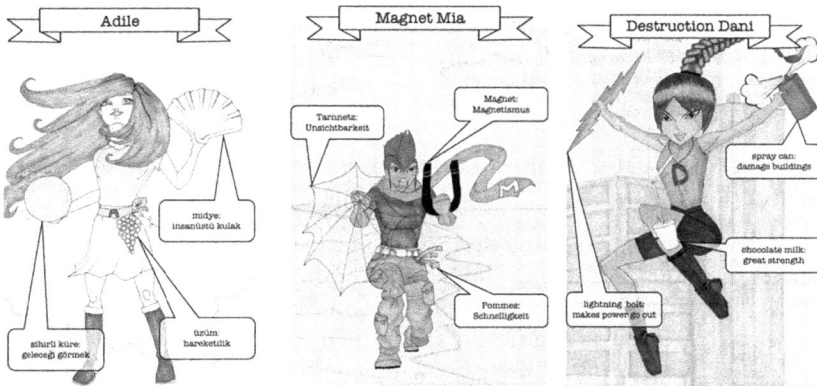

Figure 8.6 Joint support for writing strategies across languages (Marx & Steinhoff, 2020)

Promoting openness to diversity, linguistic awareness and motivation

Other approaches that promote the decompartmentalisation of languages include *Intercomprehension* between closely related languages and *language awareness/awakening to languages*, pedagogic strategies that have been developed over the last 40 years and are now the subject of a large body of literature.

Intercomprehension involves using mutual intelligibility between neighbouring languages (and others), for example being able to read and understand something in Romanian if one has learned French before or Swedish on the basis of German, when one does not yet have any knowledge of these languages. Comprehension skills are encouraged by systematically training learners in techniques such as the use of international and parallel words and the recognition of recurring linguistic patterns. This not only develops the ability to understand other languages, but also metalinguistic awareness and openness to linguistic and cultural diversity.

Language awareness/Awakening to languages activities also address these aspects, but this approach consists more globally of making learners think about languages, about what they have in common and what differentiates them, about the nature of human language, using written and audio aids that cover all the languages known and learned, but also other languages that the school does not intend to teach. It can also provide special opportunities to welcome and value the languages of migrant children. Critical language awareness aims to integrate into reflection on languages a critical dimension in relation to the issues of domination and power linked to languages.

Intercomprehension is aimed at older learners but can also be adapted to the needs of younger learners, while the opposite is true for *Awakening to languages*. Both approaches can also have a motivating effect on further language acquisition, without of course substituting for it. See more detailed information on both methods in Appendix V of the *Guide for the Development and Implementation of Curricula for Plurilingual and Intercultural Education* (Beacco *et al.*, 2016a).

Making the most of a plurilingual repertoire: Alternating languages

There is a long-standing discussion in research about alternating languages in language teaching and beyond (Lüdi & Py, 2013/1986; Grosjean, 1982). Different pedagogical approaches have been developed in recent years, called – depending on the theoretical orientation – crosslinguistic pedagogy (Cummins, 2021), pedagogical translanguaging (Cenoz & Gorter, 2021) or functional multilingual learning (Avermaet *et al.*, 2017). All approaches focus on the activation of students' whole repertoire. These include fluid practices of simultaneous use of two or more languages in oral or written production, or use of texts in one language and writing in another, and so on.

This approach supports the development of all languages used by learners and of metalinguistic awareness, while softening the boundaries between languages. On the one hand, it can be used in language learning, for example by systematically allowing students to use words in the language of schooling or other languages in their repertoire when composing texts. On the other hand, it can be used in the learning of content, and very profitably in the case of students with different first languages during conceptualisation (to be carried out, for example, in their strongest language, and then switched back to the language of schooling). Cenoz and Gorter (2021) consider that it is essential to accompany this approach with a carefully planned and implemented pedagogical framework, depending on an equally careful analysis of the educational context and learners' backgrounds, and to make learners aware of these practices.

Promoting linguistic and intercultural awareness through mobility

Educational mobility, organised in a school setting, provides particular opportunities to promote not only autonomous language learning and use, but also to encourage intercultural dialogue, social cohesion and democratic citizenship (see Figure 8.7). Short or long mobility stays, exchanges with spatial displacement and real meeting, or virtual exchanges (blogs, video conferences, e-learning platforms, etc.) without changing physical environment allow communication and co-operation with students from different cultural and linguistic backgrounds. Often, it is assumed that linguistic and intercultural learning will happen on its own. Organisational issues take precedence. However, by proper guidance before, during and after, teachers (and teacher educators) as mediators can help in enhancing learning and avoiding cultural stereotyping.

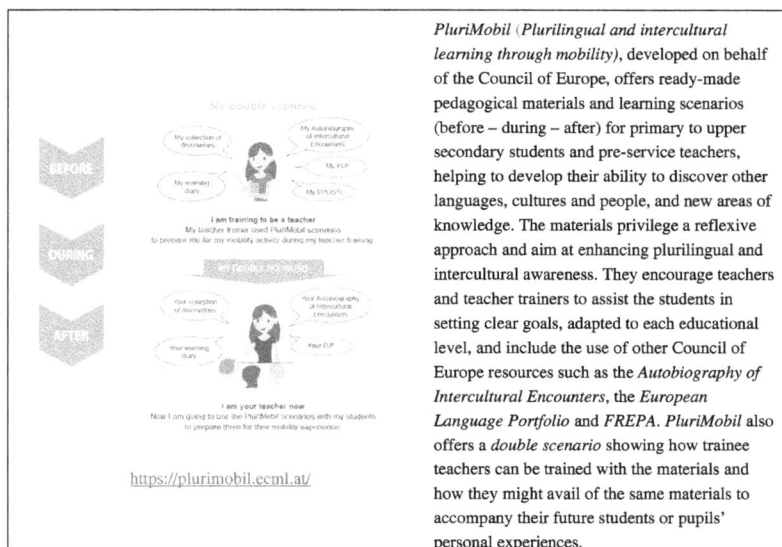

PluriMobil (Plurilingual and intercultural learning through mobility), developed on behalf of the Council of Europe, offers ready-made pedagogical materials and learning scenarios (before – during – after) for primary to upper secondary students and pre-service teachers, helping to develop their ability to discover other languages, cultures and people, and new areas of knowledge. The materials privilege a reflexive approach and aim at enhancing plurilingual and intercultural awareness. They encourage teachers and teacher trainers to assist the students in setting clear goals, adapted to each educational level, and include the use of other Council of Europe resources such as the *Autobiography of Intercultural Encounters*, the *European Language Portfolio* and FREPA. *PluriMobil* also offers a *double scenario* showing how trainee teachers can be trained with the materials and how they might avail of the same materials to accompany their future students or pupils' personal experiences.

https://plurimobil.ecml.at/

Figure 8.7 Plurilingual and intercultural learning through mobility for students and future teachers (Egli Cuenat *et al.*, 2015) © Council of Europe/ECML

Concrete methodologies include reflexive or meta-reflexive activities concerning (inter)cultural dimensions, autonomous language learning processes in informal situations, encouraging risk-taking in communication or (auto)biographical and other reflexive narratives such as logbooks/learning journals.

Conclusion

The global approach to languages proposed by the Council of Europe serves the right of all learners to an equitable, inclusive and quality education. Its major purpose is the overall education and development of the student as a person and as a social actor educated in a culture of democracy.

It has various implications for language teachers which can be summarised as follows:

- to place the student and their needs at the centre of the learning-teaching process;
- to value and take into account the plurilingual and pluricultural repertoire of all students;
- to have a global, decompartmentalised and integrated vision of language teaching while respecting the specificities of the acquisition of each individual language;
- to ensure a motivating and rewarding experience for all students in learning the languages taught in the school;
- to support students in developing competences for a culture of democracy through languages and values in plurilingual and intercultural education;
- to collaborate with language colleagues and colleagues from other disciplines on the cross-curricular dimensions of languages and cultures;
- to pay special attention to students with gaps in the language(s) of schooling and to adopt appropriate support measures.

To implement this, in addition to proven professional skills, teachers will share a common ethos to guarantee the right of all learners to quality and equity in educational opportunities across the curriculum.

Notes

(1) *Guide for the Development and Implementation of Curricula for Plurilingual and Intercultural Education* (Beacco *et al.*, 2016a: 25) and Platform of References for Plurilingual and Intercultural Education, https://www.coe.int/en/web/platform-plurilingual-intercultural-language-education/home.
(2) https://pluriliteracies.ecml.at/Home/tabid/4231/language/en-GB/Default.aspx
(3) Pedagogic materials for 5th to 7th year of schooling with video tutorials, including not only German and Turkish but also English as a Foreign Language, can be found here: https://fiona.uni-hamburg.de/4eee4dd4/texteberarbeitenmarxsteinhoff2020.pdf.

References

Auger, N. (2005) *Comparons nos langues*. Montpellier: Canopé.

Avermaet, P.V., Slembrouck, S., Gorp, K.V., Sierens, S. and Maryns, K. (2017) *The Multilingual Edge of Education*. London: Palgrave Macmillan.

Beacco, J.-C. (2013) *Specifying Languages' Contribution to Intercultural Education: Lessons Learned from the CEFR*. Strasbourg: Council of Europe. https://rm.coe.int/specifying-languages-contribution-to-intercultural-education-lessons-l/16808ae53b

Beacco, J.-C. and Byram, M. (2007) *From Linguistic Diversity to Plurilingual Education: Guide for the Development of Language Education Policies in Europe*. Main version. Strasbourg: Council of Europe. (French edn, *Guide pour l'élaboration des politiques linguistiques éducatives en Europe – De la diversité linguistique à l'éducation plurilingue*. Executive version. Strasbourg: Council of Europe, 2007.)

Beacco, J.-C., Byram, M., Cavalli, M., Coste, D., Egli Cuenat, M., Goullier, F. and Panthier, J. (2016a) *Guide for the Development and Implementation of Curricula for Plurilingual and Intercultural Education* (1st edn, 2010). Strasbourg: Council of Europe.

Beacco, J.-C., Fleming, M., Goullier, F., Thürmann, E. and Vollmer, H., with contributions by J. Sheils (2016b) *A Handbook for Curriculum Development and Teacher Training. The Language Dimension in All Subjects*. Strasbourg: Council of Europe.

Byram, M. (2006) *Languages and Identities*. Preliminary Study – Languages of Education. Strasbourg: Council of Europe.

Candelier, M., Camilleri-Grima, A., Castellotti, V., de Pietro, J.-F., Lörincz, I., Meißner, F.-J., Schröder-Sura, A., Noguerol, A. and Molinié, M. (2012) *FREPA – A Framework of Reference for Pluralistic Approaches to Languages and Cultures – Competences and Resources* (revised edn). ECML. Graz: Council of Europe.

Cavalli, M. (2005) Education bilingue et plurilinguisme. Le cas du Val d'Aoste. Paris: Didier.

Cenoz, J. and Gorter, D. (2021) *Translanguaging Pedagogy*. Cambridge: Cambridge University Press.

Coste, D. and Cavalli, M. (2015) *Education, Mobility, Otherness: The Mediation Functions of Schools*. Strasbourg: Council of Europe.

Coste, D., Moore, D. and Zarate, G. (2009) *Plurilingual and Pluricultural Competence*. With a foreword and complementary bibliography. French version originally published in 1997. Language Policy. Strasbourg: Council of Europe.

Council of Europe (2001) *Common European Framework of Reference for Languages: Learning, Teaching, Assessment (CEFR)*. Strasbourg: Council of Europe.

Council of Europe (2018) *Reference Framework of Competences for Democratic Culture* (Volume 1: Context, concepts and model; Volume 2: Descriptors; Volume 3: Guidance for implementation). Strasbourg: Council of Europe.

Council of Europe (2020) *Common European Framework of Reference for Languages: Learning, Teaching, Assessment – Companion Volume*. Strasbourg: Council of Europe.

Cummins, J. (2005) Teaching for cross-language transfer in dual language education: Possibilities and pitfalls. https://www.tesol.org/docs/default-source/new-resource-library/symposium-on-dual-language-education-3.pdf

Cummins, J. (2021) *Rethinking the Education of Multilingual Learners: A Critical Analysis of Theoretical Concepts*. Bristol: Multilingual Matters.

Egli Cuenat, M., Brogan, K., Czura, A., Muller, C., Cole, J., Szczepańska A., Bleichenbacher, L., Höchle Meier K. and Wolfer B. (2015) *PluriMobil – Plurilingual and Intercultural Learning through Mobility: Practical Resources for Teachers and Teacher Trainers*. Graz: Council of Europe. https://plurimobil.ecml.at

Fleming, M. (2010) *The Aims of Language Teaching and Learning*. Strasbourg: Council of Europe.

Forbes, K. (2021) *Cross-Linguistic Transfer of Writing Strategies: Interactions between Foreign Language and First Language Classrooms*. Bristol: Multilingual Matters.

Grosjean, F. (1982) *Life with Two Languages: An Introduction to Bilingualism*. Cambridge, MA: Harvard University Press.

Jessner, U. and Allgäuer-Hackl, E. (2020) Multilingual awareness and metacognition in multilingually diverse classrooms. *Journal of Multilingual Theories and Practices* 1 (1), 66–88. https://doi.org/10.1558/jmtp.17285

Kusters, A. and De Meulder, M. (2019) Language portraits: Investigating embodied multilingual and multimodal repertoires. *FQS* 20 (3). https://www.qualitative-research.net/index.php/fqs/article/view/3239/4452

Lüdi, G. and Py, B. (2013) *Être bilingue* (4th edn; 1st edn 1986). Bern: Peter Lang.

Marx, N. and Steinhoff, T. (2020) *Texte überarbeiten! Materialien für den Deutsch-, Herkunfts- und Fremdsprachenunterricht in der 5., 6. und 7. Klasse*. Universität Hamburg. https://fiona.uni-hamburg.de/4eee4dd4/texteberarbeitenmarxsteinhoff2020.pdf

Pottier, B. (1992) *Sémantique générale*. Paris: PUF.

Vygotsky, L.S. (1997) *Pensée et langage* (Original edn 1934, Moskva-Leningrad). Paris: la Dispute.

ECML Projects

Name	Acronym/Abbreviation	Website
Majority language in multilingual settings	MARILLE	https://www.ecml.at/ECML-Programme/Programme2008-2011/Majoritylanguage inmultilingualsettings/tabid/5451/Default.aspx
A pluriliteracies approach to teaching for learning	PLURILITERACIES	https://pluriliteracies.ecml.at/Home/tabid/4231/language/en-GB/Default.aspx
The Framework of Reference for Pluralistic Approaches to Languages and Cultures	FREPA	https://carap.ecml.at/Portals/11/documents/CARAP-version3-EN-28062010.pdf
Resources for assessing the home language competences of migrant pupils	RECOLANG	https://www.ecml.at/ECML-Programme/Programme2020-2023/Resourcesfor assessingthehomelanguagecompetencesofmigrantpupils/tabid/4297/language/en-GB/Default.aspx
A roadmap for schools to support the language(s) of schooling	ROADMAP	https://www.ecml.at/ECML-Programme/Programme2016-2019/roadmapforschools/tabid/2994/language/en-GB/Default.aspx
Language skills for successful subject learning – CEFR-linked descriptors for mathematics and history/civics	Language descriptors	https://www.ecml.at/Portals/1/mtp4/language_descriptors/documents/language-descriptors-EN.pdf
Developing language awareness in subject classes	Language in subject	https://www.ecml.at/ECML-Programme/Programme2016-2019/Languageofschooling/tabid/1854/Default.aspx
Language learning pathways of young children – Making early language learning visible	PALINGUI	https://www.ecml.at/News/TabId/643/ArtMID/2666/ArticleID/1584/PALINGUI-%E2%80%93-Language-learning-pathways-of-young-children-%E2%80%93-Making-early-language-learning-visible-webinar-recording-5-March-2020-online.aspx
Involving parents in plurilingual and intercultural education	PARENTS	https://parents.ecml.at/Home/tabid/4187/language/en-GB/Default.aspx
Plurilingual and intercultural learning through mobility – Practical resources for teachers and teacher trainers	PLURIMOBIL	https://plurimobil.ecml.at/

9 The Special Case of Education for Migrants: Children

Nathalie Auger and David Little

What do I need to do as a teacher to support children from migrant backgrounds in mastering the academic language required for school success and developing their plurilingual and pluricultural repertoires?

Introduction

This chapter describes innovative responses to two of the challenges that large-scale migration poses to education systems: the need on the one hand to develop migrants' proficiency in the language of schooling and on the other to draw their home languages into the educational process in ways that benefit all learners. The first part of the chapter explains how the *Common European Framework of Reference for Languages* (CEFR) (Council of Europe, 2001) and the European Language Portfolio (Council of Europe, 2011) were used to support the development of immigrant pupils' proficiency in English as the language of schooling in Irish primary schools. The second part of the chapter illustrates the Council of Europe's concept of plurilingual and intercultural education in action in France. The chapter also contains two vignettes. In the first, Déirdre Kirwan describes the highly successful approach to educational inclusion developed by a girls' primary school in one of Dublin's western suburbs; in the second, Anne-Laure Biales describes how a plurilingual approach to debates about literature in a French secondary school gives added value by including literature in students' home languages. We begin however with a brief overview of the Council of Europe's perspective on the education of migrant children and teenagers.

Council of Europe Policy on the Education of Migrant Children and Teenagers

Support for the educational inclusion of migrant children and teenagers is part of the Council of Europe's human rights agenda and ultimately rests on Article 2 of Protocol No. 1 to the European Convention on

Human Rights (1950): 'No person shall be denied the right to education'. The Council of Europe views educational inclusion not only as an individual right, however, but as a precondition for social cohesion. At the Third Summit of Heads of State and Government, held in Warsaw in 2005, the member states committed themselves to ensuring that cultural diversity becomes a source of mutual enrichment:

> We are determined to build cohesive societies by ensuring fair access to social rights, fighting exclusion and protecting vulnerable social groups. [...] We are also resolved to strengthen the cohesion of our societies in its social, educational, health and cultural dimensions.[1]

The European Social Charter (1961, revised 1996) recognises the role played by language in social inclusion: Parties to the Charter undertake 'to promote and facilitate the teaching of the national language of the receiving state or, if there are several, one of these languages, to migrant workers and members of their families' (Article 19.11). This is however only one side of the linguistic challenge posed by large-scale migration. The European Social Charter also recognises the importance of the mother tongue to the individual migrant's educational achievement: Parties to the Charter also undertake 'to promote and facilitate, as far as practicable, the teaching of the migrant worker's mother tongue to the children of the migrant worker' (Article 19.12). In many member states the extreme linguistic diversity of school-going populations makes it impossible to fulfil this undertaking. Some Council of Europe member states seek to avoid the challenges of inclusion altogether by educating migrants and other minorities outside the mainstream, but this practice has been sharply criticised by the Commissioner for Human Rights: 'School segregation is one of the worst forms of discrimination and a serious violation of the rights of the children concerned, as their learning opportunities are seriously harmed' (Council of Europe Commissioner for Human Rights, 2017: 5).

Two recommendations of the Committee of Ministers refer specifically to the needs of migrant pupils and students within the mainstream: Recommendation CM/Rec(2012)13, on ensuring quality education, and Recommendation CM/Rec(2014)5, on the importance of competences in the language(s) of schooling for equity and quality in education and for educational success. According to the first of these recommendations, quality education 'gives access to learning to all pupils and students, particularly those in vulnerable or disadvantaged groups, adapted to their needs as appropriate' (Appendix, 6.a); while the second recommendation states: 'Where the inability of pupils and students to follow regular educational programmes is due to temporary factors such as lack of proficiency in the language(s) of instruction [...], public authorities should ensure that those concerned are provided with opportunities to remedy the causes for their difficulty as rapidly as possible' (Appendix, 29). In parallel with these recommendations, the project *Languages in Education,*

Languages for Education produced a concept paper on the linguistic and educational inclusion of migrant pupils and students (Little, 2010) and six ancillary studies (Anderson *et al.*, 2010; Bainski *et al.*, 2010; Bertucci, 2010; Castellotti & Moore, 2010; Lengyel, 2010; Thürmann *et al.*, 2010). Containing a wide range of practical proposals inspired by Council of Europe perspectives and values, these publications provide a broader context for the projects described in this chapter.

Developing Immigrant Pupils' Proficiency in the Language of Schooling in Ireland

The context

Historically a country of emigration, Ireland has experienced unprecedented levels of immigration over the past quarter of a century. Relatively small numbers of refugees were admitted in the 1990s; larger numbers of asylum seekers and economic migrants were attracted by the booming economy in the same decade; and still larger numbers of immigrants came from eastern Europe and the Baltic states following the enlargement of the European Union in 2004 and 2007. In the 40 years from 1956 to 1996 Ireland's population increased by 25%, from 2.9 to 3.6 million; in the 20 years from 1996 to 2016 it increased by 31%, from 3.6 to 4.8 million (Central Statistics Office, 2017: 6). In 2016, 17.3% of Irish residents (0.8 million) had been born outside Ireland (Central Statistics Office, 2017: 46).

This change in Ireland's demographic posed a challenge to the education system: schools had to educate rapidly increasing numbers of primary pupils and post-primary students who lacked proficiency in English, the language of majority schooling, either because they had been born outside the country or because they had grown up speaking one of Ireland's more than 200 'new' languages at home. The official response to the challenge was to assign pupils/students for whom English was an additional language (EAL) to an age-appropriate mainstream class and to provide them with two years of specially funded English language support. Schools were free to organise this support in whatever way seemed best to them. In most cases EAL pupils/students were withdrawn from their mainstream class to attend English language lessons in small groups, usually once each day. To begin with, the Department of Education and Skills (DES) assumed that schools needed no additional support, but this turned out not to be the case. Integrate Ireland Language and Training (IILT), a non-profit campus company of Trinity College Dublin founded by David Little, was already providing English language programmes for adult refugees. In 2000 the DES commissioned IILT (i) to define benchmarks that could be used to map the linguistic development of immigrant pupils and students; (ii) to develop teaching/learning materials; and (iii) to mediate benchmarks and materials to teachers via a programme of twice-yearly in-service days. These tasks were performed separately for the primary and post-primary sectors. For reasons of space the remainder of this account focuses on the primary sector.

Making use of the CEFR: English language proficiency benchmarks

Although the CEFR was not published in its definitive version until 2001, a second draft of the document had been in circulation since 1997 and IILT used it when designing English language programmes for adult refugees. It seemed reasonable to hypothesise that in an immersion situation EAL beginners could achieve an age-appropriate version of level B1, which defines the learner as an 'independent user' of the target language, by the end of their two years of English language support (this hypothesis was subsequently confirmed by empirical research; see Ćatibušić & Little, 2014). Accordingly, the *English Language Proficiency Benchmarks* (IILT, 2003a) were based on the first three proficiency levels of the CEFR. IILT's aim was not to develop a separate EAL curriculum but to provide teachers with a lens through which to view the primary school curriculum from the perspective of EAL pupils' developing proficiency; in other words, to describe the extent to which they could participate in the activities and discourse of the mainstream classroom at levels A1, A2 and B1. At the same time, the *Benchmarks* must be a tool that teachers could easily familiarise themselves with and use on a daily basis, and they must apply to pupils across the primary school age range (4+ to 12+).

Consulting with teacher focus groups, IILT drew up a list of 13 themes ('units of work') that recurred in one way or another in each year of the primary school curriculum. It then reviewed the CEFR's illustrative scales for listening, reading, spoken interaction, spoken production and writing, identifying descriptors that could be adapted to the context of primary schooling. The adapted descriptors were collapsed into a set of 'global benchmarks of communicative proficiency' that were presented in the same way as the CEFR's self-assessment grid (Council of Europe, 2001: 26–27): proficiency levels on the horizontal axis, language activities on the vertical. Next IILT drew on the CEFR's illustrative scales of communicative language competences to create 'global scales of underlying linguistic competence', a grid containing simple age-appropriate descriptors for grammatical, lexical, phonological and orthographic competence at levels A1, A2 and B1. Finally, and again with reference to the CEFR's illustrative scales, the global benchmarks were recast for each of the 13 units of work: *Myself*; *Our School*; *Food and Clothes*; *Colours, Shapes and Opposites*; *People Who Help Us*; *Travel*; *Seasons, Holidays and Festivals*; *The Local and Wider Community*; *Time*; *People and Places in Other Areas*; *Animals and Plants*; *Caring for My Locality*. For purposes of illustration, Table 9.1 shows A2 descriptors for spoken interaction from the CEFR's self-assessment grid, the global benchmarks, and Unit of work 3, *Food and Clothes*. In their final form the *Benchmarks* ran to 24 A4 pages.

Table 9.1 Descriptors for A2 spoken interaction

	A2 Spoken interaction
CEFR self-assessment grid (Council of Europe, 2001: 26)	I can communicate in simple and routine tasks requiring a simple and direct exchange of information on familiar topics and activities. I can handle very short social exchanges, even though I can't usually understand enough to keep the conversation going myself.
Global benchmarks (IILT, 2003a: 7)	Can ask for attention in class. Can greet, take leave, request and thank appropriately. Can respond with confidence to familiar questions clearly expressed about family, friends, school work, hobbies, holidays, etc., but is not always able to keep the conversation going. Can generally sustain a conversational exchange with a peer in the classroom when carrying out a collaborative learning activity (making or drawing something, preparing a role-play, presenting a puppet show, etc.). Can express personal feelings in a simple way.
Unit of work 3, Food and clothes (IILT, 2003a: 12)	Can ask and answer basic questions about the food/drink he/she likes or dislikes and briefly report the likes and dislikes of others. Can discuss a menu and select what he/she would like. Can answer questions about items and types of clothing, e.g. what is suitable for different kinds of weather.

Using the European Language Portfolio to support teaching and learning

The Council of Europe conceived the European Language Portfolio (ELP) (Council of Europe, 2011) as a means of mediating the CEFR's ethos and proficiency levels to learners. The ELP has three components: a language passport, which summarises the owner's experience of language learning and language use; a language biography, which provides a reflective accompaniment to learning; and a dossier, in which the owner keeps work in progress and/or pieces of work that can be used as evidence of learning achievement. The ELP has two interdependent functions. In its pedagogical function it is designed to foster learner autonomy, support the development of intercultural competence, and promote plurilingualism; in its reporting function it provides evidence of learning that can be used to supplement examination grades. Goal-setting and self-assessment drive the reflective processes on which effective use of the ELP depends. They are based on checklists of 'I can' descriptors arranged according to the communicative language activities and proficiency levels of the CEFR; in most ELPs the checklists are included in the language biography because they guide learning. Periodically owners update the summary of their proficiency contained in the language passport, usually with reference to the CEFR's self-assessment grid.

Although IILT's ELP for primary EAL learners (IILT, 2003b) was designed to support the learning of English, it took full account of pupils' plurilingual and pluricultural identities. Teachers were encouraged to get parents to translate headings into their home language, and the language passport and language biography both contained pages that enabled pupils to summarise their experience of language in their lives outside school. The dossier contained a contents page, open pages related to units of work in the *Benchmarks* and a number of worksheets to which teachers were encouraged to add. Figure 9.1 shows the checklist of 'I can'

Figure 9.1 Irish ELP for EAL primary pupils: goal-setting and self-assessment checklist for *Weather*

descriptors for the unit of work, *Weather*. Teachers used the *Benchmarks* and the ELP to plan their English classes. Every two or three weeks they would refer to the checklists in a review of the work they had been doing and pupils would show that they could perform the relevant checklist tasks. They would then colour in the icons beside the relevant descriptors, against which the teacher would stamp the date. In this way pupils' ELPs provided a detailed chronological record of their progress. Periodically the teacher would help them to update the equivalent of the self-assessment grid in their language passport (an abbreviated version of the global benchmarks), where they could indicate their ability to perform language activities at each level, first 'with a lot of help', then 'with a little help', and finally 'with no help'.

Between 2000 and 2008 IILT developed a large corpus of learning materials and a suite of communicative language tests based on the *Benchmarks*. In each of the last two years of its existence (2006–2007 and 2007–2008) IILT supplied the Irish primary sector with 5000 ELPs and 2000 copies of a pre-literate version, *My First English Book* (IILT, 2005). These figures show that the great majority of pupils entitled to English language support were using one of these instruments and their teachers were using the *English Language Proficiency Benchmarks*. Thanks to the *Benchmarks*, teachers, school principals and school inspectors had a clearly articulated description of the trajectory of proficiency development achievable by two years of English language support. Thanks to the ELP and *My First English Book*, awareness of progress was central to each EAL pupil's language learning experience and easily communicated to parents.

IILT was an early casualty of Ireland's financial crisis and funding was withdrawn in 2008. The system IILT had built in collaboration with teachers around the country quickly fell into disuse, and today the *English Language Proficiency Benchmarks*, the ELP for EAL pupils and *My First English Book* have largely been forgotten. Although IILT's commission was to provide a framework and resources to support the English language proficiency development of EAL pupils and students, its ELPs were designed to make pupils aware of their plurilingual repertoires and its in-service seminars for teachers stressed the importance of home language maintenance, encouraging schools to celebrate the plurilingualism of their pupils in classroom displays. This was the starting point for the innovative approach to plurilingual and intercultural education developed by Scoil Bhríde (Cailíní) (St Brigid's School for Girls), Blanchardstown, which quickly went a long way beyond anything IILT or the Department of Education had envisaged. Scoil Bhríde is the subject of this chapter's first vignette.

Vignette 1

The integrated approach to language teaching developed by Scoil Bhríde (Cailíní) – Déirdre Kirwan

Integration (social integration, inclusion) is understood as a two-sided process and as the capacity of people to live together with full respect for the dignity of each individual, the common good, pluralism and diversity, non-violence and solidarity, as well as their ability to participate in social, cultural, economic and political life.

(*White Paper on Intercultural Dialogue, 'Living Together as Equals in Dignity'*; Council of Europe, 2008: 11)

Introduction

In 1987 I was appointed principal of Scoil Bhríde (Cailíní) (SBC; St Brigid's School for Girls), an English-medium primary school for girls in a western suburb of Dublin. From the mid-1990s, the school experienced unprecedented change. By the time I retired in 2015, 80% of the pupil cohort came from more than 50 linguistic and cultural backgrounds. Most of these children had little or no English when they started school.

In order to ensure that all pupils were fully included in the school and to support them in reaching their full potential, it was necessary to adopt a whole-school approach to meeting their needs. A language policy was formulated and endorsed by the Board of Management, which includes parent representatives. As teachers, we recognised the importance of home languages (HLs) for children's learning, the HL being central to each pupil's sense of self and her principal cognitive tool, the default medium of her discursive thinking, ever present in the unspoken stream of her consciousness (European Commission, 2020: 14). We also saw the linguistic diversity of the school as a resource to be exploited for the benefit of all pupils.

Classroom discourse

We realised that dealing with linguistic diversity was less about devising new approaches and more about being flexible in using current practices to include what learners bring with them. Knowing that 'the child's existing knowledge and experience form the basis for learning' (Government of Ireland, 1999: 8), 'the child is an active agent in his or her learning' (Government of Ireland, 1999: 8) and 'the life of the home is the most potent factor in [the child's] development during the primary school years' (Government of Ireland, 1999: 24), we developed an approach to language education that sought to include the plurilingual repertoires of all our pupils and to support social cohesion. SBC's language policy encouraged pupils to use their HLs at school, inside the classroom as well as outside. As one teacher remarked: 'When you bring in the home languages the lights come on!' While teachers were always in control of classroom discourse, pupils had the right to offer initiatives. A strong emphasis was placed on the development of literacy skills in English, Irish, French (in the last two grades) and HLs.

Although they were unknown to the teachers, the pupils' HLs performed three important functions in the classroom: as the medium of reciprocal communication between pupils with the same or closely related HLs; as a means of display – 'This is what we say in my language'; and as a source of linguistic intuition and insight that encouraged cross-linguistic comparisons and promoted language awareness.

Learning to write in home languages

Regular use of English, Irish and HLs in SBC's classrooms allowed children to use their plurilingual skills to communicate orally. But as writing is closely associated with self-expression, we believed that pupils should learn to write in their HL as well as in English, Irish and French. While we could not teach them to do this, we understood that literacy skills acquired in English could be transferred to Irish and HLs. The support of immigrant parents was crucial to the successful development of their daughters' emerging HL writing skills. The ability to write opened new vistas of cognitive and communicative potential in pupils, resulting in the autonomous production of stories, diaries, autobiographical texts, poems, etc. in multiple languages. Reading aloud the texts they had written in the language(s) of their choice, led to further exploratory talk. Both discussion and written expression developed in complexity as pupils' proficiency in these skills developed.

Being familiar with their own and their classmates' plurilingual skills and with the print-rich environment of their classrooms, where English and Irish are visible, Junior Infant pupils (age 4½) begin to recognise words and phrases. As Senior Infants (5½) they progress to using teacher-designed worksheets, based on classroom discussion. These texts are completed in English and Irish/HLs. Simple identity texts in English and HLs in First Class (6½) become more elaborate in Second Class (7½), while in Third Class (8½) some pupils begin to write texts in English, Irish and their HL. Pupils use their ingenuity to show off their developing language skills; for example, a Romanian pupil in Fourth Class (9½) filled six pages of her copybook with a story in English where the characters speak Romanian. In Fifth Class (10½) French is added to English, Irish and HLs, resulting in texts in three or four languages. In Sixth Class (11½) pupils engage in sophisticated language play and write confidently in English, Irish, French and their HL. The English and Russian texts shown in Figure 9.2 were written by a 7-year-old pupil (First Class) from Latvia; both texts were composed in class without assistance in either language. Figure 9.3 shows four parallel texts, in English, Irish, French and Mandarin, that describe a fictitious teenager, Marceline; they were written by a 12-year-old pupil (Sixth Class) from China.

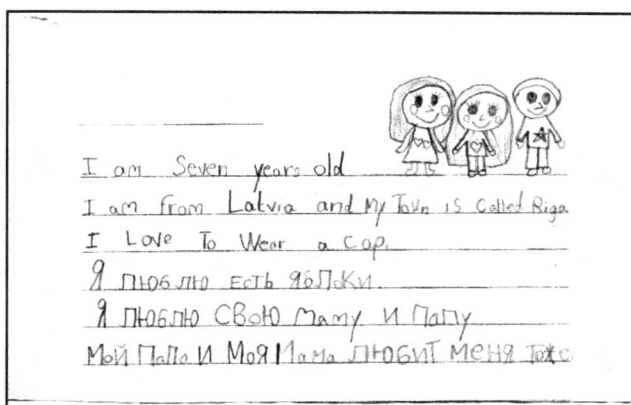

Figure 9.2 Texts in English and Russian written by a 7-year-old pupil from Latvia

A word about Irish

In English-medium schools, Irish provides a level playing field for indigenous Irish and immigrant pupils: they all have their first contact with the language when they start school. As all pupils are beginners, Irish becomes the glue that connects the other languages in the room, including English – teachers have found that pupils contribute more in their HLs during Irish lessons. Pupils' plurilingualism is strengthened by the fact that in SBC, Irish is used as a means of communication outside Irish lessons. Our experience with Irish makes us wonder whether English could play a similar role in countries where it is taught as the first foreign language in primary schools.

Conclusion

Key features of the innovative approach to language learning developed in SBC derive from a view of primary education that is

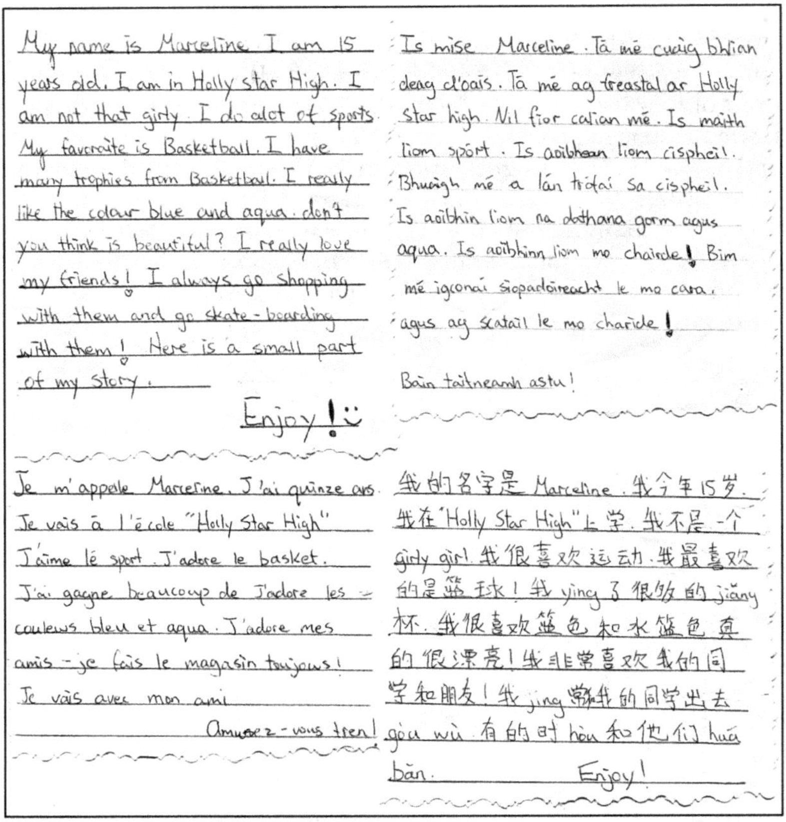

My name is Marceline. I am 15 years old. I am in Holly star High. I am not that girly. I do alot of sports. My favorite is Basketball. I have many trophies from Basketball. I really like the colour blue and aqua. don't you think is beautiful? I really love my friends! I always go shopping with them and go skate-boarding with them! Here is a small part of my story.

Enjoy! :)

Is mise Marceline. Tá mé cúig bhlian deag d'aois. Tá mé ag freastal ar Holly star high. Níl fíor cailín mé. Is maith liom spórt. Is aoibhean liom cispheil. Bhuaigh mé a lán trófaí sa cispheil. Is aoibhin liom na dathana gorm agus aqua. Is aoibhinn liom mo chairde! Bím mé igconaí siopadóireacht le mo cara, agus ag scátaíl le mo chairde!

Bain taitneamh astu!

Je m'appelle Marceline. J'ai quinze ans. Je vais à l'école "Holly Star High". J'aime le sport. J'adore le basket. J'ai gagne beaucoup de J'adore les couleurs bleu et aqua. J'adore mes amis – je fais le magasin toujours! Je vais avec mon ami.

Amusez-vous bien!

我的名字是 Marceline. 我今年15岁. 我在 "Holly Star High" 上学. 我不是一个 girly girl. 我很喜欢运动. 我最喜欢的是篮球! 我 yíng 了很多的 jiǎng 杯. 我很喜欢篮色和水篮色真的很漂亮! 我非常喜欢我的同学和朋友! 我 jing 常我的同学出去 gòu wù. 有的时 hòu 和他们 huá bǎn.　Enjoy!

Figure 9.3 Parallel texts in English, Irish, French and Mandarin written by a 12-year-old pupil from China

child-centred, so that reflective and analytical dimensions of learning are firmly rooted in what pupils themselves contribute. Because classroom interaction takes account of their existing knowledge, skills and interests, pupils tend to be fully engaged. We have found that even very young children can be trusted to know how to use their HL autonomously as a tool of learning and self-evaluation. Finally, the development of literacy in English as the principal language of schooling feeds into, but also depends on, the development of pupils' literacy in their HL, Irish and (in Fifth and Sixth Class) French. Developing oral proficiency, literacy and language awareness is a complex process, in which all language skills support one another.

In SBC, we have found that a plurilingual approach leads to enhanced pupil motivation, an unusual degree of language awareness, a fascination with language and languages that results in autonomous learning, and high levels of literate proficiency in multiple languages. The final word rests with the pupils: 'to be able to say that I went to a school that supports all different languages and cultures is a great thing to have'; 'sometimes it's not really about which language you're learning, it's how to learn a language'; 'your own language [is] what makes you *you* – it's like having an arm or a leg, you can't take it away from you'. (For a full account of SBC's version of plurilingual and intercultural education, see Little & Kirwan, 2019.)

Plurilingual Language Education

This part of the chapter addresses the role of home languages in the implementation of plurilingual and intercultural education in contexts of great linguistic diversity, illustrated by reference to France.

Although the CEFR and more recently its Companion Volume (Council of Europe, 2020) describe proficiency in relation to an unspecified individual language, they assume that language users/learners develop integrated plurilingual repertoires. One of the preparatory studies for the CEFR, by Daniel Coste, Danièle Moore and Geneviève Zarate, explains that the learner's plurilingual and pluricultural competence is not to be thought of as 'the superposition or juxtaposition of distinct competences, but rather as the existence of a complex or even composite competence on which the social actor may draw' (Coste *et al.*, 1999: 11). In 2001, the CEFR argued that plurilingual and pluricultural competence 'promotes the development of linguistic and communication awareness, and even metacognitive strategies which enable the social agent to become more aware of and control his or her own "spontaneous" ways of managing tasks and in particular their linguistic dimension' (Council of Europe, 2001: 134). The experience of learning a new language cannot therefore be conceptualised without taking into account the languages already present in the learner's repertoire, in other words their 'plurilingual competence'. The Council of Europe's (2016) Platform for Plurilingual and Intercultural Education (Figure 9.4) gives practical and concrete indications for operationalising the synergies between the languages present at school for a better acquisition of the language of schooling and of curriculum content. Thus, the language of schooling (in this case, French) can be seen in relation to regional languages, family languages, languages of migration, modern foreign languages, and ancient languages, in any class, whatever the subject is. The management of this repertoire implies that the varieties which compose it do not remain isolated from one another but constitute an integrated communicative competence (Beacco & Byram, 2007: 71).

In practice, it is noticeable that there is still a clear separation between classes hosting newly arrived pupils and mainstream classes, and between the different school subjects where home languages are still not much used.

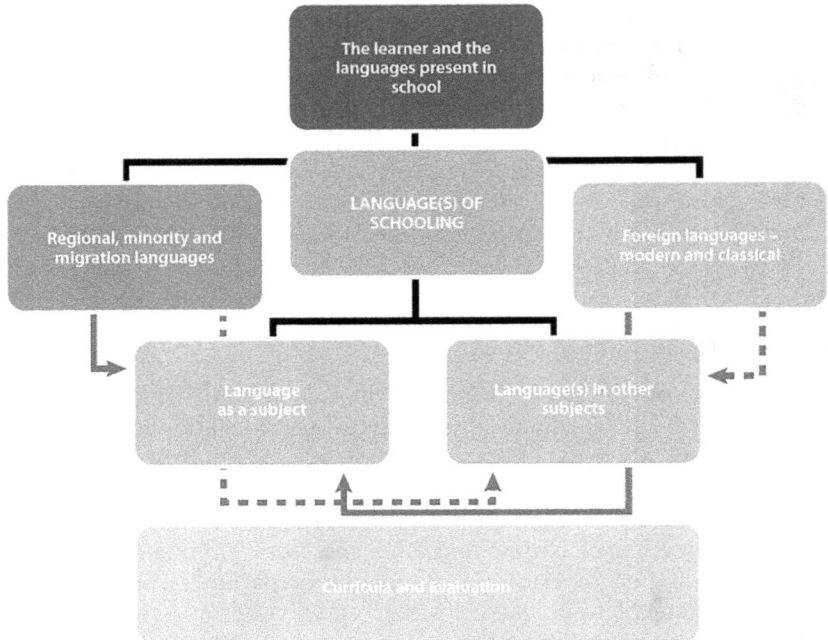

Figure 9.4 Platform of resources and references for plurilingual and intercultural education

In order to bridge these divides and 'make a connection between various aspects, even contrary ones' in Edgar Morin's (2004) sense, it is necessary to start from the students – their language and cultural experiences – which can serve as a springboard for learning the language of schooling and engaging with the language dimension of different curriculum subjects. The focus will be on finding ways to help learners from immigrant families to use their home language(s) to support and enhance their engagement in formal learning at all levels of schooling, from pre-school to upper secondary. After nearly 20 years of research on the subject (Auger, 2014), we have fashioned a diamond-shaped model for developing plurilingual language education to promote an inclusive approach to plurilingual repertoires and cultural diversity in the classroom (Figure 9.5; Auger, 2021a, 2021b). The diamond figure was chosen because we identified seven facets of plurilingual inclusion. These facets should be taken as a whole and are not designed to be treated in a linear way (e.g. facet 4 before facet 6). Each facet of the diamond offers concrete support to teachers, teacher trainers and administrators. The diamond is structured around (1) identifying students' languages and cultural experiences; (2) using all the languages and cultural experiences in the classroom as a resource for teaching and learning (using techniques such as translation,

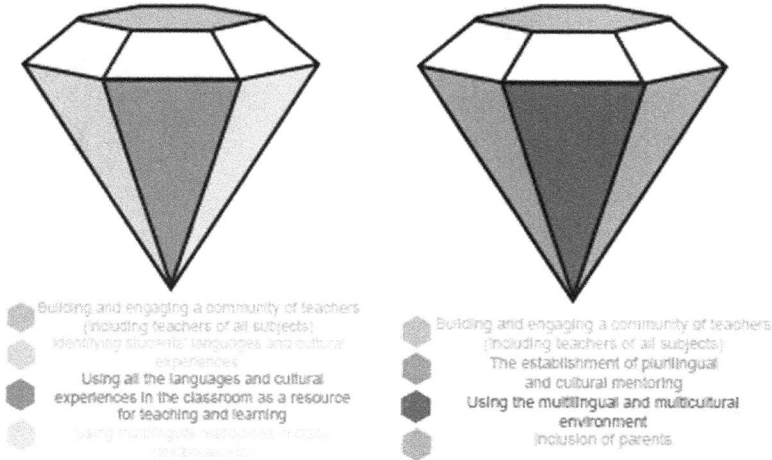

Figure 9.5 Diamond-shaped model for developing plurilingual language education

comparing language and cultural experiences, and creating plurilingual texts); (3) using multilingual resources in class (textbooks etc.); (4) the establishment of plurilingual and cultural mentoring; (5) using the plurilingual and pluricultural environment; (6) inclusion of parents; and (7) building and engaging a community of teachers (including teachers of all subjects) and other educational staff (such as directors etc.) to share a vision of plurilingual and intercultural inclusion.

We have chosen the image of the diamond for its complex qualities, as well as the plurilingualism that strengthens the diversity and complexity of each person's identity which builds the multilingualism of the classroom and allows for better relationships and understanding of others. Moreover, the bonds between the atoms of the diamond give the diamond its meaningful qualities. In our conceptualisation, the links, the synergy between the different activities proposed for each facet give coherence to the model.

In the popular imagination, owning a diamond means being rich! This representation is intended to imply that this conception of plurilingualism 'strengthens the cohesion of our societies in its social, educational, health and cultural dimensions', as stated earlier.

Facet 1: Identifying and highlighting the linguistic repertoire of the class

Identifying the languages of the classroom and the school is a way of making visible the repertoires that are often ignored by teachers who are under pressure to ensure that their students succeed academically in French, which would mean forgetting all other languages and previous cultural experiences.

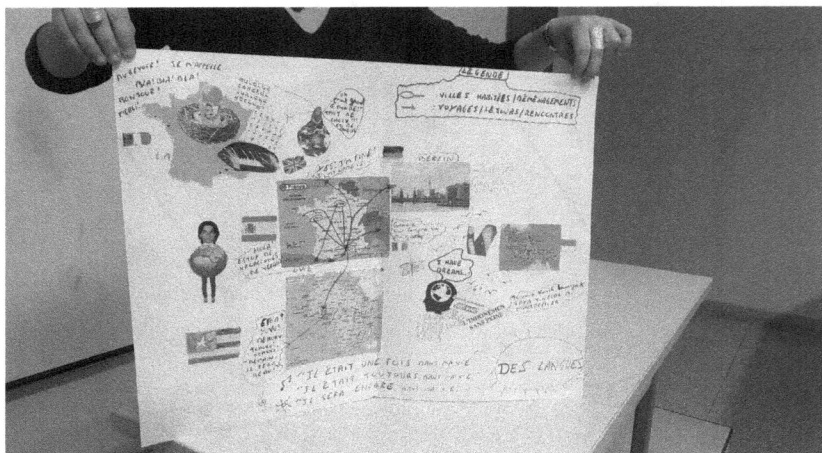

Figure 9.6 Example of a language biography in a high school (languages, mobility, cultural experiences)

To identify the languages present in the classroom, there are very simple activities that can be carried out, such as language biographies (see Figure 9.6) – see the resource 'Maledive – Majority Language and Diversity'[2] developed by the European Centre for Modern Languages (ECML). These language biographies, according to Busch's (2006) assumptions, are intended for all ages and levels of competence. Their aim is to empower students by helping them to identify their linguistic repertoire, reflect on their experience of language and develop a greater sense of language security and confidence, being aware of their own linguistic identity and multiple language resources when learning a new language.

The aim is by no means to know pupils' languages in order to 'correct' them. On the contrary, the important thing is to recognise these languages in order to promote linguistic benevolence (Beacco & Byram, 2007: 75). This also enhances the identity of the students in the classroom, which in turn can lead to increased engagement, as noted by Cummins (2001/2020).

Facet 2: Using all languages as a resource for teaching and learning

Performing learning tasks in the language of schooling, in other modern languages taught in school and in different subjects, is crucial for pupils (Auger, 2017). It is easy to translate school contents (class instructions, text activities etc.) into languages with which pupils are more comfortable to enable them to better understand instructions for example, or texts to be studied. There are various possibilities: dictionaries, digital translators on phones, tablets or computers. Getting help from speakers of the same languages, whether adults or children, is also valuable.

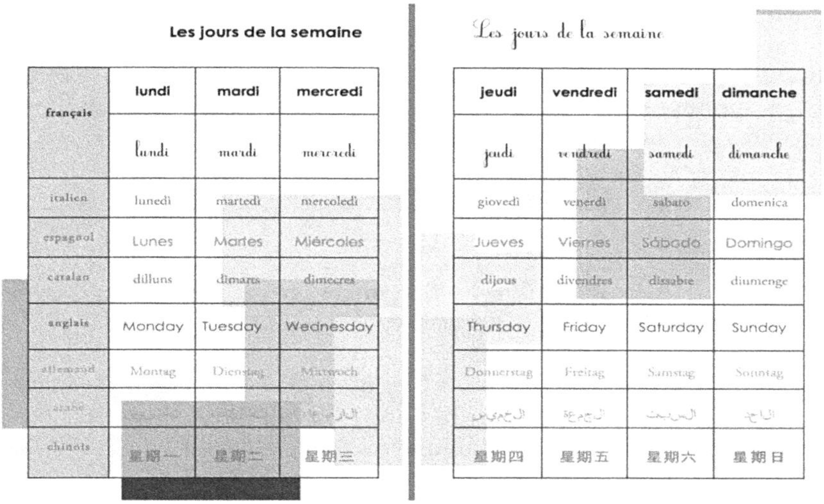

Les jours de la semaine			
français	lundi	mardi	mercredi
	lundi	mardi	mercredi
italien	lunedì	martedì	mercoledì
espagnol	Lunes	Martes	Miércoles
catalan	dilluns	dimarts	dimecres
anglais	Monday	Tuesday	Wednesday
allemand	Montag	Dienstag	Mittwoch
arabe			الأثنين
chinois	星期一	星期二	星期三

Les jours de la semaine			
jeudi	vendredi	samedi	dimanche
jeudi	vendredi	samedi	dimanche
giovedì	venerdì	sabato	domenica
Jueves	Viernes	Sábado	Domingo
dijous	divendres	dissabte	diumenge
Thursday	Friday	Saturday	Sunday
Donnerstag	Freitag	Samstag	Sonntag
الخميس	الجمعة	السبت	الأحد
星期四	星期五	星期六	星期日

Figure 9.7 Days of the week. 'A plurilingual book in French and a variety of students' diverse languages in Sète, France'[4] (Prasad & Auger, 2013)

'Let's compare our languages',[3] on the ECML website (Auger, 2005), is an activity that allows pupils to compare their family languages (or other known languages of their choice – it is advisable, of course, not to assign the pupil to a language) with the language of schooling (French) in order to activate transfers but also to reflect on language and languages and to build skills in French (e.g. Figure 9.7).

These activities for observing the similarities and specificities of each language can be carried out in all subjects – in Geography, for example, students can draw on their plurilingual repertoires to talk about borrowings and exchanges between languages regarding the oceans.[5]

Facet 3: Using plurilingual and pluricultural materials

The introduction of linguistically and culturally diverse materials into the classroom is important for our multilingual and multicultural classrooms in the 21st century (UNESCO, 2018). It also promotes the intercultural approach in the classroom valued by the Council of Europe and strengthens the relation between the pupils in the class and the teacher.

Offering multilingual and multicultural material such as books, manuals, children's literature videos, audio documents, and documents translated into the pupils' family languages also allows for a better understanding of the subject content. Pupils should not wait until they are fully competent in the language of schooling before engaging with the various school subjects. One should not hesitate to use online documents in family languages or documents translated by the pupils themselves as resources for the class. It is about encouraging pupils to bring in material that they have in their possession to share with others, as in the literature example described by Anne-Laure Biales in our second vignette.

Vignette 2

Using literature in family languages in a French course – Anne-Laure Biales

In French secondary schools, because each school subject is taught by a different teacher, plurilingual and pluricultural competence finds its place only in language programmes. My PhD research focused on the fact that pupils speak more than two languages and sometimes have a different home language than French. In order to spotlight their plurilingual and pluricultural competence, teachers have to be aware of the existence of this linguistic and cultural wealth in their class and use it. Thus, as a teacher of French, I work on my students' literary culture. As they speak more than one language, they may also read in these languages. I wanted to create a multilingual and multicultural environment in my French classes.

Holding debates about literature in different languages

After questioning my students about their relationships with their languages (home languages, languages learned at school, languages learned on their own), I invited them to share their multilingual and multicultural knowledge with their classmates during a specific activity: holding debates about literature. In order to participate, students had to explore their own literary culture, which comprised not only French books or books read and studied at school but books from home and written in their family languages.

Reading in other languages: a common practice among pupils

At the beginning of the school year, I asked my students which kind of books they liked to read, where and in which languages. I was surprised to learn that some of them read a lot at home, but a few of them had read a book in a language other than French. By giving them the opportunity to bring their books into the French class – books written in their home languages or languages they had learnt in the course of migration – I gave them the confidence to share their plurilingual culture with classmates who in turn could share the same or a different culture (see Figure 9.8). If, at the beginning of my PhD study, students did not use their plurilingual knowledge in class, more and more of them did so as my study progressed.

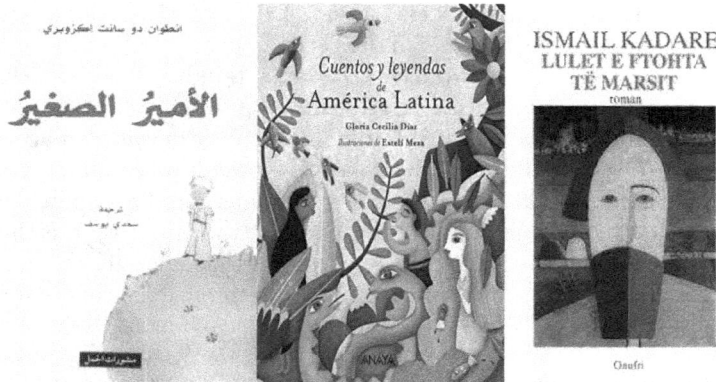

Figure 9.8 Student's selection of books in different languages (Arabic, Spanish, Albanian)

Of my students, 65.2% said they wanted to try to read in a language other than their home language. Of course, they were put off by the difficulty of reading in another language. They were not sure about their plurilingual abilities given that they were not conscious of them. Moreover, reading in another language in a French class disrupts the monolingual and monocultural ideology shared most of the time unconsciously by teachers and students in French schools.

Towards training teachers

For teachers who worked with me on my research, it was a surprise to discover that their students could own this plurilingual culture. Unfortunately, even if they wanted to use it in their own teaching, they did not know how to do so because of a lack of training. Giving the students the opportunity to share their plurilingual and pluricultural knowledge, new relationships develop in class: like the teacher, students are expert in their language and culture. My PhD research demonstrated that using home language literature and speaking about it in class is an interesting way of improving students' competences in French language and literature as well as creating a climate of confidence regarding diversity in the class.

Facet 4: Setting up mutual mentoring

Tandem language learning is a form of mutual mentoring. For example, a child who has recently arrived in France offers to exchange French lessons for lessons in his or her language. However, French-speaking students do not always wish to learn the languages of other children. It is therefore important that students always have experiences to share, even beyond languages. A student can thus exchange help in French for help in music, art, sport, other modern languages taught at school, etc. It is important to ensure that the relationship is symmetrical because if the student is always in a mentoring role, he/she may develop an attitude of contempt to other children with a relatively lower level of competence. On the other hand, the student who is regularly mentored may perceive himself as incompetent and no longer dare to take the initiative. It is therefore important for the teacher to create activities that mitigate this potential dynamic, based on the objectives of the programme, ensuring that opportunities for reciprocity arise for sustainable mutual mentoring.

Facet 5: Using multilingual and multicultural environments (outside the classroom, school) as a resource

We live in multilingual environments that are not always explored at school. This may be as simple as street names, shop signs, shopkeepers who are themselves plurilingual, signage (as in Figure 9.9).

Educational projects that take linguistic and cultural diversity into account can therefore take place in public spaces as well as in museums or libraries where different languages and cultures are represented.

Facet 6: Including parents in the life of the school

Comparative studies (UNESCO, 2018) show that parents are not always included in the life of schools. In this respect, awareness-raising

Figure 9.9 Street sign in French and Occitan near Montpellier

information aimed at promoting bi/plurilingualism as an opportunity and not a 'danger' to the child's development is important.[6] It may also be possible to involve parents in concrete ways in classroom projects. Pioneering projects in this area come from the Swiss with their 'story bags' concept. In this project, the aim is to provide books in the language of schooling (French) and in other family languages (in written and audio versions) which the children read in class and at home with their parents (those who cannot read, listen to them). Afterwards, parents are invited to help with the translation of other books.

In the European Romtels[7] project in France, parents and pupils have written placards for a museum of fine arts in Romani, Romanian and French. In summary, such projects represent an infinite number of examples that can be adapted to the objectives of teachers and school programmes.

Facet 7: Building a community of teachers of all subjects and other school staff sharing a vision of plurilingual and intercultural inclusion

Teachers, head teachers and other staff dealing with pupils are encouraged to embrace this perspective. The aim is to ensure that everyone feels included in the process, that there is a connection between teachers, classes, pupils, subjects, parents, and the in-school and out-of-school environment.

The training of teachers, educational staff and parents is the key to the success of the schooling of migrant children, and more generally, of all pupils who benefit from these inclusive approaches which advocate living together in our multilingual and multicultural contexts. However, any training must anticipate a number of challenges. Teachers' beliefs about languages can be an obstacle. Moreover, teaching French is not just about the teacher of French but about all teachers who use language both as an object and as a means of learning, as in the Listiac[8] project. Teachers also need to be trained to share their expertise with their students, to understand what resources they have in terms of knowledge, lived experience and languages and how they can make efficient use of those resources to support their learning.

Conclusion

In this chapter we have described projects in Ireland and France that began to take shape at the turn of the millennium; in other words, they are not new. They were inspired by or are easily linked to the Council of Europe's work on language education and one of them adapted Council of Europe instruments to local needs. In one way or another they demonstrate the feasibility of implementing plurilingual and intercultural education as a means to effective inclusion in our increasingly diverse societies. Essentially, however, the projects are bottom-up initiatives in the sense that they were undertaken without official guidance or support (although Integrate Ireland Language and Training was acting on behalf of the Irish government, its work quickly disappeared from view when IILT itself ceased to exist). The projects all feature in academic publications and are well-known to specialists, and yet they are not widely imitated. This is unlikely to change without significant developments in national language education policies and corresponding transformations in pre-service teacher education. On the other hand, these projects demonstrate that teachers can make a difference and develop their own projects for the benefit of their learners. We therefore conclude by returning briefly to the question in our title: 'What do I need to do as a teacher to support children from migrant backgrounds in mastering the academic language required for school success and developing their plurilingual and pluricultural repertoires?'

To support children with an immigrant background you can rely on policy texts from international organisations, including the Council of Europe, to understand their rights but also the responsibilities incumbent on them. In addition, it is important to have theoretical knowledge about what learning a new language implies for migrant pupils. Our list of references provides access to the work we have described and to the Council of Europe publications we have cited. You will also find a large number of relevant documents on the Council of Europe's platform of resources for plurilingual and intercultural education[9] and further resources on the website of the European Centre for Modern Languages.[10] It is important to remember that whatever steps you take to develop migrant learners' proficiency in academic language and thus expand their plurilingual repertoires will also benefit learners who do not speak languages other than those they learn at school.

Notes

(1) Summit Declaration; https://www.coe.int/t/dcr/summit/20050517_decl_varsovie_en.asp
(2) https://maledive.ecml.at/ (accessed 22 July 2021).
(3) https://www.ecml.at/ECML-Programme/Programme2008-2011/Majoritylanguageinmultilingualsettings/Trainingkit/tabid/5452/language/en-GB/Default.aspx (accessed 22 July 2021).
(4) https://issuu.com/gprasad/docs/setejours?embed_cta=embed_badge&embed_context=embed&embed_domain=www.iamplurilingual.com&utm_medium=referral&utm_source=www.iamplurilingual.com
(5) https://conbat.ecml.at/DidacticUnits/Motionintheocean/tabid/2697/language/en-GB/Default.aspx (accessed 22 July 2021).
(6) https://maledive.ecml.at/Studymaterials/Society/Dealingwithfactsmyths/tabid/3650/language/en-GB/Default.aspx (accessed 22 July 2021)
(7) https://nuvision.ncl.ac.uk/Play/17830 (accessed 22 July 2021).
(8) https://listiac.univ-montp3.fr/videotheque; http://listiac.org/ (accessed 22 July 2021).
(9) https://www.coe.int/en/web/language-policy/platform
(10) https://www.ecml.at

References

Anderson, J., Hélot, C., McPake, J. and Obied, V. (2010) Professional development for staff working in multilingual schools. Strasbourg: Council of Europe. https://rm.coe.int/CoERMPublicCommonSearchServices/DisplayDCTMContent?docu mentId=09000016805a1cb4 (accessed 22 June 2021).

Auger, N. (2005) *Comparons nos langues, Démarche d'apprentissage du français auprès d'enfants nouvellement arrivés.* Éditions CNDP. Coll. «Ressources Formation Multimédi», DVD (26 min.) et guide pédagogique (15 pages). 'Let's compare our languages' video with English subtitles. https://www.ecml.at/ECML-Programme/ Programme2008-2011/Majoritylanguageinmultilingualsettings/Trainingkit/tabid/ 5452/language/en-GB/Default.aspx (accessed 22 July 2021).

Auger, N. (2014) Exploring the use of migrant languages to support learning in mainstream classrooms in France. In D. Little, C. Leung and P. Van Avermaet (eds) *Managing Diversity in Education: Languages, Policies, Pedagogies* (pp. 223–242). Bristol: Multilingual Matters.

Auger, N. (2017) Developing competence for French as a foreign language within a plurilingual paradigm. In S. Coffey and U. Wingate (eds) *New Directions in Foreign Language Education Research* (pp. 151–164). New York: Routledge.

Auger, N. (2021a) Translanguaging: How to take account of ALL pupils' languages for improved results! Brussels: European Commission. https://www.schooleducation-gateway.eu/da/pub/latest/news/translanguaging-improvedresult.htm (accessed 26 July 2021).

Auger, N. (2021b) Examining the nature and potential of plurilingual language education. Towards a seven-step plurilingual language education framework. In E. Piccardo, A. Germain-Rutherford and G. Lawrence (eds) *The Routledge Handbook of Plurilingual Language Education* (pp. 465–483). New York: Routledge.

Bainski, C., Kaseric, T., Michel, U., McPake, J. and Thompson, A. (2010) Cooperation, management and networking: Effective ways to promote the linguistic and educational integration of children and adolescents from migrant backgrounds. Strasbourg: Council of Europe. https://rm.coe.int/CoERMPublicCommon SearchServices/DisplayDCTMContent?documentId=09000016805a1cb5 (accessed 22 June 2021).

Beacco, J.-C. and Byram, M. (2007) *From Linguistic Diversity to Plurilingual Education: Guide for the Development of Language Education Policies in Europe.* Strasbourg: Council of Europe. https://www.coe.int/en/web/language-policy/from-linguistic-diversity-to-plurilingual-education-guide-for-the-development-of-language-education-policies-in-europe (accessed 16 July 2021).

Bertucci, M.-M. (2010) Migrant pupils and formal mastery of the language of schooling: Variations and representations. Strasbourg: Council of Europe. https://rm.coe.int/ CoERMPublicCommonSearchServices/DisplayDCTMContent?documentId=09000 016805a1cb0 (accessed 22 June 2021).

Busch, B. (2006) Language biographies: Approaches to multilingualism in education and linguistic research. In B. Busch, A. Jardine and A. Tjoutuku (eds) *Language Biographies for Multilingual Learning* (pp. 5–19). Cape Town: PRAESA.

Castellotti, V. and Moore, D. (2010) Capitalising on, activating and developing plurilingual and pluricultural repertoires for better school integration. Strasbourg: Council of Europe. https://rm.coe.int/CoERMPublicCommonSearchServices/DisplayDCTM Content?documentId=09000016805a1cb2 (accessed 22 June 2021).

Ćatibušić, B. and Little, D. (2014) *Immigrant Pupils Learn English: A CEFR-related Empirical Study of L2 Development.* Cambridge: Cambridge University Press.

Central Statistics Office (2017) *2016 Census Summary Results, Part I.* Dublin: Central Statistics Office. https://www.cso.ie/en/media/csoie/newsevents/documents/census-2016summaryresultspart1/Census2016SummaryPart1.pdf (accessed 8 July 2021).

Coste, D., Moore, D. and Zarate, G. (1999) *Plurilingual and Pluricultural Competence.* Strasbourg: Council of Europe. https://rm.coe.int/168069d29b (accessed 23 July 2021).

Council of Europe (2001) *Common European Framework of Reference for Languages: Learning, Teaching, Assessment* (CEFR). Strasbourg: Council of Europe. www.coe.int/t/dg4/linguistic/source/framework (accessed 9 July 2021).

Council of Europe (2008) White Paper on Intercultural Dialogue: 'Living Together as Equals in Dignity'. Strasbourg: Council of Europe. https://www.coe.int/t/dg4/intercultural/source/white%20paper_final_revised_en.pdf (accessed 9 July 2021).

Council of Europe (2011) European Language Portfolio (ELP) Principles and Guidelines, with added explanatory notes. Strasbourg: Council of Europe. https://rm.coe.int/CoERMPublicCommonSearchServices/DisplayDCTMContent?documentId=09000016804586ba (accessed 8 July 2021).

Council of Europe (2012) Recommendation CM/Rec(2012)13 of the Committee of Ministers to member States on ensuring quality education. Strasbourg: Council of Europe. https://www.ecml.at/Portals/1/documents/CoE-documents/CMRec2012-13_quality_EN.pdf?ver=2016-11-29-113145-700 (accessed 22 June 2021).

Council of Europe (2014) Recommendation CM/Rec(2014)5 of the Committee of Ministers to member States on the importance of competences in the language(s) of schooling for equity and quality in education and for educational success. Strasbourg: Council of Europe. https://search.coe.int/cm/Pages/result_details.aspx?ObjectID=09000016805c6105 (accessed 22 June 2021).

Council of Europe (2016) *Platform of Resources and References for Plurilingual and Intercultural Education.* Strasbourg: Council of Europe. https://www.coe.int/en/web/platform-plurilingual-intercultural-language-education (accessed 22 July 2021).

Council of Europe (2020) *Common European Framework of Reference for Languages: Learning, Teaching, Assessment. Companion Volume.* Strasbourg: Council of Europe. https://rm.coe.int/common-european-framework-of-reference-for-languages-learning-teaching/16809ea0d4 (accessed 22 July 2021).

Council of Europe Commissioner for Human Rights (2017) *Fighting School Segregation in Europe through School Education: A Position Paper.* Strasbourg: Council of Europe. https://rm.coe.int/fighting-school-segregation-in-europe-throughinclusive-education-a-pos/168073fb65 (accessed 22 June 2021).

Cummins, J. (2001/2020) *Negotiating Identities: Education for Empowerment in a Diverse Society.* Los Angeles: California Association for Bilingual Education.

European Commission (2020) *Education Begins with Language.* Brussels: European Commission. https://op.europa.eu/en/publication-detail/-/publication/6b7e2851-b5fb-11ea-bb7a-1aa75ed71a1/language-en/format-PDF/source-148560937 (accessed 9 July 2021).

Government of Ireland (1999) *Primary School Curriculum: Introduction.* Dublin: Stationery Office. https://www.curriculumonline.ie/Primary/Curriculum/ (accessed 9 July 2021).

Integrate Ireland Language and Training (IILT) (2003a) *English Language Proficiency Benchmarks for non-English-speaking pupils at primary level.* Dublin: Integrate Ireland Language and Training. https://ncca.ie/media/2064/english_language_proficiency_benchmarks.pdf (accessed 8 July 2021).

Integrate Ireland Language and Training (IILT) (2003b) European Language Portfolio, Primary: Learning the language of the host community. Dublin: Integrate Ireland Language and Training. https://www.ecml.at/Portals/1/ELP_Portfolios/ea920271-a832-4a71-9957-07ac5f9e9ffb.pdf?ver=2011-09-13-160442-523 (accessed 8 July 2021).

Integrate Ireland Language and Training (IILT) (2005) *My First English Book.* Dublin: Integrate Ireland Language and Training. https://ncca.ie/media/2077/first_english-book.pdf (accessed 8 July 2021).

Lengyel, D. (2010) Language diagnostics in multilingual setting with respect to continuous assessment procedures as accompaniment of learning and teaching. Strasbourg: Council of Europe. https://rm.coe.int/CoERMPublicCommonSearchServices/Displa yDCTMContent?documentId=09000016805a1cac (accessed 22 June 2021).

Little, D. (2010) The linguistic and educational integration of children and adolescents from migrant backgrounds. Strasbourg: Council of Europe. https://rm.coe.int/the-linguistic-and-educational-integration-of-children-and-adolescents/16805a0d1b (accessed 22 June 2021).

Little, D. and Kirwan, D. (2019) *Engaging with Linguistic Diversity: A Study of Educational Inclusion in an Irish Primary School*. London: Bloomsbury Academic.

Morin, E. (2004) La méthode 6 – *Éthique*. Paris: Le Seuil.

Prasad, G. and Auger (2013) Les jours de la semaines. https://www.iamplurilingual.com/

Thürmann, E., Vollmer, H. and Pieper, I. (2010) Languages of schooling: Focusing on vulnerable learners. Strasbourg: Council of Europe. https://rm.coe.int/ CoERMPublicCommonSearchServices/DisplayDCTMContent?documentId=09000 016805a1caf (accessed 22 June 2021).

UNESCO (2018) Global Education Monitoring Report. Paris: UNESCO. https:// en.unesco.org/gem-report/taxonomy/term/209 (accessed 22 July 2021).

10 Education for Integration: The Case of Adult Migrants

Cecilie Hamnes Carlsen, Lorenzo Rocca and
Joseph Sheils

Introduction

Social inclusion, respect for diversity and the dignity of all are important goals for Council of Europe actions concerning migration (see
Introduction to this book). The Council of Europe's (CoE) human rights
standards in this area underline the CoE vision of Europe 'as a multinational and multicultural society, where immigrants take part as equal
members, on the basis of equality of rights and opportunities in return for
equality of obligations' (Council of Europe, 2003). Integration is seen as
a process leading to active participation on equal terms in all areas of
society: economic, social, cultural and political. High-quality education
is not only an important means to reach these goals, but a fundamental
right in itself. This right is not restricted to children and young learners
but applies to adult learners alike, as currently reflected in UN Sustainable
Development Goal 4 concerning Education (United Nations, 2018).
Indeed, many adults will need to complement their competences throughout life and will benefit from access to lifelong learning opportunities.
This is not least the case for adult migrants and refugees, in particular
those who for various reasons may not have completed their basic education. High-quality adult education can compensate for a lack of education
in earlier life and thus promote social mobility, social cohesion, equity and
equality as well as active citizenship, democracy and participation.[1]

The experiences and current life situations of adult migrants are
extremely diverse. Access to education tailored to their complex needs is
therefore crucial for quality education benefiting the individual migrants in
their integration process. Education provision for adult migrants often takes
place in an ongoing tension between the real, and often quite urgent, needs
of the individual and the expectations and requirements of the host society.
As more and more states are introducing language and knowledge of society
(KoS) requirements for residency, family reunion and citizenship, this tension becomes critical. The CoE plays an important role in guiding member
states in how to handle the challenges related to migration, while at the

same time respecting the dignity and human rights of the individual migrant. In order to promote intercultural understanding and counteract discrimination, the CoE has prepared reports, and issued papers and recommendations, raising awareness of the important role of language learning and education in the integration process. These policy statements and guidelines, and the core values which underpin them, are central to this chapter, with a particular focus on vulnerable groups such as asylum seekers, refugees and low-literate adults (Council of Europe, 2021).

This chapter focuses, accordingly, on the specific characteristics of adult migrants and how to best meet their learning needs. Respecting learners' linguistic and cultural diversity, personal circumstances and educational biographies, is key to achieving these goals. We will provide concrete examples through four *vignettes* that present tools and suggestions for teachers of adult migrants. These vignettes are framed as outcomes within the broader action plan developed by the Linguistic Integration of Adult Migrants (LIAM) project at the CoE in Strasbourg.[2] The aim of LIAM is to support policymakers and professionals in member states in their actions to develop inclusive language policies and practical resources within a human rights culture. The role, actions and concrete results of the LIAM project based on CoE shared values and guiding principles represent the backbone of this chapter.

Adult Learners and Adult Learning within the Migration Context

Education systems are typically organised on the assumption that all learners start with somewhat similar backgrounds, knowledge of the world, cultural attitudes, values, beliefs and needs. In the context of adult migrants, this assumption is a poor starting point for successful education (Krumm & Plutzar, 2008; Douglas Fir Group, 2016). Adult migrants are a vastly heterogeneous group. They include both refugees and labour migrants, who not only face different challenges, but also have varying learning, teaching and assessment needs and entitlements. In addition, there are substantial differences in the migrant population when it comes to prior schooling, literacy profiles and digital skills. Treating everybody in the same way, does not ensure equal opportunities for the diverse group of adult learners. On the contrary, the importance of tailoring language courses to adult migrants' diverse needs, taking into account their mental and psycho-social situation, has been repeatedly stressed (Richterich, 1983; Rossner, 2008). Education policymakers and language teachers need to consider at least the following three characteristics of adult migrants' learning situation, as identified by Little (2012).

Firstly, adult migrants acquire the language of their new country not only via formal teaching but also in non-formal learning environments outside the classroom. The extent to which migrants get the opportunity to practise language outside school, however, varies according to their different family and job situations.

Secondly, language learning in the migration context typically takes place under a high level of social, economic and legal pressure. Migrants are often well aware of the fact that they need to learn the majority language(s) not only in order to get access to labour and education, but also to obtain family reunification, permanent residency, and citizenship (see section on language and KoS requirements below). Language learning in the migration context is therefore a high-stakes activity responding to very concrete, basic needs related to fundamental rights.

A third distinguishing characteristic of the adult migrant learning environment is its multilingual nature. As opposed to the foreign language classroom (e.g. the teaching of foreign languages to majority pupils in a school setting), the second language classroom in the migration context is typically characterised by a high level of linguistic variation: learners master different languages to a different degree, some only orally; the linguistic context varies between learners, some of whom use different languages in families and outside the classroom; and there are different external pressures and degrees of personal motivation to learn. Therefore, language education in the migration context needs to reflect learners' varying language biographies, language abilities and prior learning and life experiences more generally (Krumm & Plutzar, 2008).

These characteristics reflect important principles of adult education as described by Malcom Knowles (1978a, 1978b) and others. Knowles used the term *andragogy* to raise awareness of the significant differences between the ways adults and children learn. His learning theory is based on a series of assumptions about adult learners, such as a high degree of self-directedness, an ability to draw on life experience to aid learning, a readiness to learn according to new roles in life, a problem-centred attitude, a wish to apply new learning immediately, and a tendency to be motivated by internal rather than external factors.

These assumptions lead to concrete implications for teaching practice: adult learners want to know why they are learning something; therefore, teachers should explain why they teach specific skills in a certain way. Since adults learn by doing,[3] adult education should focus on real-life tasks that adults can perform, rather than on exercises intended to improve knowledge *per se*. As adults are problem-oriented and learn best when what they learn is of immediate use, instruction is most effective when relating learning to learners' needs involving learners in dealing with problems relevant for their lives. Knowles's approach emphasises adult learners as genuinely self-driven and adult learning as self-directed. The concept of self-directed learning, or learner autonomy, has been central to the CoE's thinking about language teaching and learning since the end of the 1980s (Holec, 1981; Little, 2009) for both adults and children. It should be noted, however, that learner autonomy is not equally easy for all, and especially not for adults who lack prior schooling and literacy skills. These learners may need specific support in relation to learning to learn as we will illustrate below.

Linguistic Integration of Adult Migrants

The CoE defines integration as a two-way process, meaning equality of rights and opportunities in return for equality of obligations. Integration is thus a shared endeavour requiring an effort from migrants as well as from different levels of the host society at the political level as well as the local community. As underlined by the CoE, the aim should be to provide migrants with the means to function in society and develop their potential while preserving their cultural and ethnic identity. Integration as a two-way process also means familiarising the non-immigrant population with the rights, culture, traditions and needs of the migrant population (Council of Europe, 2003). The ultimate aim of integration is to enable migrants to take part in the political, public, economic and cultural life of their new country, and eventually live under the same legal, social and financial conditions as members of the majority population (Krumm and Plutzar, 2008: 2). There is little doubt that knowing the language of the host country is a facilitating factor in the integration process and in achieving equal opportunities. But what does it mean to know a language?

In Europe today, knowing a language, or having language proficiency, both in the context of teaching and assessment, is typically defined as a person's ability to use language appropriately and effectively in concrete language use situations, defined as *communicative competence* (Hymes, 1972; Canale & Swain, 1980; Bachman, 1990). The conceptualisation of language proficiency as communicative competence has been further promoted in Europe through the widespread adoption of the *Common European Framework of Reference for Languages* (CEFR) (Council of Europe, 2001) and its recently published update, the Companion Volume (CEFR-CV) (Council of Europe, 2020).[4] In the last 20 years, the CEFR has been translated into more than 40 languages and is used in almost every CoE member state as a reference source. Even though the CEFR was not developed with migrants or vulnerable refugees and low-literate learners in mind, its language proficiency levels are increasingly used in migration contexts, as the basis for curricula, teaching material and tests (Rocca *et al.*, 2020).

An important aspect highlighted in the CEFR (2001) and the CEFR-CV (2020) is the fact that all language users, first language (L1) and second language (L2) users alike, normally do *not* perform equally well across the different language skills. On the contrary, it is quite natural to perform at a higher level in the receptive skills (reading and listening), than in the productive skills (writing and speaking). Learners with little prior schooling and low levels of literacy often perform better in the oral modes (oral reception, production and interaction) than in the written modes (written reception, production and interaction) (Carlsen, 2017). Accordingly, CoE (LIAM project) encourages users of the CEFR to recognise learners' differentiated profiles in teaching as well as in assessment (Council of Europe, 2020: 39). One of the reasons the CEFR includes so

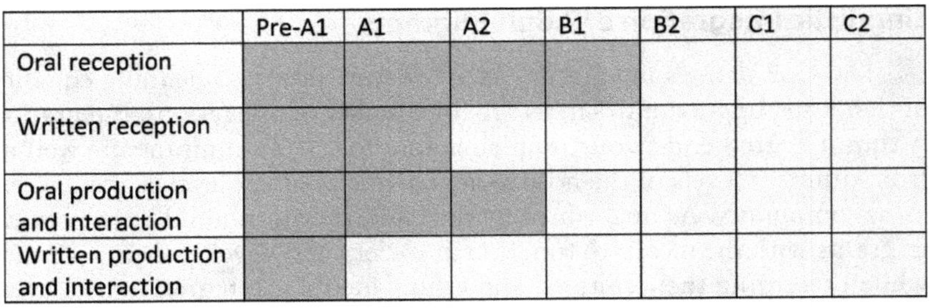

	Pre-A1	A1	A2	B1	B2	C1	C2
Oral reception							
Written reception							
Oral production and interaction							
Written production and interaction							

Figure 10.1 Uneven language profiles

many descriptor scales is precisely to encourage users to develop differentiated profiles, as illustrated in Figure 10.1.

When using the CEFR as the basis for curriculum development, teaching and assessment, it is critical to start from the real-life language needs of migrants in terms of the main competences required for the workplace. Similarly, when employers set language requirements for L2-users, they would secure a more inclusive job market by setting differentiated language requirements rather than an even language level for all language skills. In the opposite case, if the same level of proficiency is required in all skills for practical occupations (perhaps including unnecessarily high levels of reading and writing), there is a risk that vulnerable learners with low levels of literacy will be disproportionally discriminated against in the job market.

Another issue raised in the CEFR-CV is the importance of not comparing L2-use with the language of an idealised native speaker. It is explicitly stated in the CEFR-CV that 'the CEFR illustrative descriptors do not take an idealised native speaker as a reference point for the competence of a user/learner' (Council of Europe, 2020: 243). This view is in line with that of several prominent SLA-researchers who warn against using the native speaker as a point of reference when describing or assessing L2-language use. Twenty years ago, Davies (2003) pointed to the potential racist use of the term as it can be used to exclude highly proficient L2-users and users with a slight foreign accent even though their pronunciation is fully intelligible, and their language proficiency is otherwise fully adequate. Hulstijn (2015) stresses the fact that it is an illusion that all L1-users (e.g. 'native users') of a language master the language to perfection, while a similar level is unattainable for L2-users. Significantly, he demonstrates that there is large variation between L1-users when it comes to breadth of vocabulary, pragmatic appropriateness, writing and reading skills etc., and that the perfect native speaker is a mere myth.

The idea of the idealised native speaker mastering the L1 to perfection stems in part from a time when language competence was defined narrowly as grammatical competence, a linguistic area where indeed the

L1-users can be said to have a level of control normally superior to L2-users (Chomsky, 1965). This limited view no longer reflects a common conception of language competence. Rather, within the dominating paradigm of communicative competence also represented in the CEFR, it is not only possible, but quite likely that not all L1-users can be placed at the upper levels of the CEFR, just as it is fully possible for L2-learners to obtain academic language skills in an L2 and reach the highest levels of the CEFR scale. Dewaele *et al.* (2020) strongly encourage the second language acquisition (SLA) field to abandon the terms native speaker (NS) and non-native speaker (NNS) altogether and adopt more neutral terms that emphasise the equal status of first and foreign language users, since as they put it: 'We will argue that continued use of NS/NNS is an obstacle in the pursuit of equality and equity in education and research. It is fundamentally unjust to judge a person's linguistic competence solely on the fact that they were born into the language' (Dewaele *et al.*, 2020: 25).

In fact, respecting adult migrants' learning situation and life challenges within a multilingual context is only possible if the majority society fully accepts that migrants may speak the majority language(s) with a foreign accent. Tolerance for spoken varieties that deviate from the so-called native spoken norm(s) is necessary in order to avoid linguistic discrimination. If an accent-free pronunciation is upheld as the ideal, adult migrants may never be accepted as competent speakers of the majority language even if their pronunciation is quite comprehensible and their lexical and pragmatic abilities fully adequate. In an important update of the description of phonological control in the CEFR-CV, it is underscored:

> In language teaching, the phonological control of an idealised native speaker has traditionally been seen as the target, with accent being seen as a marker of poor phonological control. The focus on accent and on accuracy instead of on intelligibility has been detrimental to the development of the teaching of pronunciation. Idealised models that ignore the retention of accent lack consideration for context, sociolinguistic aspects and learners' needs. (Council of Europe, 2020: 133)

Of equal importance, valuing migrants' plurilingualism as a resource for society as well as for the individual is necessary in order to prevent a situation in which migrants' first language(s) is devalued and plurilingualism is understood as a resource only when the plurilingual speaker is a member of the majority population (Flores *et al.*, 2020), as discussed in more detail below.

Plurilingual Education within the Migration Context

Plurilingual education is oriented towards enlarging individuals' linguistic repertoires according to their needs, expectations and interests. It sustains a person's feeling of belonging within a multilingual environment, while at the same time increasing acceptance of linguistic varieties within the majority society, thus preventing specific repertoires from becoming a sign of marginality (Freire, 2005; Yosso, 2005).

Adult migrants are typically plurilingual. Many come from multilingual countries and have been using their first language(s) at home and a lingua franca (or other languages) in the public domain; and they may have acquired additional languages on their migration journey. Moreover, their plurilingual repertoires may include elements of the majority language and/or a regional language of the new country of residence, or languages of other migrant groups with whom they are in contact in everyday settings, for example at the workplace.

Migrants' first language(s) is of value in itself, and CoE initiatives in this domain have drawn attention to the importance of using the first language(s) as a natural support and recourse both when learning the language of the host country – perhaps learning to read and write for the first time or in a new alphabet – and when acquiring knowledge of the new society (Rocca et al., 2020).

Assuming that plurilingual competence is the manifestation of the capacity to communicate which, as Beacco recalls, is part of the genetic make-up of all human beings and which can be used in several languages in succession throughout a person's lifetime, learning a language implies an ongoing reorganisation of one's linguistic repertoire. This less evident but significant aspect of the complex integration process has been described as follows: 'In the case of migrants, the reorganisation is more complicated, because acquiring the majority language is an important issue [...], a fundamentally identity-based process that takes place in full public view in the host country, and which is usually called linguistic integration (although this over-simplifies matters)' (Beacco, 2014: 2).

Education for Democratic Participation

Democracy is a core value promoted by the CoE, which attaches particular importance to the participation of all individuals as active citizens in democratic societies. Being an active citizen entails more than voting, yet having the right to vote, and using that right, is fundamental to democratic participation for the individual and for a democratic society as such. Accordingly, the CoE emphasises that 'the disenfranchisement of millions of migrants from voting and citizenship is arguably the largest democratic deficit in our democracies today' (Huddleston, 2016: 10).

As the CoE/ALTE 2018 survey[5] revealed, it has become the rule rather than the exception that CoE member states provide migrants with courses on knowledge of society (KoS). In many countries, there are also formal KoS tests for migrants. Such courses and tests typically cover topics concerning history and geography, constitution and law, customs and traditions, rights and duties, education, employment and services (Rocca et al.,

2020). The CoE stresses the importance of teaching knowledge of society in a manner that is respectful and life-relevant for adult learners, focusing on topics such as education, labour, democratic participation, access to welfare, housing, health, and care for children (Little, 2012). The content of the KoS courses and tests should facilitate migrants' integration into society, while at the same time valuing their diversity and intercultural competence (Byram, 1997; Byram & Zarate, 1997) with the aim of fostering intercultural dialogue (Council of Europe, 2008).[6]

To equip individuals with the competences needed to take an active part in a democratic society, hence, to act as a plurilingual-and-interculturally competent democratically active citizen, the CoE has developed a *Reference Framework of Competences for Democratic Culture* (RFCDC) (Council of Europe, 2018; Barrett and Byram, 2020). While the RFCDC (Chapters 1, 7 above) was not developed primarily with adult migrant education in mind, it offers a comprehensive description of intercultural and democratic competences which KoS course developers and teachers may wish to consult in their work to support active participation by migrants. The RFCDC descriptors are divided into four categories: *values, attitudes, skills* and *knowledge and critical understanding*. The descriptors for values and attitudes reflect shared European values rather than a set of particular national values or culture-specific moral attitudes. These values are concerned with *valuing human dignity and human rights*, *valuing cultural diversity*, and *valuing democracy, justice, fairness, equality and the rule of law*. In a similar fashion, descriptors relating to attitudes focus on shared European attitudes such as *openness to cultural otherness*, *respect*, *civic-mindedness*, *responsibility* and *self-efficacy*.

The relationship between democratic competence and intercultural competence is clear from the RFCDC:

> A fundamental principle of democracy is that those affected by political decisions are able to express their views when decisions are being made, and that decision makers pay attention to their views. Intercultural dialogue is, first, the most important means through which citizens can express their views to other citizens with different cultural affiliations. It is, second, the means through which decision makers can understand the views of all citizens, taking account of their various self-ascribed cultural affiliations. In culturally diverse societies, intercultural dialogue is thus crucial for ensuring that all citizens are equally able to participate in public discussion and decision making. Democracy and intercultural dialogue are complementary in culturally diverse societies. (Council of Europe, 2018: 24)

As neither a curriculum nor a test can ever be value-neutral (McNamara, 2006; McNamara & Roever, 2006), it is important to examine critically the underlying values inherent in KoS courses and KoS tests, and the extent to which they may be reduced to so-called 'national' values (Anderson, 2016).

Users of CoE values-oriented reference instruments such as the RFCDC and the CEFR may wish to reflect critically on their adaptation and use to meet the needs of migrants, while also aiming to ensure that they are not exploited as a potential barrier to active democratic and intercultural citizenship, as discussed further in the next part of this chapter.

Language and KoS Requirements as Potential Barriers to Integration

As underlined above, a certain level of communicative competence in the language(s) of the host country as well as civic knowledge is without doubt a facilitator in the integration process. However, if we accept integration as a two-way process, a chapter on linguistic integration should not only focus on migrants' learning and integration efforts and opportunities, but also consider possible barriers on their road to integration. The CoE, as well as numerous researchers, language testers, lawyers and social scientists, have pointed to formal language and KoS requirements as barriers with very real exclusionary power, especially for those individuals who are less likely to pass formal language and KoS tests (Strik, 2013; Huddleston, 2016; Shohamy, 2007, 2008; Shohamy & McNamara, 2009; Khan & McNamara, 2017; van Oers, 2013; Goodman, 2010, 2014). As shown in the four surveys carried out by the CoE on both language and KoS requirements in CoE member states since the turn of the millennium, it has become more and more common to make residency rights, family reunification and citizenship dependent upon the ability to pass a language and KoS test (see Council of Europe project: "Linguistic Integration of Adult Migrants" see Council of Europe https://www.coe.int/en/web/language-policy/adult-migrants). The most recent CoE/ALTE survey from 2018 revealed that setting such requirements has not only become the norm in Europe today, the requirements have also grown gradually stricter over the years (Rocca et al., 2020). In 2018 as many as four of the responding countries required that migrants applying for citizenship pass a language test at the B2-level, a level commonly used for university admission (Deygers et al., 2018). In general, B1 has replaced A2 as the most commonly required level for citizenship.

The CoE has expressed serious concern that this use of tests may be hindering integration and represent an infringement of basic human rights, such as the right to respect for private and family life (European Convention on Human Rights, Article 8) and the prohibition of discrimination (Article 14). It is of particular concern that an individual's secure residence rights and the possibility to reunite with children and partner through family reunification has come to depend on a test score (Council of Europe, 2004; Huddleston, 2016; Carrera & Vankova, 2019). It is repeatedly stressed by the CoE that uncertainty about one's future status and security of residence may inhibit migrants' ability, as well as their motivation, to invest in their integration process (Strik, 2013; Huddleston, 2016), a point also supported from research (Brekke *et al.*, 2019; Dansk Flygtningehjælp, 2019). Importantly, the CoE warns against reducing European standards and acceptable norms of integration policy by making it more difficult to obtain permanent residence permits, citizenship and family reunion in an attempt to make European countries appear 'less attractive' to potential migrants abroad and thereby discouraging asylum flows (Huddleston, 2016). These restrictions not only run counter to Europe's shared values but may also affect integration negatively while having a disproportionately harmful impact on vulnerable and discriminated groups (Huddleston, 2016).

Furthermore, there is the paradox that the CEFR and the related language proficiency levels, developed specifically to acknowledge and facilitate the idea of a multilingual Europe and to promote plurilingualism, mobility and communication, are being used as a tool to justify monolingual policies based on the requirement of given national languages (Bruzos *et al.*, 2017: 423). The Council of Europe LIAM group explicitly warns against this kind of misuse of the CEFR, underscoring that '[t]he CEFR was not intended for this purpose. [...] Its inappropriate use can have serious consequences that may include the infringement of migrants' human rights', hence underlining that this use of the CEFR runs counter to its original purpose as well as to CoE values of human rights and democracy (Little, 2012).

To understand the logic behind the widespread linking of language to residency rights and citizenship today, we must recognise the fact that language is not only a means to communicate efficiently, it also has a significant symbolic role. Language is a marker of social and cultural identity as well as of group belonging and can therefore be a sign through which we distinguish 'us' from 'them' and friends from foes (Slade & Möllering, 2010; McNamara & Roever, 2006). In the migration context, the ability to speak the national language(s) has become a symbol of national belonging (Blackledge, 2009; Extra & Spotti, 2009), with mastering the national language identified as a 'symbol for unity, loyalty, patriotism, inclusion and legitimacy' (Shohamy, 2006: xvi). Similarly, the inability to speak the national language has become embedded with the social value of nonbelonging and may even be interpreted as an unwillingness to integrate (Van Avermaet & Gysen, 2009: 119).

This double role of language as both a means to communicate efficiently and as a symbol of belonging is what is in play when language requirements are introduced for residency rights (Carlsen & Rocca, 2021). As Goodman (2014: 237) importantly points out, even though the language requirements for migration purposes are *per se* symbolic, the consequences for migrants are very real and concrete indeed.

The (mis-)use of language tests as gatekeepers preventing migrants from availing of basic human rights underlines the high-stakes nature of language and KoS learning and testing in the migration context and imposes a serious ethical responsibility on language test developers (Shohamy, 2001; Carlsen, 2018; Carlsen & Rocca, 2021). This is a responsibility for which the ethical guidelines for language testing professionals, such as the ILTA codes of ethics, the ALTE code of practice and the EALTA guidelines for good practice, are only partly suitable (Deygers & Van Cauwenberge, 2022).

This policy also represents new challenges for teachers who might find themselves part of a system of gatekeeping where their decisions as raters and/or their roles as teachers can have very serious and direct consequences for their learners' lives and future (IMPECT, 2022), as underlined by Krumm and Plutzar:

> Language teachers need to create an atmosphere of confidence and openness, so that learning can take place. If language testing is compulsory in an integration context, they as testers judge their learners in ways which decide on inclusion or exclusion. If a language test decides whether a migrant can stay or has to leave the country or through citizenship gains democratic rights in that society, the ethical dimension is overwhelming. (Krumm & Plutzar, 2008: 9)

In any discussion of 'requirements' and 'barriers', it is essential to bear in mind how learning a language and acquiring other skills and competences necessary for integration is not equally easy for all. Such requirements and their discriminatory power may form part of a more or less visible system of structural racism leading to the exclusion of particular groups of migrants from social justice and equal rights and opportunities, whether these consequences are intentional or not (Carlsen, 2021). Accordingly, to ensure social justice, inclusion and non-discrimination, it is of paramount importance that member states facilitate integration and avoid creating insurmountable barriers on the road to integration, as underlined in several CoE recommendations and action plans (Rocca *et al.*, 2020; Council of Europe, 2021). (For an illustration, see Vignette 1 below.)

CoE Tools for the Facilitation of Integration

The next part of this chapter presents concrete tools and outcomes of CoE work produced with the specific aim of facilitating the learning and integration processes of adult migrants, not least with a particular focus on low-literate adult learners. A representative sample of these tools is illustrated in a number of *vignettes* at the end of the chapter. These deal with language and KoS requirements for residence and citizenship (Vignette 1); developing communicative language scenarios (Vignette 2); the individual learner's linguistic repertoire (Vignette 3); a self-assessment grid for low-literate adult migrants (Vignette 4).

In order to address the complex issues of migrant integration and language learning, the Language Policy Division of the CoE initiated the Linguistic Integration of Adult Migrants (LIAM) project in 2006, dedicated specifically to the linguistic challenges imposed by migration flows. This includes an ongoing focus on responsible and appropriate use of existing CoE tools, in particular the *European Language Portfolio* (ELP) and CEFR. LIAM has regularly highlighted the importance of considering the CEFR as an open and flexible reference tool to be appropriately adapted when taking into account the target group, in this instance adult migrants as social agents (Coste, 2007; Little, 2007).

This crucial process implies actions reflecting the approaches adopted in the CEFR (particularly the concept of communicative competence), to the specificities of the migration context. Such actions may include improving the reference to the social domain, by inviting teachers to propose situations, themes and texts addressing training and job opportunities, accommodation, public services, healthcare and educational system, rights and duties related to daily life, or inviting the reader not to take for granted the learners' understanding of behaviours and situations characterised by a high European cultural connotation. As Krumm points out: 'The very heterogeneous groups of migrants are totally different from the learners originally targeted by the CEFR. [...] Migrants in a new society primarily have to use the language [...] in administrative contexts, and these environments of use are not currently the focus of the CEFR' (Krumm, 2007: 668).

Over the years, LIAM activities have increasingly focused attention on the needs of vulnerable migrants, i.e. refugees and low-literate learners who not only need to learn the majority language(s), but also need basic literacy training as part of their education. Below, we will look more closely at two important LIAM outcomes related to the linguistic support of refugees: a toolkit to assist volunteer teachers, and a reference framework to support teachers of low-literate learners (LASLLIAM), on which we are going to focus.

The LIAM Toolkit[7]

The LIAM Toolkit, which seeks to assist organisations that provide language support for refugees within non-formal learning environments, is available in seven languages (English, French, Dutch, German, Greek, Italian and Turkish). Many such organisations draw on the services of volunteers who have little or no training in language teaching and the toolkit aims to help such people in particular.

The 57 different tools of the toolkit are divided into three main sections:

(1) The *introduction*, addressing intercultural and ethical issues, as well as insights on language awareness and language learning.

(2) The *preparation and planning* section, containing tools which deal with the practical aspects of preparing for and delivering language support to a diverse group of refugees. It offers guidance to prepare the field: how to manage mixed groups of learners; how to select teaching materials; how to analyse users' needs, their literacy and linguistic profiles; how to support and value the use of other languages.
(3) The *learning activities* section has five parts beginning with important advice on getting started in the initial meetings with refugee learners. Other parts deal with concepts and support reflection about language learning, raising refugees' awareness of their learning process.

The next set of tools provides theme-based scenarios focusing on practical communicative situations typical of the daily challenges faced by refugees. Each scenario provides a set of real-world situations, with activities presented in a strategic order to satisfy a specific need. A scenario can be defined as a sequencing of real-life tasks aimed at developing the communicative competence needed to address a concrete need identified by the learners. (See Vignette 2 and 3 below.)

The LASLLIAM Reference Guide

In the context of its increasing focus on vulnerable learners, in 2018 the CoE (LIAM) decided to develop a tool specifically addressing the needs of those migrants who face the complex and demanding task of learning a new language while learning to read and write for the first time (https://rm.coe.int/prems-008922-eng-2518-literacy-and-second-language-learning-couv-te xte/1680a70e18).

LASLLIAM stands for *Literacy and Second Language Learning for the Linguistic Integration of Adult Migrants* – a CoE Reference Guide offering competence descriptors for designers of curricula, as well as teaching guidance and materials, portfolios and assessment tools for teachers in their daily work with adult migrants who have low levels of literacy. The Guide, conceived as a complement to the CEFR descriptor scales, addresses the twin, non-linear process of acquiring literacy as well as oracy in a second language with a strong focus on the didactic dimension (Kurvers *et al.*, 2010; Tarone, 2010).

In LASLLIAM the notion of literacy is understood as a person's capacity to deal with the written code. It refers to the ability of migrants, as social agents, to identify, understand, interpret and produce written texts, which can be handwritten, printed, digital and multi-modal (Condelli and Wrigley, 2006). Digital literacy is seen as an integral part of literacy. Based on the European Digital Competence Framework for citizens (DigComp), the LASLLIAM digital descriptors provide an example of the kind of skills needed to be able to participate in a digital society, with particular regard to three areas: communication and collaboration, content creation and management, and safety (Sokolowsky, 2022).

LASLLIAM builds on the concept of linguistic profiles, going beyond linguistic profiles (only), to literacy-and-linguistic profiles. Stakeholders such as teachers, assessors and others are invited to use LASLLIAM descriptor scales to reduce the fragmentation of a learning process that might occur when migrants move through various countries. It can support the mutual recognition of segments within the ongoing learning process by different providers (e.g. volunteers in a camp, teachers in an integration course system) and at different places (e.g. different cities or countries), or at different phases (e.g. first or second place of refugee). The need to put pieces together in order to sustain commitment and progression of the learner is fundamental, for instance when learning has started in a member state, is continuing in another and will be completed in yet another. In other words, a Portfolio drawing on LASLLIAM descriptors can offer a concrete response to the reciprocal need of migrants and teachers to make visible the achievement of learning goals. In this respect, an important added-value of LASLLIAM is its potential for representing a bridge, linking the drop-out in one learning environment with the drop-in in another.

The need for a guide such as LASLLIAM became even more apparent when the results of the CoE-ALTE survey in 2020 revealed that less than one third of CoE member states provide courses addressing literacy challenges. Low-literate migrants rarely receive sufficient instruction in terms of hours of tuition or benefit from the most appropriate teaching approaches, yet are very often requested to pass a compulsory written test, with very few exemptions.

LASLLIAM is not designed to serve as an instrument for developing high-stake examinations. On the contrary, it aims to put into practice what is highlighted in Recommendation 5.1 and 5.3 of the CoE-ALTE report mentioned above, and to support PACE Recommendation 2034[8] (Council of Europe, 2014): 'Rather than promoting testing, offering language courses [...] may offer greater advantages without running the risk of excluding migrants'.

In LASLLIAM the use of checklists is also strongly recommended as a practical way of implementing the European Language Portfolio, for example by listing *Can-do statements* that tend to expand the general descriptors of the self-assessment grid into a detailed inventory of communicative activities that can be used for regular goal-setting and self-assessment. (See Vignette 4 below.)

Conclusion

In this chapter, we have addressed some of the challenges in relation to the linguistic integration of adult migrants, with a particular focus on the central role of education in achieving the CoE goals of social justice and equal rights for all. As emphasised in earlier chapters of this book

(Chapters 1 and 2 in.particular), the concepts of quality and equity in education are derived from CoE values and are closely related. Equity implies taking measures tailored to the specific needs and personal circumstances of migrants, while quality implies that courses for migrants need to be practical and effective, and underpinned by educational policy and practices that build on and reflect shared values. We have focused on migrants' learning rights and opportunities and on CoE values, including respect for linguistic and cultural diversity. In pursuing the CoE aims of inclusion and social justice, we have echoed SLA-researchers in stressing the importance of challenging the myth of the perfect native speaker, underscoring what language competence means in practice. It is particularly important to correct the mistaken idea that a language user speaking with a foreign accent is a less competent user.

The CoE, and its LIAM group in Strasbourg in particular, plays an important role in promoting the dignity and rights of the individual within the migration context, focusing special attention on the most vulnerable migrants such as refugees and low-literate learners. Our intention has been to underline the importance of the CoE core values in migration contexts, and integration as a two-way process where respect for the migrant's language and culture is central, while bearing in mind the statement by the Parliamentary Assembly of the CoE that 'where integration tests are a barely veiled migration management measure, they inhibit and are detrimental to integration and they should be discontinued' (Strik, 2013: 3).

When addressing the question of migrant integration into all areas of the new society, it is important to look into migrants' opportunities for learning as well as barriers on their path to integration. We have therefore also looked at the use of language and KoS requirements as gatekeepers to residency, family reunification and citizenship, a practice that is gaining ground in CoE member states and is of a matter of growing concern to the CoE and professionals working in the field of migrant teaching, assessment and integration alike. As we have seen, the language proficiency levels required for these contexts are gradually increasing, often exceeding A2 in speaking and A1 in writing, considered an absolute maximum in order not to exclude vulnerable learner groups from democratic participation and a secure future (Strik, 2013).

Finally, we have presented the important work of the CoE LIAM group in developing practical and concrete tools for teachers. As underlined by Philia Thalgott, former head of the CoE Language Policy Unit, learning a language is potentially a lifelong process (Thalgott, 2017). Therefore, to foster language learning and integration, allowing migrants to participate as full members of society with equal rights and opportunities, European societies should provide rich language learning opportunities tailored to migrants' diverse and complex learning needs rather than introducing formal language requirements, which may function as barriers on the path to integration.

Vignettes

Vignette 1 suggests questions related to the role of teachers within the context of language and KoS-requirements for residency and citizenship. The questions can be used either for personal reflection or for discussion with teacher colleagues.

Vignette 1: Questions for reflection and/or discussion with colleague teachers

(1) Has your role as a teacher changed due to language requirements for residency and citizenship? If yes,
    (1a) How has it changed? For the worse or for the better?
    (1b) Do the requirements affect the content and focus of your teaching?
    (1c) Do you feel that your role vis-à-vis your learners have changed with the requirements?
(2) Are you involved in making high-stakes decisions about your learners' legal status, such as residency and citizenship? If yes,
    (2a) Do you find this problematic in any way? (ethically, pedagogically, socially, practically?)
(3) How do you experience your learners being affected by language requirements for residency and citizenship? Is it a source of motivation for them to learn the language? Or a source of concern and anxiety? Are different learner groups affected differently?

Vignette 2 illustrates the structure and the key features of a scenario, while giving indications to teachers on how to adopt this methodology in developing scenarios related to the concrete needs of their learners.

Vignette 2: How to develop a communicative language scenario

Title – referring to the concrete and contextualised need of the learners.

    Aims – specifying language learning goals.

    Communicative situations – specifying the relevant situations, topics, text types and types of communication.

    Materials – exemplifying the necessary teaching materials.

    Language activities – exemplifying relevant language activities.

    The language activities can be used separately (in a learning session, in any order) or in combination (as a series, in the suggested order) as further specified below.

Features of the language activities:

We recommend that those involved learners start with a brain-storming session related to the concrete need highlighted by the title of the scenario. In this round it is important to support inter-cultural dialogue and appreciate the contributions of all participants.
According to the learning need, the aim is to come up with lan-guage activities related to reception, production and, above all, interaction, mainly spoken.
Ideally, at least one activity should imply the use of digital devices (smart phone, iPad and similar), in order to improve digital skills as well (see section 'The LASLLIAM Reference Guide', above). These activities should include both individual tasks and tasks where learners interact in small groups, which would support peer learning as well as peer assessment.

With regard to the small group tasks, we recommend providing two kinds of activities:

Firstly, one could carry out similar activities (same topic, same skill), but provided at different levels of difficulty. This would allow teachers to better manage a group of learners at different levels of language proficiency, which is so often the case. To foster interaction and learning, it is an advantage to put learners together in small groups with other learners at more or less the same level of language proficiency.
The aim is that through this approach there will be an increased feeling of solidarity between peer learners, and one that may even lead participants to feel responsible not only for their own learn-ing, but also for the learning of their peers. In fact, accepting that weaker classmates need more support and more time is a matter of valuing equity, and respecting these needs and being willing to help others is a consequence of and, at the same time, evidence of valuing each person's right to equal opportunities.

Regarding the small group tasks, we recommend providing two kinds of activities:

As suggested above, one could carry out similar activities, but provided at different levels of difficulty.
In addition, one could organise the small groups in a different way, this time taking as the starting point a learner with a sufficient level

of L2 proficiency and collaborative behaviour taking on the role of mediator in a group of classmates. When possible, it is highly recommended to pass on the role of mediator from the teacher to the learners, in order to raise awareness about peer mediation (of texts, concepts, communication) within the learning environment.

Vignette 3 illustrates the *Plurilingual Portrait* aimed at making visible the individual's linguistic repertoire.

Vignette 3: The Plurilingual Portrait

The *Plurilingual Portrait* is presented as a reflective task for refugees, a very inclusive activity that supports learners in becoming aware of the *linguistic capital* they possess, thereby enhancing their self-esteem, especially in circumstances where they seem to be defined by the languages they do *not* know rather than the languages they know.

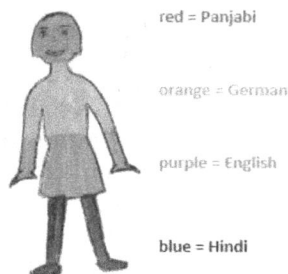

red = Panjabi

orange = German

purple = English

blue = Hindi

Source: H.-J. Krumm (Hgg. H.-J. Krumm/E.M. Jenkins: *Kinder und ihre Sprachen – lebendige Mehrsprachigkeit*. Vienna 2001) in Council of Europe Toolkit for Adult Refugees. See also Tools16 and 38. http://www.coe.int/lang-refugees

After having shown the example above, volunteers are invited to ask learners to draw a blank figure and create their own language portrait by assigning a colour, a position within the body and a space to each language present in their repertoire.

The colouring of the figure is meant to be a spontaneous, intuitive activity: the time for reflection is after they have created their language portrait.

In addition, it is important to encourage learners to include all linguistic varieties: dialects have the same value as standard languages.

Finally, the message should be that:

- the competence levels are not important at all: even a very low competence will allow a language to be visible;
- learners can draw their body as they like, as the outcome below aims to highlight.

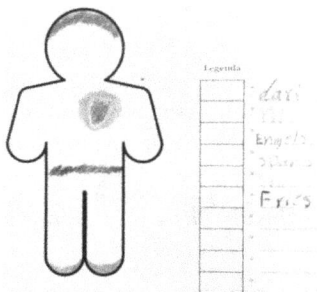

Source: Soares, C.T., Duarte, J. and Günter-van der Meij, M. (2020) 'Red is the colour of the heart': Making young children's multilingualism visible through language portraits. Language and Education 35 (1), 22-41.

Vignette 4 illustrates a self-assessment grid for low-literate adult migrants.

Vignette 4: Example of checklist targeted to low-literate adult migrants at LASLLIAM levels

As in CEFR (Appendix C), all statements start with the incipit 'I can' and are the result of a partial adaptation of the corresponding LASLLIAM descriptors, with a direct reference to the concrete outcomes achieved thanks to the communicative language activity just completed within the learning environment.

With regard to the vulnerable target group of LASLLIAM, the teacher should not expect learners to assess themselves without assistance. Therefore, the teacher is asked to present orally the meaning of each descriptor and have it mediated (using as necessary the learner's first language(s) or other languages familiar to them), paying particular attention to the symbols used to label the columns where the learner has to place a tick. It is also possible to insert facilitating elements, such as pictures or icons.

According to the migrant's profile the checklist invites the learner to specify the degree of help needed to be able to carry out the action described in the *Can-do* and whether this is confirmed by appropriate feedback given by the teacher.

A fair assessment based on LASLLIAM should always highlight outcomes in a positive way. For this reason, only smileys are provided, even in the case of 'a lot of help' (column refers to one smiley, while two smileys mean some help and three smileys mean without any help).

By marking the relevant column, the learner indicates that the teacher has confirmed the related *Can-do*, underlining once more the importance of using LASLLIAM within a learning environment, with the presence of a supportive teacher to guide and encourage the learner.

LASLLIAM LEVEL	COMMUNICATIVE LANGUAGE ACTIVITY WRITTEN PRODUCTION
4	I can write the name of the sports I like.
4	I can describe what my room looks like.
3	I can write the names of the main square of my village in map of public transportation.
2	I can write down a shopping list with few words.
2	I can note down date and time of appointment with doctor.
1	I can copy the lesson time into my agenda.

(Adapted from CEFR-CV) © Council of Europe

Notes

(1) European Association for the Education of Adults, https://eaea.org/.
(2) Linguistic Integration of Adult Migrants (LIAM), https://www.coe.int/en/web/lang-migrants/.
(3) This is of course also true for children.
(4) It should be noted that the CEFR (2001) contains content on language teaching, learning and assessment and pedagogical use of the CEFR. To equate the CEFR and the CEFR-CV only with the proficiency scales is therefore a rather reductionist use of the CEFR/CEFR-CV.
(5) https://rm.coe.int/the-2018-council-of-europe-and-alte-survey-on-language-and-know ledge-o/16809c88f9
(6) 'Intercultural dialogue is understood as an open and respectful exchange of views between individuals, groups with different ethnic, cultural, religious and linguistic backgrounds and heritage on the basis of mutual understanding and respect. [...] It operates at all levels – within societies, between the societies of Europe and between Europe and the wider world' (Council of Europe, 2008: 10–11).
(7) https://www.coe.int/en/web/language-support-for-adult-refugees/home
(8) The Parliamentary Assembly of the Council of Europe (PACE) is a deliberative body composed of representatives of the 46 national parliaments.

References

Anderson, B. (2016) *Imagined Communities: Reflections on the Origin and Spread of Nationalism* (3rd edn). London: Verso.
Bachman, L. (1990) *Fundamental Considerations in Language Testing*. Oxford: Oxford University Press.
Barrett, M. and Byram, M. (2020) Errors by Simpson and Dervin (2019) in their description of the Council of Europe's Reference Framework of Competences for Democratic Culture. *Intercultural Communication Education* 3 (2), 75–95.
Beacco, J.-C. (2014) *Language Repertoire*. Strasbourg: Council of Europe. https://www.coe.int/it/web/lang-migrants/repertoire-language-
Blackledge, A. (2009) 'As a country we do expect': The further extension of language testing regimes in the United Kingdom. *Language Assessment Quarterly* 6 (1), 6–16.
Brekke, J.-P., Birkvad, S.R. and Erdal, M.B. (2019) *Losing the Right to Stay. Revocation of Immigrant Residence Permits and Citizenship in Norway – Experiences and Effects*. Oslo: Institute for Social Research.

Bruzos, A., Erdocia, I. and Khan, K. (2017) The path to naturalization in Spain: Old ideologies, new language testing regimes and the problem of test use. *Language Policy* 17 (4), 419–441.

Byram, M. (1997) *Teaching and Assessing Intercultural Communicative Competence* (1st edn). Bristol: Multilingual Matters.

Byram, M. and Zarate, G. (1997) Defining and assessing intercultural competence: Some principles and proposals for the European context. *Language Teaching* 29, 14–18.

Canale, M. and Swain, M. (1980) Theoretical bases of communicative approaches to second language teaching and testing. *Applied Linguistics* 1, 1–47.

Carlsen, C.H. (2017) Giving LESLLA learners a fair chance in testing. In M. Sosinski (ed.) *Proceedings from LESLLA 2016 12th Annual Symposium* (pp. 135–148). Granada: Universidad de Granada.

Carlsen, C.H. (2018) Justice in practice – what it means and why it is our responsibility. Invited plenary. *ALTE 53rd Conference*, Gent, 24–26 April.

Carlsen, C.H. (2021) Social justice and structural racism: The role of language, language tests and language testers. *Presentation at ALTE 1st International Digital Conference*, 28–30 April.

Carlsen, C.H. and Rocca, L. (2021) Language test misuse. *Language Assessment Quarterly* 18 (5), 477–491. https://doi.org/10.1080/15434303.2021.1947288

Carrera, S. and Vankova, Z. (2019) Human rights aspects of immigrant and refugee integration policies. *Council of Europe Issue Paper*. Strasbourg: Council of Europe.

Chomsky, N. (1965) *Aspects of the Theory of Syntax*. Cambridge, MA: The MIT Press.

Condelli, L. and Wrigley, H. (2006) The *What Works Study*: Instruction, literacy and language learning for adult ESL literacy students. In I. van de Craats, J. Kurvers and M. Young-Scholten (eds) *Low-educated Adult Second Language and Literacy Acquisition. Proceedings of the Inaugural Symposium Tilburg* (pp. 111–133). Utrecht: Lot.

Coste, D. (2007) Contextualising uses of the Common European Framework of Reference for Languages, paper presented at a Council of Europe Intergovernmental Language Policy Forum on the uses of the CFER. Strasbourg: Council of Europe.

Council of Europe (2001) *Common European Framework of Reference for Languages: Learning, Teaching, Assessment*. Strasbourg: Council of Europe.

Council of Europe (2003) Parliamentary Assembly (PACE) recommendation 1625. Policies for the integration of immigrants in Council of Europe member states. Strasbourg: Council of Europe.

Council of Europe (2004) Parliamentary Assembly (PACE) recommendation 1686. Human mobility and the right to family reunion. Strasbourg: Council of Europe.

Council of Europe (2008) *White Paper on Intercultural Dialogue: Living Together as Equals in Dignity*. Strasbourg: Council of Europe.

Council of Europe (2014) Parliamentary Assembly (PACE) recommendation 2034. Integration tests: Helping or hindering integration? Strasbourg: Council of Europe.

Council of Europe (2018) *Reference Framework of Competences for Democratic Culture (RFCDC), Vol. 1*. Strasbourg: Council of Europe.

Council of Europe (2020) *Common European Framework of Reference for Languages: Learning, Teaching, Assessment – Companion Volume*. Strasbourg: Council of Europe.

Council of Europe (2021) *Council of Europe Action Plan on Protecting Vulnerable Persons in the Context of Migration and Asylum in Europe (2021–2025)*. Strasbourg: Council of Europe.

Dansk Flygtningehjælp (2019) Vi tager jo drømmerne fra dem! (We are taking their dreams away from them!) Report published by Danish Refugee Council. https://prod.drc.ngo/media/oqlnvauu/vi-tager-jo-droemmene-fra-dem-undersoegelse_lovaendringer_2019.pdf

Davies, A. (2003) *The Native Speaker: Myth and Reality*. Clevedon: Multilingual Matters.

Dewaele, J.-M., Bak, T.H. and Ortega, L. (2020) Why the mythical 'native speaker' has mud on its face. In N. Slavkov, S. Melo-Pfeifer and N. Kerschhofer-Puhalo (eds) *The Changing Face of the 'Native Speaker': Perspectives from Multilingualism and Globalization* (pp. 25–46). Berlin: De Gruyter Mouton.

Deygers, B. and Van Cauwenberge, D. (forthcoming 2022) Language testing ethics, and our place in the ecosystem. *Language Testing*.

Deygers, B., Zeidler, B., Vilcu, D. and Carlsen, C.H. (2018) One framework to unite them all? Use of the CEFR in European university entrance policies. *Language Assessment Quarterly* 15 (1), 3–15.

Douglas Fir Group (2016) A transdisciplinary framework for SLA in a multilingual world. *The Modern Language Journal* 100 (S1), 19–47.

Extra, G. and Spotti, M. (2009) Testing regimes for newcomers to the Netherlands. In G. Extra, M. Spotti and P. van Avermaet (eds) *Language Testing, Migration and Citizenship: Cross-national Perspectives on Integration Regimes* (pp. 128–147). London: Continuum.

Flores, N., Tseng, A. and Subtirelu, N. (2020) Bilingualism for all or just for the rich and white? Introducing a raciolinguistic perspective to dual language education. In N. Flores, A. Tseng and N. Subtirelu (eds) *Bilingualism for All? Raciolinguistic Perspectives on Dual Language Education in the United States* (pp. 1–18). Bristol: Multilingual Matters.

Freire, P. (2005) *Pedagogy of the Oppressed*. New York: Continuum. (First published in Portuguese in 1968.)

Goodman, S.W. (2010) Integration requirements for integration's sake? Identifying, categorising and comparing civic integration policies. *Journal of Ethnic and Migration Studies* 36 (5), 753–772.

Goodman, S.W. (2014) *Immigration and Membership Politics in Western Europe*. Cambridge: Cambridge University Press.

Holec, H. (1981) *Autonomy and Foreign Language Learning*. Oxford: Pergamon. (First published 1979, Strasbourg: Council of Europe.)

Huddleston, T. (2016) *Time for Europe to Get Migrant Integration Right. Issue paper*. Strasbourg: Council of Europe.

Hulstijn, J. (2015) *Language Proficiency in Native and Non-native Speakers: Theory and Research*. Amsterdam: John Benjamins Publishing Co.

Hymes, D. (1972) On communicative competence. In J.B. Pride and J. Holmes (eds) *Sociolinguistics: Selected Readings*. Harmondsworth: Penguin.

IMPECT (2022) Linguistic Integration of Adult Migrants with Poor Education and the Consequences of Migration Tests. https://www.hvl.no/forsking/prosjekt/impect/

Khan, K. and McNamara, T. (2017) Citizenship, immigration laws, and language. In S. Canagarajah (ed.) *The Routledge Handbook of Migration and Language* (pp. 451–467). London: Routledge.

Knowles, M.S. (1978a) *The Adult Learner: A Neglected Species*. Houston: Gulf Publishing Company.

Knowles, M.S. (1978b) Andragogy: Adult learning theory in perspective. *Adult and Student Learning* 5 (3), 9–20.

Krumm, H.-J. (2007) Profiles instead of levels: The CEFR and its (ab)uses in the context of migration. *The Modern Language Journal* 91 (4), 667–669.

Krumm, H.-J. and Plutzar, V. (2008) *Tailoring Language Provisions and Requirements to the Needs and Capacities of Adult Migrants*. Strasbourg: Council of Europe.

Kurvers, J., Stockmann, W. and van de Craats, I. (2010) Predictors of success in adult L2 literacy acquisition. In T. Wall and M. Leong (eds) *Low-Educated Second Language and Literacy Acquisition. Proceedings of the 5th Symposium* (pp. 64–79). Calgary: Bow Valley College.

Little, D. (2007). The Common European Framework of Reference for Languages: Perspectives on the making of supranational language education policy. *The Modern Language Journal* 91 (4), 645–655.

Little, D. (2009) Learner autonomy in action: Adult immigrants learning English in Ireland. In F. Kjisik, P. Voller, N. Aoki and Y. Nakata (eds) *Mapping the Terrain of Learner Autonomy: Learning Environments, Learning Communities and Identities* (pp. 51–85). Tampere: Tampere University Press.

Little, D. (2012) *The Linguistic Integration of Adult Migrants and the Common European Framework of Reference for Languages.* Strasbourg: Council of Europe. https://rm.coe.int/16802fc1ca

McNamara, T. (2006) Validity in language testing: The challenge of Sam Messick's legacy. *Language Assessment Quarterly: An International Journal* 3 (1), 31–51.

McNamara, T. and Roever, C. (2006) *Language Testing: The Social Dimension.* Malden, MA: Blackwell.

Richterich, R. (1983) *Case Studies in Identifying Language Needs.* Oxford: Pergamon.

Rocca, L., Carlsen, C.H. and Deygers, B. (2020) *Linguistic Integration of Adult Migrants: Requirements and Learning Opportunities.* Strasbourg: Council of Europe.

Rossner, R. (2008) *Quality Assurance in the Provision of Language Education and Training for Adult Migrants – Guidelines and Options.* Strasbourg: Council of Europe. https://www.eaquals.org/resources/quality-assurance-in-the-provision-of-language-education-and-training-for-adult-migrants-guidelines-and-options/

Shohamy, E. (2001) *The Power of Tests: A Critical Perspective on the Uses of Language Tests.* London: Pearson.

Shohamy, E. (2006) *Language Policy: Hidden Agendas and New Approaches.* London: Routledge.

Shohamy, E. (2007) Language tests as language policy tools. *Assessment in Education* 14 (1), 117–130. https://doi.org/10.1080/09695940701272948

Shohamy, E. (2008) Language policy and language assessment: The relationship. *Current Issues in Language Planning* 9 (3), 363–373. https://doi.org/10.1080/14664200802139604

Shohamy, E. and McNamara, T. (2009) Language tests for citizenship, immigration, and asylum. *Language Assessment Quarterly* 6 (1), 1–5. https://doi.org/10.1080/15434300802606440

Slade, C. and Möllering, M. (2010) *From Migrant to Citizen: Testing Language, Testing Culture.* London: Palgrave Macmillan.

Sokolowsky, C. (2022) Digital learning opportunities for second language learning and basic education: Key criteria and experiences for development, operation and use. In M. D'Agostino and E. Mocciaro (eds) *Languages and Literacy in New Migration. Research, Practice, and Policy. Literacy Education and Second Language Learning for Adults (LESLLA): Proceedings of the 14th Annual Meeting of LESLLA*, Palermo, 4–6 October (pp. 385–399). Palermo: UniPa Press.

Strik, T. (2013) Integration tests: helping or hindering integration. Council of Europe Parliamentary Assembly report, Doc. 13361. Strasbourg: Council of Europe.

Tarone, E. (2010) Second language acquisition by low-literate learners: An understudied population. *Language Teaching* 43, 75–83.

Thalgott P. (2017) Foreword. In J.-C. Beacco, H.-J. Krumm, D. Little and P. Thalgott (eds) *The Linguistic Integration of Adult Migrants.* Berlin: De Gruyter.

United Nations (2018) United Nations Sustainable Development Goals: Pathways to Success – A Systematic Framework for Aligning Investments. https://www.citivelocity.com/citigps/un-sustainable-development-goals/

Van Avermaet, P. and Gysen, S. (2009) One nation two policies: Language requirements for citizenship and integration in Belgium. In G. Extra, M. Spotti and P. Van Avermaet (eds) *Language Testing, Migration and Citizenship: Cross-national Perspectives on Integration Regimes* (pp. 107–124). London: Advances in Sociolinguistics.

van Oers, R. (2013) *Deserving Citizenship: Citizenship Tests in Germany, the Netherlands and the United Kingdom.* Leiden: Martinus Nijhoff.

Yosso, T.J. (2005) Whose culture has capital? A critical race theory discussion of community cultural wealth. *Race, Ethnicity and Education* 8 (1), 69–91.

11 As the Leader of a Language-Friendly Educational Institution, What Do I Need to Know about Policymaking for Language and Literacy Education in a Coherent Whole-School Approach?

Jonas Erin and Waldemar Martyniuk

Introduction

This chapter differs somewhat from previous ones written primarily for teachers in classrooms. The following text analyses the school principal's particular role in promoting a whole-school policy for plurilingual and intercultural education. What teachers can do is dependent on how an institution and its curriculum are organised, with the principal being an important actor.

This chapter deals with a number of curricular principles and practices in ensuring quality and equity in education. These include creating a plurilingual curriculum as proposed in the Council of Europe *Guide for the Development and Implementation of Curricula for Plurilingual and Intercultural Education* (Beacco *et al.*, 2016a), facilitating teacher collaboration on language(s) of schooling, including content and language integrated learning (CLIL), promoting a whole-school approach to the development of competences for democratic culture, and to the inclusion of all children independent of their social or socioeconomic background.

The whole-school approach is explained in its various dimensions and in terms of its impact on school development and the management of change, taking into account significant developments such as the digitalisation of education, and bearing in mind the social responsibility of schools since plurilingual and intercultural competences and competences for democratic culture are essential for social inclusion and cohesion.

A whole-school approach helps to combine all dimensions of language education and to engage all actors in the school community. This chapter highlights the principal's role in each domain and illustrates strategies to develop and implement a whole-school approach to languages.

What Could a Whole-School Approach Be from the Point of View of School Principals?

The concept of a whole-school approach refers to three complementary dimensions:

- the learning environment and its cultural, personal and structural features;
- a holistic management that takes into account the different levels (learning, teaching, managing, making decisions);
- a global approach to language education which considers the combination of formal, informal and non-formal learning spaces.

These three dimensions are complementary as they contribute to establishing a language-friendly environment in terms of the coherence of the school management, the convergence of all efforts and the synchronisation of all actions.

Language learning environments

Language learning environments can be defined as a combination of cultural (values, content, projects, events, habits, etc.), structural (time, spaces, facilities, equipment, funding, etc.) and personal (networks, partners, teams, training, etc.) features. Due to the history and specificity of different school systems, we note that efforts made by schools to set up language-friendly learning environments frequently focus on one or two aspects but rarely simultaneously on all three. The focus is often on equipment and funding ('structure') and targets, values or content-based goals ('culture'). Learners' needs are often considered in isolation from adults' needs (parents, teachers, staff, partners) and hardly connected to the other considerations. Figure 11.1 describes a European Centre for Modern Languages of the Council of Europe (ECML) project that seeks to balance all three aspects.[1] The project illustrates the school's mediation function in and through languages.[2]

The EOL website and project offers a method and various tools to help school principals and staff to consider all three aspects in a synchronic way. More than 100 schools throughout Europe have been involved in the project. The André Chénier lower secondary school in southern France set up a "walk and talk" project in which students guide tourists through a local museum.

This project shows an exemplary balance between cultural, structural and personal aspects. The content of the exhibition is prepared in the foreign language class with the help of teachers of other subjects; students guide tourists in the target language and a formal agreement underpins the partnership between the school, the museum, and the tourist office.

Culture
The content of the exhibition is related to modern language classes.

People
Students guide tourists in their own languages through the city and the museum.

Structure
A partnership between the school and the museum gives students the availability to be at the museum once a week.

Collège Chénier, Carcassone – France, 2019

This approach changed the image of foreign language classes. It helped to promote an action-based approach where learners' individual and collective agency, their self-esteem and sense of belonging is at the heart of learning. Being ambassadors of the local culture and adapting to the cultural references of foreign tourists are two pillars of citizenship building. Moreover, this project highlights the school's mediation function through and for languages.

Figure 11.1 A project showing a balance between cultural, structural and personal aspects © Council of Europe/ECML

The principals' role, for example in the EOL approach illustrated above, is to identify key features of language learning environments. The 'TrEOL' tool is a card game that encompasses cultural, structural and personal aspects. Its interactive version[3] helps school staff to focus on strengths and priorities.

Combining all three features (cultural, structural and personal) is an effective way to overcome the usual disconnections such as the lack of continuity of language learning pathways, an isolated approach to each language, no transfer between formal and non-formal language education, etc. This combination can also support human resource management, i.e. professional development, cross-subject approach, project-based innovation, etc.

Example: The Lycée Lumière, a vocational upper secondary school in Luxeuil in France, relied on a reflexion about language learning environments to improve its educational offer. The team discussions led to the following challenge: 'How to optimise the school's network of both educational and non-educational partnerships in order to enrich vocational curricula through mobility and increased exposure to foreign languages'.[4]

Considering the language learning environment is an essential step towards a whole-school approach.

A holistic view on language education

Depending on the school system, school management often focuses on one particular level: either on content and methodology or on communication and human resource management. Language education requires both: content and communication, methodology and professional skills, individual needs and collective approaches.

The school management is also very dependent on the educational authorities and the degree of their proximity to the school. The capacity of educational authorities to be engaged with the local reality as well as to create opportunities for international partnerships has a major influence on school management. In Europe, there are municipal, regional and national educational bodies with local, federal or centralised educational policies. Whatever the school system is and whatever the degree of proximity, language education needs to cope simultaneously with individual and collective needs, with personal initiatives and international programmes, with local cultures and global goals.

Setting up a holistic view on language education embraces all levels of education: learners, teachers, schools and school systems. In order to generate a coherent and efficient approach, the EOL matrix explores five recurrent dimensions of language education through all levels (see Figure 11.2).

The matrix supports schools in the development of language-friendly learning environments and the identification of new opportunities for and through languages. The EOL website[5] offers an interactive version of the matrix, and has been translated into nine languages.

The principals' role is to involve all actors in language education through a coherent plan. Considering all levels of education increases the chance for a high impact on quality in education.

	NANO : learner	MICRO : class	MESO : schools	MACRO : system
1. Language and languages *operational dimension*	1.1. Supporting language skills	1.2. Strengthening communicative skills	1.3. Setting up school communication policy	1.4. Fostering global language awareness
2. Valuing languages *ethical dimension*	2.1. Sensitizing learners towards languages	2.2. Evaluating and assessing	2.3. Setting up a whole-school language policy	2.4. Ensuring and widening language diversity
3. Intercultural dialogue *experiential dimension*	3.1. Learning with others	3.2. Implementing a sensitive approach to languages and cultures	3.3. Developing international networks	3.4. Enhancing interconnections for inclusion
4. Enriching curricula *curricular dimension*	4.1. Valorizing language biographies and repertoires	4.2. Fostering cross subject approaches	4.3. Ensuring cross curricular continuity	4.4. Promoting collective intelligence
5. Everyday languages *existential dimension*	5.1. Enriching language repertoires	5.2. Using all learning fields	5.3. Exploring linguistic landscape	5.4. Building multilingual environment

Figure 11.2 Matrix showing dimensions of language education © Council of Europe/ ECML

The matrix can be used in two different ways:

- either to set up a global language plan at school level by combining two entries…

  Example: If a school wants to promote a global language education (see below) especially through social networks, gaming, etc. the staff should discuss the combination 5.2. *Using all learning fields* and 2.3. *Setting up a whole-school language policy.*

- …or as an orientation table helping principals to value existing projects and widen their impact.

  Example: If intercultural dialogue is the main target of the educational plan, then the school should look to synchronise all levels: learning (3.1. *Learning with others*), teaching (3.2. *Implementing a sensitive approach to languages and cultures*), the school's priorities (3.3. *Developing international networks*) and the educational policy level (3.4. *Enhancing interconnections for inclusion*).

In both cases, the matrix supports school principals and school staff in moving towards a holistic approach in order to develop more coherence and convergence within the school policy and communication.

Coherence and convergence are key strategies to set up a whole-school approach.

A global approach to language education

A global education offer integrates formal, informal and non-formal learning spaces. This is becoming essential with the development of digital learning environments. The delimitation between formal and non-formal learning is vanishing with increasingly playful online language learning platforms. Even informal learning tools such as intuitive online games in which players need to communicate in various languages play a growing role in everyday exposure to various languages. Moreover, it is important to mention here social networks or online TV providers which make it very easy to write in, speak about or listen to various modern languages.

In this context, school language policies should not focus only on formal learning but also support learners in their capacity to use all possible opportunities to develop their plurilingual and pluricultural repertoire. The principals' role is therefore to identify what digital equipment, resources and services the school could offer.

To go even further, language education should be considered as an asset to change schools into 'service institutions',[6] that is to say, places likely to welcome public audiences and promote social cohesion and inclusion. Outside school time, a school's resources can offer significant conditions to support digital literacy among the whole community, to foster intercultural

In 2018, the lycée Evariste Gallois organized a Europe Day (journée de l'Europe) with the aim to promote the European identity among the whole community.

Using all learning spaces: during the day of Europe the students transformed the stairs into a map of Europe. [viii]

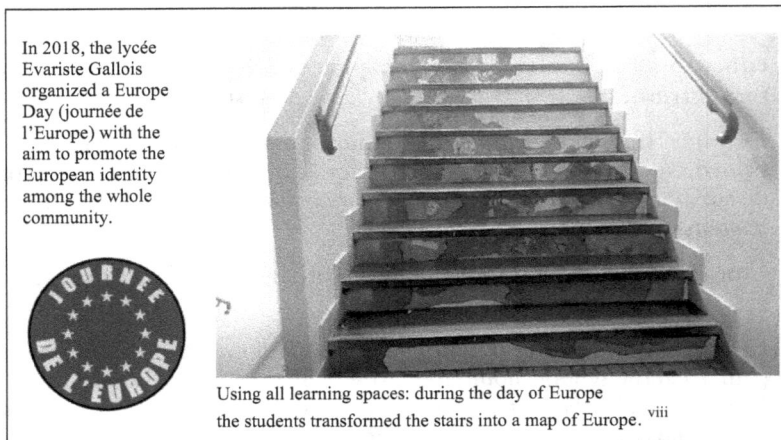

Figure 11.3 A school European Day[8] © Council of Europe/ECML

meetings for parents, to promote international mobility, to develop the school community's identity through sports or cultural events, etc.

Language education plays a major role when it comes to the mediation function of schools.[7]

Example: In order to facilitate the transition from the collège (lower secondary school) to the lycée (upper secondary school), the Lycée Evariste Gallois in France organises every year a plurilingual and intercultural day to welcome students and teachers from various surrounding collèges (see Figure 11.3). Everyone participates in the organisation of workshops and concerts: students, teachers, parents. This approach raises the awareness of all stakeholders of the diversity of languages and cultures but also of the importance of intercultural competences.

Conclusion

Creating, maintaining and cultivating 'learning environments where languages flourish' – as in the title of the EOL project presented briefly above – seems to be the most challenging but at the same time potentially most rewarding task for principals wishing to adopt a coherent whole-school approach to language and literacy education. The challenge is to convince all stakeholders in the educational processes – not just learners and teachers but also parents, partners in society, networks, administrators, etc. – of the value, the importance, and the power of language ability, and to engage them in a common effort to provide good quality education that is inclusive and based upon all linguistic resources available to all learners in the system. The rewarding outcome will most certainly be visible in a growing level of educational satisfaction and success of all learners, essential for social prosperity, stability and cohesion.

How to Adapt the Different Guides and Frameworks for Whole-School Management?

By whole-school management, we mean the school management takes into account all formal and non-formal education opportunities when designing language learning pathways and supporting a transversal approach to language education. In order to do this, language education has to be considered as a consistent part of the school's identity (as outlined below in the section 'School Communication and Inclusion') with a focus on the importance of school communication and the way a school highlights its values through language education.

Language education and curricula for plurilingual and intercultural education

A whole-school approach is essential when it comes to considering all teachers as language teachers and to setting up in-service training programmes with a focus on the linguistic dimension of all learning. The schema of the Council of Europe's Platform for Plurilingual and Intercultural Education (see Figure 11.4) represents the key links across

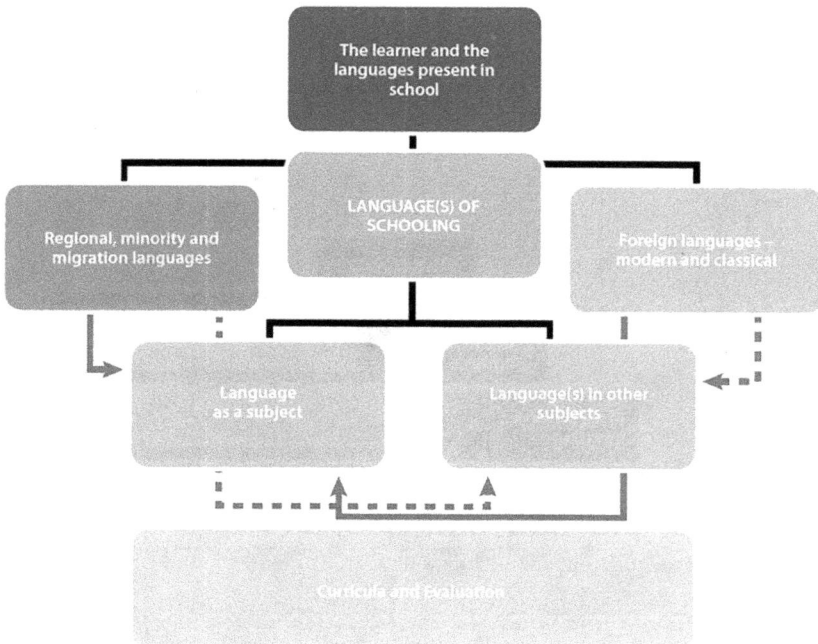

Figure 11.4 Platform of resources and references for plurilingual and intercultural education[9] © Council of Europe

languages and highlights the importance of language competences across the curricula.

The whole-school approach carried out by the ECML project PlurCur shows how schools might embody the transversal nature of language matters in their policy. 'The proposed whole-school policy is designed in such a way that languages taught as subjects are not treated in isolation and language and non-language instruction overlap so that all subject teaching is also language teaching. This consistent implementation of content-based language(s) instruction is transferable to all non-language content lessons.'[10]

There are two major steps towards plurilingual and intercultural education that need to be taken and for which a whole-school management is essential:

- **Supporting teachers**
  The first step is to help teachers with monolingual qualifications to set up plurilingual classrooms. In addition to a coherent language learning pathway in which each new language builds on the previous language learning experience, schools should offer learners the opportunity to develop plurilingual and intercultural strategies through cross-language teaching formats. The arrow in Figure 11.5 illustrates the concrete progression of a possible individual school career.

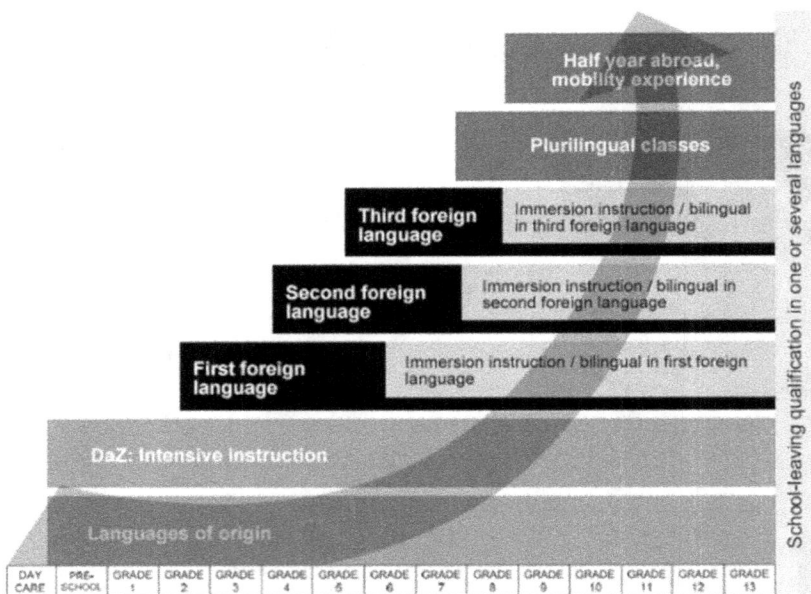

Figure 11.5 A possible plurilingual whole-school curriculum[11] © Council of Europe/ ECML

Often the formal curriculum leaves no possibility for multilingual settings. This is why informal multilingual teaching such as multilingual drama, plurilingual café or intercultural projects can be a transitional solution.

- **Supporting learners**

  The second step is to develop learners' sensitivity towards language diversity. Making language and cultural diversity not only acceptable but also enjoyable should be seen as a main educational objective. Enactive pedagogies (Aden and Eschenauer, 2020) offer various ways (speaking, moving, making gestures, etc.) to explore the sensory universe of languages and to make learners aware of their plurilingual repertoire. Giving learners the opportunity to value their own plurilingualism through an aesthetic experience as an actor is at the very heart of performative pedagogies that might correspond to the desire for social commitment of the younger generations.

The principals' role is to place teachers in the best possible conditions to go beyond their own plurilingual repertoire and to develop opportunities for learners where they can explore various ways to learn and use all languages. Flexible school management is essential to achieve this.

Language learning pathways and school policymaking

The diversity of the language offer contributes to the attractiveness of a school. This means not only the diversity of the languages offered but also the consistency (richness + continuity) of the language learning pathways. Bilingual, immersive and CLIL teaching is essential when it comes to raising the eventual level of the students in one or more languages. It gives students more opportunities to use the languages they learn in diverse contexts and subjects.[12]

One of the main challenges of educational policies is to foster CLIL teaching.[13] Among the main barriers, we can mention here:

- On a political level, CLIL is seen in some countries as being in competition with the language of schooling which can become an issue when the country has few speakers of the national language;
- It is still a challenge to resist the common belief among parents, decision makers and politicians that exploring one or more subjects in a foreign language might slow down the learners' progression;
- In several countries, CLIL can only be offered through an official procedure that requires an additional certificate which can lead to a human resource bottleneck. The lack of plurilingual competences among teachers is either due to procedural or cultural issues. Sometimes school authorities don't even know that some teachers have plurilingual competences and could offer CLIL teaching.

For these three reasons, it is often necessary to set up a global process over several years to implement CLIL teaching as a central part of plurilingual and intercultural education. Here are seven key steps:

(1) Motivate teachers and sensitise parents through an intercultural event that combines various subjects and languages.
(2) Offer the staff common training on language-sensitive teaching.
(3) Foster international cooperation through a plurilingual project in science or fine arts subjects.
(4) Offer professional development in foreign languages through school exchange programmes, and other ways.
(5) Facilitate team-teaching which includes foreign language teachers.
(6) Set up an offer to learners of CLIL.
(7) Emphasise the value of CLIL teaching as a central contribution to plurilingual and intercultural education in school communications, including social networks.

The principals' role is to set up a medium-term strategy for human resource management in which languages play a central role.

School communication and inclusion

Foreign languages offer great flexibility when it comes to lesson content, but only a minority of educational authorities have established a specific cultural content in their curricula. Nonetheless, the cultural objectives still offer a major opportunity to combine language education and media education. This can be done in various ways:

- Highlighting the role of language education by expanding the range of digital uses (communicating, searching for information, setting up new digital content, etc.);
- Supporting individual and collective agency through school exchange and mobility programmes where students are empowered, e.g. in communication management;
- Making the school's website a platform for intercultural communication within the school community and beyond. This can offer great opportunities for students to experience their role as intercultural mediators and/or webmasters, etc.

Furthermore, plurilingualism as such should also be part of the school curriculum. Instead of organising separate language lessons, a school could also set up plurilingual classrooms, which means that during some lessons or in a project more than one language is used for instruction. This step is essential for the capacity of a school to move towards the inclusion of all languages.

> The ECML project *Plurilingual whole school curricula* offers various examples to set up 'Mehrsprachenunterricht' (Plurilingual teaching): https://www.ecml.at/ECML-Programme/Programme2012-2015/ PlurCur/PlurCurvideos/tabid/1780/language/en-GB/Default.aspx

The principals' role is to generate as many opportunities as possible to offer students the possibility to contribute to and be involved in educational and social inclusion through multilingual communication.

Conclusion

Since all education goes through language(s) it is perhaps high time to reconsider the standard educational model which offers languages only as separate 'school subjects' and viewing areas such as Geography, History or Sciences as 'non-language subjects'. It seems quite obvious that educational content – both in terms of knowledge, skills and attitudes – is always language-mediated. It is also quite evident that language instruction is most efficient when it is driven by and offered through interesting content. The challenge for principals may be to overcome the traditional divisions and encourage not only teachers but also their learners to perceive each subject class as an important part of language development, and vice versa – each language class as a valuable part of content education.[14]

How to Foster School Development and Change Management through Language Education?

In the previous paragraphs, we have tried to show that a global, whole-school approach relies on both a specific and a transversal approach to languages. Language education should therefore not be considered in isolation from further considerations (other subjects, social issues, the school's context, etc.). This global approach is essential for school management and justifies a reflexion on how to combine goals (symbiotic approach), engage all actors (project-based approach) and monitor a project (quality assurance approach).

The symbiotic approach

Symbiosis can be defined as a mutually beneficial interaction that relates each other's needs. The symbiotic approach to language learning environments developed by the EOL project simultaneously takes into account a school's strengths and its needs. Highlighting the strengths of a school in the area of language education in order to target its priorities in other areas is a key strategy for change management. School development can be fostered through languages if it also makes sense to non-specialists. Here are some examples of various challenges formulated by EOL partner schools based on the symbiotic approach:

- Using languages and other subjects for school guidance to help pupils to choose the direction in which they want to study and work: How to support school orientation through languages and international partnerships?
- Supporting general language education building on collaborative teaching: How to foster language awareness thanks to collaborative thinking between teachers?
- Fostering intercultural learning and civic education through school networking: How can a common language project promote collaborative approaches to teaching within a school network?

Through the symbiotic approach, the principals' role is to find ways to support collective intelligence.

A project-based approach

One of the best ways to motivate the school staff is the project-based approach that gives the opportunity to make various actors converge towards a common goal. If the project's aim is formulated properly in terms of concrete targets, steps and schedule, it will foster both team spirit and cross-subject process.

Example: The Adam Mickiewicz Gymnasium in Vilnius is an upper secondary school in which Polish is the language of instruction, Lithuanian the state language, English the first foreign language and Russian the second (optional) foreign language. The staff set up a whole-school project in order to support language awareness, culture and values through all the activities at school. The team made this project concrete through various cultural events that engaged the whole community: Celebration of the International Languages Day; Ecological week in English and Russian; International project 'Lodz and Vilnius are multicultural cities'; Celebration of 100 years of Lithuanian independence; etc.

Sharing the project management through a project-based approach to language education helps to motivate the staff and fosters team spirit.

A quality assurance approach

Addressing quality assurance is essential when it comes to engaging all actors in a sustainable way in language education. Hans-Günther Rolff (2013) set up a 'three-way model' (see Figure 11.6) which can easily be adapted to a global approach to languages.[15] His model for school development relies on the same three pillars – people (personal development),

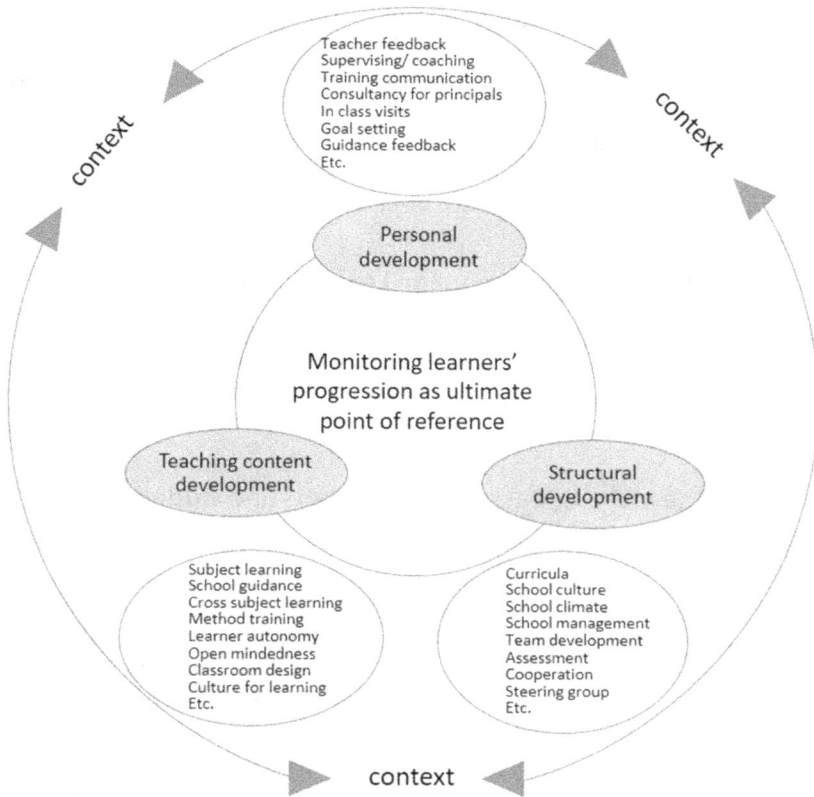

Figure 11.6 A model for a global approach to languages

structure (organisational development) and culture (teaching content) – as we defined for language learning environments (see above).

Another key element for the success of project management is to establish a common internal (staff) and/or external (school community and school authorities) recognition. Attributing a quality label to both the process and the result of a school project supports the motivation of the staff and highlights everyone's contribution. The EOL tool called 'labelling procedure' gives an input on the process in three steps: (1) Identification; (2) Recognition; (3) Quality control.

The principals' role is to ensure that language education is part of the school development process, integrated in the school's educational plan and valued in internal and external assessment procedures.

Conclusion

Introducing and managing change in an institutional environment is not an easy task. School principals may, however, discover significant potential in turning to language education as the area upon which to build school development and cohesion. The enhanced curricular coherence offered by a plurilingual and intercultural approach to education as promoted by the Council of Europe offers an opportunity to overcome the usual compartmentalisation of actions for the benefit of a more symbiotic interaction of all those involved in school work, in turn leading to a more efficient use of resources and a stronger team spirit.

How to Set Up a Digital Language Learning Environment

The digital paradigm shift in education has a great impact on language education. It puts language education, communication skills, oral and written interaction at the heart of education. It also offers new opportunities to use modern languages in authentic communication situations.

What are the main digital needs of teachers and students?

Younger generations are characterised by their quest for meaning and their desire for engagement. Social networks meet these needs. However, the linguistic dimension is fundamental in the use of social networks. The school must therefore not only support learners in developing their language proficiency but also foster interaction skills, intercultural competences, media education, network management and project management, all with a critical reflection dimension.[16] In parallel, while the digitalisation of education is a challenge for many teachers, it also creates an opportunity to share cross-curricular objectives such as using news tools and devices, supporting interaction at a distance, connecting formal and non-formal education, etc.

The principals' role is to invest in the school's digital equipment and offer professional development sessions in order to help teachers to bridge the generational gap.

What can we learn from home schooling in times of pandemic?

UNESCO, in cooperation with different partners, developed a learning continuity toolkit to help decision makers in the context of the pandemic. The UNESCO approach offers a set of grids and schemas to help prioritise issues and considerations in different contexts, and explains why hybrid learning is a central element in ensuring continued learning. The illustration in Figure 11.7 paves the way for a differentiated approach to subjects and age groups for hybrid teaching.

This approach also highlights the importance of language in distance-learning solutions and how much the learning format relies on the learners' capacity to take up the linguistic load, e.g. the importance of scaffolding in asynchronous learning, the importance of language for

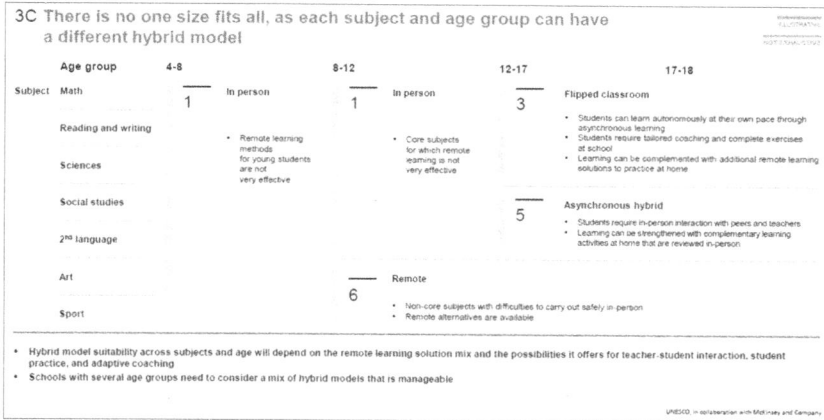

Figure 11.7 Covid-19 response: a differentiated approach to hybrid learning[17]

distant interaction, the importance of the language dimension in each subject, etc. We believe that a similar method could be used to differentiate the contribution of each subject to language education during the whole-school career.

Principals need to find strategies to develop a common understanding and development of the language dimension in all subjects.[18]

What could the language-friendly school of the future look like?

Digital tools and media have a great impact on our modes of communication. The development of written interaction, the constraint of a 180-character message (tweet), the impact of a hashtag on our syntax, etc. change the way we communicate. Our mobile devices also give us access nearly everywhere in the world and create opportunities to use all the languages of our repertoire more frequently. 'Wikis' give the opportunity to share knowledge with others and use modern languages in authentic communication situations called the 'social-interactional approach' (see Figure 11.8). The

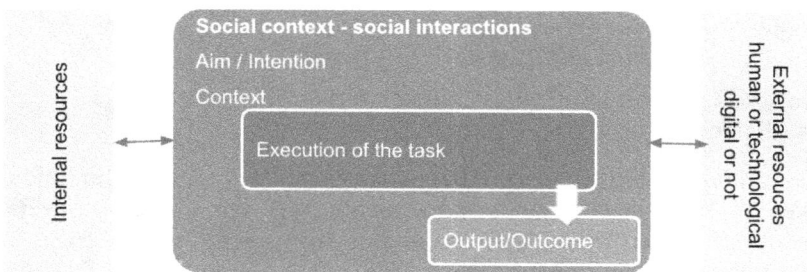

Figure 11.8 Scheme from an ECML (2016) project showing a didactic framework[19] © Council of Europe/ECML

internet has changed access to knowledge if we know how to use it ethically and linguistically. Language education in general – communication skills, linguistic flexibility, plurilingualism, etc. – has become even more important.

The next revolution is coming from the emergence of artificial intelligence (AI) in education. AI already helps learners to select training tools, to monitor their learning progress and to find learning partners in a reciprocal approach to language learning. All these considerations have a great impact on the way languages are taught in school.

Digital tools ease the implementation of flipped classrooms and help teachers to individualise the learning process. Mutual classrooms give teachers the opportunity to share a common approach with a colleague abroad. This interaction reinforces the role of intercultural skills in education.

Principals can promote innovation in and through language education. Various ECML projects such as ICT-REV[20] offer concrete tools, tutorials and examples.

Conclusion

The outbreak of the COVID-19 pandemic in 2020 and the rapid shift to an online modus of operation as the only way to keep the educational processes ongoing mark a significant change in the perception, the role and the use of technology in education. Technology can no longer be viewed only as 'support' or 'innovation'; it has become an integrated educational standard in most 'developed' countries. For principals, the challenge is how to keep abreast of rapidly progressing technological development and provide an adequate school infrastructure and, at the same time, maintain a high level of expertise and know-how among school personnel. The challenge will also be how to keep a balanced approach to the level of technological demands and ensure *equal access to quality education for all learners in the system*, not just those from advantaged socioeconomic contexts. This includes a shift from 'digital resource' towards 'digital service' as a strategy to compensate for possible social inequities.

How to Connect Language Learner Autonomy and the Mediation Function of Schools?

Immanuel Kant connected the concept of *Mündigkeit* (individual agency) with the idea of modern societies' enlightenment (collective agency).[21] Making each learner act autonomously is an essential cog in the general mechanics of plural societies. Plurilingual and intercultural education makes an important contribution to the school's mediation function in terms of social cohesion and inclusion.[22]

Language education, above all plurilingual and intercultural education, can play an essential role in supporting schools in their social role to offer equal access to good quality education for all learners. Through democratic instances, partnerships, networks, etc. but also through quality standards in curricula, schools can offer key opportunities that learners might not find elsewhere in their own environment.

In times of increased mobility and migration, providing equal opportunities for all learners is a major challenge for both teachers and administrators. There is evidence, however, that diversity can become an asset in education rather than an obstacle. A Flemish research project *Multilingual Assessment Education* (MulAe) highlighted for example the importance of referring to learners' plurilingual competences regardless of the subject matter of a given test or task (De Backer *et al.*, 2017). The focus of the project was to explore how plurilingual children who are not yet proficient in the language of schooling can be assessed in a fair and valid way and achieve considerable success in content-related areas (see Chapters 1 and 9).

What links autonomy and linguistic proficiency?

B1 (Threshold Level) of the CEFR is described as the entry level for an independent user of the language. At this key level, the language user can deal with most familiar communication situations[23] and the corresponding communicative language strategies, e.g. planning, framing, inferring, compensating, cooperating, etc. All these strategies are essential when it comes to supporting learners' autonomy and their capacity to plan their learning, to define their own learning objectives and to evaluate and assess their work. As such, plurilingual education, and particularly being aware of one's language profile, contributes to both the process and the development of a metalanguage that describes one's own learning goals. Integrating in a formal way the linguistic proficiency needed to achieve every single task in each subject is an efficient approach to making learners' autonomy become a cross-subject aim.

The principals' role is to encourage and support co-operation between language and subject teachers.

What links autonomy and school democracy?

Plurilingual and intercultural education helps each learner to develop the skills that make individuals contribute to social cohesion and inclusion: showing interest in other cultures, respecting minorities, taking into account other perspectives, mediating between persons with different cultural backgrounds, preventing intercultural misunderstandings etc., are essential social skills. More generally, language education plays a major role in the democratic culture of schools. It promotes respectful communication and supports individual and collective expression which are central to school democracy; listening to others, expressing a point of view, participating in a conversation or a debate, reframing various expressions, formulating a compromise, etc. have to be part of the education offered by a school. Accordingly, it is crucial to give learners opportunities to develop plurilingual communication skills and act as intercultural mediators through group work, project-based approaches and social engagement.

Principals have to generate opportunities to empower students in their citizenship through mobilisation in democratic structures and processes at school, in partnerships and network management, associative commitment, etc.

What links learners' autonomy and 21st-century skills such as leadership?

Language education is essential for 21st-century skills either intrinsically as a key component to develop a skill or extrinsically when language plays an indirect role to implement and use a skill. Table 11.1 is designed to make more explicit the language dimension that underpins each skill and the role of language education when supporting learners' autonomy.

The focus on languages and language education illustrates their importance for social cohesion and inclusion, a common thread to all those 21st-century skills listed in Table 11.1. A glance at the model of competences for democratic culture (Figure 11.9) confirms the importance of languages (Council of Europe, 2018).

Principals can foster the social function of schools where plurilingual and intercultural education underpins a school's language plan.

Conclusion

Fostering the schools' mediation function and supporting the learners' autonomy are closely interrelated. Plurilingual and intercultural education

Table 11.1 The language dimension in underpinning skills

Skills	Role of language education		Skills	Role of language education	
	Intrinsically	Extrinsically		Intrinsically	Extrinsically
Critical thinking	V	V	Technological literacy		V
Creativity		V	Flexibility		V
Collaboration	V	V	Leadership	V	V
Communication	V	V	Initiative		V
Information literacy	V		Productivity		V
Media literacy		V	Social skills		V

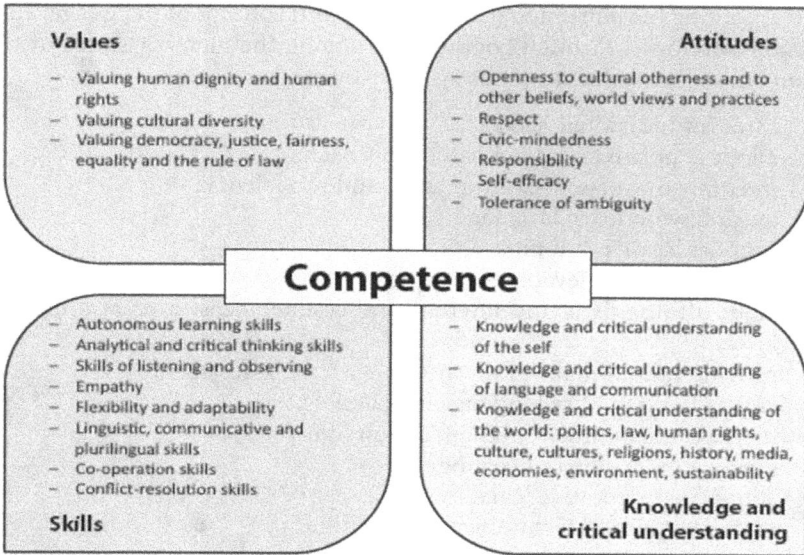

Values
- Valuing human dignity and human rights
- Valuing cultural diversity
- Valuing democracy, justice, fairness, equality and the rule of law

Attitudes
- Openness to cultural otherness and to other beliefs, world views and practices
- Respect
- Civic-mindedness
- Responsibility
- Self-efficacy
- Tolerance of ambiguity

Competence

Skills
- Autonomous learning skills
- Analytical and critical thinking skills
- Skills of listening and observing
- Empathy
- Flexibility and adaptability
- Linguistic, communicative and plurilingual skills
- Co-operation skills
- Conflict-resolution skills

Knowledge and critical understanding
- Knowledge and critical understanding of the self
- Knowledge and critical understanding of language and communication
- Knowledge and critical understanding of the world: politics, law, human rights, culture, cultures, religions, history, media, economies, environment, sustainability

Figure 11.9 Model of competences for democratic culture (Council of Europe, 2018: 38) © Council of Europe

offers the opportunity to promote common values and social cohesion through individual and collective agency. Promotion of democratic cultural and educational policies should not only focus on the learner but also on the process that underpins school democracy.

In Summary

Creating and cultivating language-friendly learning environments in a coherent whole-school approach means – in general terms – raising awareness of the linguistic nature of being and acting in the world. Supporting learners in their development of plurilingual competence means enhancing their opportunities for citizenship and participation, linked to the development of a person as an individual within the community. The goal of language education should not be only to transfer knowledge about languages, but above all to create conditions for effective linguistic development as well as learning about and exploring the world. Language education enhances the learner's personality, and leads to better orientation in the world. The development of language ability goes hand in hand with careful, critical analysis of reality and one's own place in it. It leads to the development of such character traits as curiosity about the world, the desire to explore it, sensitivity, openness to what is new, different and unknown, tolerance and respect, but also critical reflection, creativity, readiness to act, self-confidence and responsibility.

Adopting the plurilingual and intercultural concept of (language) education developed through cooperation among the member states of the Council of Europe means, among other things, to:

- cater for individual needs;
- adopt a 'positive', 'added-value' approach;
- integrate out-of-school experience and proficiency;
- teach how to learn languages;
- support learner autonomy;
- set clear and achievable objectives;
- value all linguistic and intercultural competences, even at a modest level;
- provide valid, reliable, fair and transparent assessment;
- ensure good quality language instruction;
- increase the number of languages on offer;
- support independent learning;
- support co-operative learning;
- make wise use of technology and media.[24]

In a given context, school principals – as leaders of a language-friendly educational institution, interested in the implementation of a coherent whole-school approach to language and literacy education, may wish, among other things, to consider:

- identifying and reflecting upon key features of language learning environments;
- involving all actors in language education through a coherent plan;
- focusing not only on formal learning but also supporting learners in their capacity to use all possible opportunities to develop their plurilingual and pluricultural repertoire;
- developing opportunities for learners where they can explore various ways to learn and use all languages;
- generating as many opportunities as possible to offer students the possibility to contribute to scholarly and social inclusion through multilingual communication;
- generating opportunities to empower students in their citizenship;
- considering language education as part of the school development process;
- setting up a medium-term strategy for human resource management in which languages play a central role;
- sharing project management through a project-based approach to language education which helps to motivate the staff and foster team spirit;
- finding strategies to develop a common culture of language dimension in all subjects;
- finding ways to support collective teaching intelligence;
- supporting co-operation between language and subject teachers;

- putting teachers in the best possible conditions to go beyond their own plurilingual repertoire;
- promoting innovation through language education;
- investing in the school's digital equipment and offering professional development sessions in order to help teachers to bridge the generational gap;
- identifying what digital equipment, resources and services the school can offer;
- establishing and maintaining equal access to good quality education for all learners in the system.

Notes

(1) 'Learning environments where modern languages flourish' is an ECML project and training and consultancy offer. EOL stands for the French name: Environnements Optimisés pour et par les Langues; https://www.ecml.at/ECML-Programme/Programme2016-2019/Learningenvironmentswhereforeignlanguagesflourish/tabid/1865/language/en-GB/Default.aspx

(2) 'Teacher mediation is required to deal with real situations of interpersonal, intergroup and even intergenerational tension and dissension, providing opportunities to develop relational and conflict resolution skills' (Coste and Cavalli, 2015: 50). 'At ISCED level 2 the pupil's choice of direction begins to take the form of a plan whose effectiveness depends on the taking of appropriate steps and initiatives: meetings with school principals and upper secondary students; interviews with workers in various occupations, employees, entrepreneurs, artists, craftsmen or shop owners, or visits to schools. Through their teaching activities, teachers can help each pupil to outline a life plan – for the very short term – which provides them with various openings in the longer term and without leading them into dead ends' (Coste and Cavalli, 2015: 51). 'In every community of practice at school, relational mediation impacts, from an educational perspective, on everything to do with "coming together as a community", creating a sense of belonging and the motivation to "be with" and to "be part of", with all that entails in terms of awareness through reflexivity' (Coste and Cavalli, 2015: 52).

(3) https://tools.ecml.at/eol/

(4) From 'Learning environments where modern languages flourish' – ECML project 2016–19, https://www.ecml.at/ECML-Programme/Programme2016-2019/Learningenvironmentswhereforeignlanguagesflourish/Projectoverview/tabid/4265/language/en-GB/Default.aspx.

(5) https://www.ecml.at/ECML-Programme/Programme2016-2019/Learningenvironmentswhereforeignlanguagesflourish/Concept/Matrix/tabid/4259/Default.aspx

(6) From the French 'établissement de service'.

(7) https://rm.coe.int/education-mobility-otherness-the-mediation-functions-of-schools/16807367ee

(8) ECML/CELV > ECML-Programme > Programme 2016-2019 > Learning environments where foreign languages flourish > Examples from schools

(9) https://www.coe.int/en/web/platform-plurilingual-intercultural-language-education/home. See also Appendix IV: 'Instruments and resources for developing and implementing curricula for plurilingual and intercultural education' in the Council of Europe *Guide for the Development and Implementation of Curricula for Plurilingual and Intercultural Education* (Beacco *et al.*, 2016a).

(10) PlurCur – 'Towards whole-school language curricula', ECML project 2012–2015, https://www.ecml.at/ECML-Programme/Programme2012-2015/PlurCur/tabid/1750/language/en-GB/Default.aspx

(11) Allgäuer-Hackl *et al.* (2017). 'DaZ' in Figure 11.5 stands for: Deutsch als Zweitsprache (German as a second language).

(12) As indicated in Figure 11.4 a possible plurilingual whole-school curriculum includes foreign languages and languages of origin which include languages of minorities (both old and new) subject to Council of Europe language policy normative standards such as the European Charter for Regional or Minority Languages, the Framework Convention for the Protection of National Minorities (which since 2016 also includes the languages of established migrant communities), and the European Commission against Racism and Intolerance. School principals are responsible for implementing policy in this respect and Council of Europe member states are monitored on implementation with strong importance attached to language education policy and practices. For additional reading see Piccardo *et al.* (2022).

(13) European Framework for CLIL teacher education, https://www.ecml.at/Resources/ECMLPublications/tabid/277/ID/35/language/en-GB/Default.aspx

(14) As suggested in chapter 8 on Linguistic diversification and curriculum of the Council of Europe's *Common European Framework of Reference for Languages: Learning, Teaching, Assessment*, school principals may wish to reflect upon:
– how to fit learning concerned with a particular language or culture coherently into an overall curriculum in which the experience of several languages and several cultures is developed;
– how to encourage, for the learners concerned, the decompartmentalisation and establishment of an effective relationship among the different components of plurilingual and pluricultural competence in the process of being developed; in particular how to focus attention on and draw on the learners' existing transferable and transversal knowledge and skills (Council of Europe, 2001: 176).

(15) *Schulentwicklung* with a focus on the *Drei-Wege-Modell der Schulentwicklung*, in Rolff (2013: 20) (translated into English); also online: https://www.fachportal-paedagogik.de/literatur/vollanzeige.html?FId = 1108004.

(16) *The Autobiography of Intercultural Encounters* (AIE) (Byram *et al.*, 2009) and *Images of Others: An Autobiography of Intercultural Encounters through Visual Media* (AIEVM) (Barrett *et al.*, 2013) are tools developed by the Council of Europe which support the learners' effort to learn from intercultural encounters. Both could be used to develop awareness of the benefits of intercultural learning – https://www.coe.int/en/web/autobiography-intercultural-encounters.

(17) UNESCO, 'COVID-19 response – hybrid learning', December 2020, COVID-19 recovery: Education: from school closure to recovery.

(18) See Beacco *et al.* (2016b) and Fleming (2010). See also Corson (1999).

(19) See Christian (2018).

(20) See inventory tool at https://ict-rev.ecml.at/

(21) 'Aufklärung ist der Ausgang des Menschen aus seiner selbstverschuldeten Unmündigkeit. Unmündigkeit ist das Unvermögen, sich seines Verstandes ohne Leitung eines anderen zu bedienen.' Quotation, Immanuel Kant, 1784.

(22) See Coste and Cavalli (2015).

(23) At B1 level, the user: 'Can understand the main points of clear standard input on familiar matters regularly encountered in work, school, leisure, etc. Can deal with most situations likely to arise whilst travelling in an area where the language is spoken. Can produce simple connected text on topics which are familiar or of personal interest. Can describe experiences and events, dreams, hopes & ambitions and briefly give reasons and explanations for opinions and plans.' Global scale – Table 1 (CEFR 3.3): Common Reference levels, Council of Europe (2001).

(24) See Annual Report by the Council of Europe Secretary General (Council of Europe, 2021): 'Over the next four years the main thematic priorities should include...highlighting the role of education, itself transformed by digital technologies, in helping our societies take advantage of the possibilities and avoid the pitfalls of digital transformation, including a growing use of artificial intelligence, ensuring that their use is rooted in democratic values and promotes democratic practice...'.

References

Aden, J. and Eschenauer, S. (2020) Une pédagogie enactive-performative de la translangageance en milieu plurilingue. In B. Shadlich (ed.) *Perspektiven auf Mehrsprachigkeit im Fremdsprachenunterricht – Regards croisés sur le plurilinguisme et l'apprentissage des langues* (pp. 177–199). Berlin: Springer. https://hal.archives-ouvertes.fr/hal-03224336/file/2020_Aden%26Eschenauer_Translangageance_DEF.pdf

Allgäuer-Hackl, E., Brogan, K., Henning, U., Hufeisen, B. and Schlabach, J. (2017) *More Languages? – PlurCur! Research and Practice Regarding Plurilingual Whole School Curricula.* Graz: Council of Europe. First published in German in 2015. https://www.ecml.at/Portals/1/documents/ECML-resources/PlurCur-EN-final.pdf

Barrett, M., Byram, M., Ipgrave, J. and Seurrat, A. (2013) *Images of Others: An Autobiography of Intercultural Encounters through Visual Media.* Strasbourg: Council of Europe. https://www.coe.int/en/web/autobiography-intercultural-encounters/images-of-others

Beacco, J.-C., Byram, M., Cavalli, M., Coste, D., Cuenat, M., Goullier, F. and Panthier, J. (2016a) *Guide for the Development and Implementation of Curricula for Plurilingual and Intercultural Education.* Strasbourg: Council of Europe. https://www.coe.int/en/web/language-policy/guide-for-the-development-and-implementation-of-curricula-for-plurilingual-and-intercultural-education

Beacco, J.-C., Fleming, M., Goullier, F., Thürmann, E. and Vollmer, H.J., with contributions by J. Sheils (2016b) *The Language Dimension in All Subjects: A Handbook for Curriculum Development and Teacher Training.* Strasbourg: Council of Europe. https://www.coe.int/en/web/language-policy/a-handbook-for-curriculum-development-and-teacher-training.-the-language-dimension-in-all-subjects

Byram, M., Barrett, M., Ipgrave, J., Jackson, R. and Mendez-Garcia, M. (2009) *The Autobiography of Intercultural Encounters.* Strasbourg: Council of Europe.

Christian, O. (2018) *Towards a Socio-interactional Approach to Foster Autonomy in Language Learners and Users.* Graz: Council of Europe (ECML). https://www.ecml.at/Portals/1/documents/ECML-resources/elang-EN-A5_28112018_112721.pdf?ver=2018-11-28-112721-473

Corson, D. (1999) *Language Policy in Schools – A Resource for Teachers and Administrators.* Mahwah, NJ: Lawrence Erlbaum Associates. Reprinted 2008, Routledge.

Coste, D., and Cavalli, M. (2015) *Education, Mobility, Otherness: The Mediation Functions of Schools.* https://rm.coe.int/education-mobility-otherness-the-mediation-functions-of-schools/16807367ee

Council of Europe (2001) *Common European Framework of Reference for Languages: Learning, Teaching, Assessment.* Strasbourg: Council of Europe.

Council of Europe (2018) *Reference Framework of Competences for Democratic Culture.* Strasbourg: Council of Europe.

Council of Europe (2021) *State of Democracy, Human Rights and the Rule of Law: A Democratic Renewal for Europe.* Report by the Secretary General of the Council of Europe. Strasbourg: Council of Europe.

De Backer, F., Van Avermaet, P. and Slembrouck, S. (2017) Schools as laboratories for exploring multilingual assessment policies and practices. *Language and Education* 31 (3), 217–230.

European Centre for Modern Languages (2019) *EOL: Approach, Process and Outcomes.* Graz: Council of Europe. (An output of the project 'Learning environments where modern languages flourish', 2016–2019). https://www.ecml.at/Portals/1/5MTP/Erin%20Jonas/documents/EOL-Approach-Process-and-Outcomes.pdf?ver=2020-02-06-104037-240

Fleming, M. (2010) *The Aims of Language Teaching and Learning.* Strasbourg: Council of Europe. https://rm.coe.int/09000016805a09ce

Piccardo, E., Germain-Rutherford, A. and Lawrence, G. (eds) (2022) *The Routledge Handbook of Plurilingual Language Education.* London: Taylor & Francis.

Rolff, H.-G. (2013) *Schulentwicklung kompakt.* Weinheim: Beltz Verlag. https://www.fachportal-paedagogik.de/literatur/vollanzeige.html?FId=1108004

Summary

Michael Byram and Joseph Sheils

The vision of the Council of Europe is that education is a fundamental right, and is located within the Council of Europe's general, overall vision of Europe as a democratic and legal area within which human rights and respect for, and dialogue with, others are crucial. Education needs to be founded on quality and equity, on equal access for all, whatever their characteristics, and on recognizing and meeting the particular needs of diverse learners in the best possible ways.

Language plays a crucial but not exclusive role in learners' experience of education. Where a mismatch exists between the language of learners – because their home language or language variety is different from the language needed in learning – there is inequity and reduced access to the full potential of learning. In addition to linguistic competence, however, other factors play a role since learning is dependent on interaction with others – whether teachers or other mediators and facilitators of learning – and on the effect of power in relationships. Learners need, too, the capacity to recognise and overcome such factors with the help of teachers. Furthermore, some learners are particularly vulnerable because of their status in society, not least those learners, young and adult, who are migrants.

The vision of the Council of Europe for all learners is that they become plurilingual, intercultural and democratic citizens. The purpose of the preceding chapters is to help teachers and all those responsible for education to recognise and respond to the connection between quality and equity and their work in classrooms and beyond, so that their learners become the citizens the Council of Europe envisages.

Given the crucial role of language, the preceding chapters analyse the potential for all teachers to ensure that learners acquire the necessary language – be it the language of mathematics or any other school subject – for successful learning. Those who are language teachers – of foreign and minority languages or languages of schooling – have particular expertise and can cooperate with other teachers to implement appropriate approaches and methods. They can also and not least do so to facilitate the learning of the vulnerable such as child and adult migrants.

Learning needs to be assessed and the principles of quality and equity need to be followed here too. An effective approach to ensure these principles is through portfolio assessment, which encompasses both cognitive and affective dimensions of learning.

Teachers work in contexts, and contexts affect their possibilities of ensuring quality and equity. The most immediate context is the educational institution within which they work. Principals of educational institutions need therefore to take into consideration and support the linguistic dimensions of all learning, providing the appropriate curricular and institutional structures.

In short, where teachers and principals recognise, understand and respond to the linguistic dimensions of learning they will provide the necessary and appropriate conditions for quality and equity in the education of Europe's plurilingual, intercultural and democratic citizens.

Appendix: The Council of Europe

Democracy, Human Rights and the Rule of Law

The Council of Europe (CoE), an international organization with its headquarters in Strasbourg, was founded in 1949, in the immediate aftermath of the Second World War, to promote democracy, and to protect human rights and the rule of law. From an initial ten member states – Belgium, France, Luxembourg, the Netherlands, the United Kingdom, Ireland, Italy, Denmark, Norway, Sweden – the organization grew to 18 members by 1970. The fall of the Berlin Wall in 1989 and the ensuing process of democratization in Central and Eastern Europe led to the steady enlargement of the Council of Europe, today a pan-European organization with 46 member states.[1]

As Europe's leading human rights organization, the Council has developed common democratic and legal principles. The Convention for the Protection of Human Rights and Fundamental Freedoms, more commonly known as the European Convention on Human Rights (ECHR, 1950), is designed to ensure respect for the rights and freedoms of all. Its ratification by all member states represents a binding commitment to democracy, justice and peace, and to the civil and political rights of each individual. Of particular note in the context of this book is that the right to education is stated in the ECHR (art. 2 of Protocol no. 1).

The European Court of Human Rights (ECtHR, Strasbourg) oversees the implementation of the Convention, a living instrument which continues to evolve through the case law of 'the Court'. The Court's judgments are binding and have resulted in member states amending their legislation and practice in a number of areas.

Implementation of the Court's judgments is monitored by the Committee of Ministers, the statutory decision-making body representing the Ministers of Foreign Affairs of member states.[2]

The civil and political rights enshrined in the ECHR are complemented by the European Social Charter (ESC, 1961; Revised Charter, 1996) which guarantees fundamental social and economic rights related to employment, health, housing, education, social protection and welfare. Often referred to as the 'Social Constitution of Europe', the ESC places particular emphasis on the rights of vulnerable persons (elderly people, children, people with disabilities, migrants). The effectiveness of the right to education in the ECHR is developed in detail in the ESC. Monitoring of the Charter's implementation in member states is ensured by the European Committee of Social Rights (ECSR).

While the Council of Europe and the European Union (EU) are distinct organizations, they share the same fundamental values. For example, the Charter of Fundamental Rights of the EU includes a number of social rights based on relevant articles of the CoE's European Social Charter, and the European Union regularly refers to Council of Europe standards and monitoring work in its dealings with non-EU countries, many of which are Council of Europe member states. The European Court of Justice (Luxembourg) is responsible for the interpretation and application of EU legislation in its member states.

The Council of Europe includes all (currently 27) European Union states and no country has so far joined the EU without already being a member of the Council of Europe. There is regular legal and technical cooperation between the two entities, for example in Joint Programmes to promote human rights and social inclusion.

The Council of Europe and the European Union also cooperate on education and language policy activities. They jointly organized the European Year of Languages (2001) campaign to promote language learning and linguistic diversity in Europe, and continue to promote its aims through the annual European Day of Languages (26 September).

Linguistic and Cultural Diversity

In addition to the instruments mentioned above, Council of Europe member states can ratify a range of other treaties designed to further support effective enjoyment of the rights and freedoms guaranteed by the ECHR. These include the European Charter for Regional or Minority Languages and the Framework Convention for the Protection of National Minorities which play a significant role in the implementation of CoE values underpinning language policy and practice.

Ratification of the European Charter for Regional or Minority Languages (ECRML), which entered into force in 1998, commits states which decide to ratify it to protecting and actively promoting the languages of traditional minorities in public and private life, without prejudice to official languages. Commonly known as the 'language charter', the ECRML promotes regional and minority languages as a key aspect of Europe's cultural heritage. It complements the existing rights of minority language speakers by placing obligations on states to take active promotional measures in education, administration, the courts, media culture, and economic and social life, at the same time ensuring that official and regional or minority language each have their rightful place. Monitoring of commitments is undertaken by a Committee of Experts consisting of representatives of the ratifying states.

Furthermore, the Framework Convention for the Protection of National Minorities (FCNM), which entered into force in 1998, establishes legal principles and provisions concerning the effective protection of national minorities and of persons belonging to such minorities. This legally binding instrument addresses, *inter alia*, the teaching of and in minority languages in public and private schools, at all levels, and includes intercultural education. States which have chosen to ratify this Convention undertake to promote equal opportunities for access to education at all levels for persons belonging to national minorities, and to recognize that every person belonging to a national minority has the right to learn their minority language.

In addition, the European Commission against Racism and Intolerance (ECRI, 1994) monitors the situation in each state and prepares reports and recommendations to deal with any problems of racism and discrimination in key areas, including racism and discrimination on grounds of language.

Intergovernmental Education Programmes

Cooperation among member states in the domain of education is carried out within the framework of the European Cultural Convention (1954). This instrument has been ratified by the 46 member states of the Council of Europe, and by Belarus, the Holy See and Kazakhstan; it can also be ratified by other non-member states in Europe. The Convention seeks to develop mutual understanding among the peoples of Europe and reciprocal appreciation of their cultural diversity. It encourages the study of the languages and cultures of other member states in support of Council of Europe values.[3]

Programmes are overseen by a Steering Committee composed of representatives of ministries of education and associated bodies, and a number of NGOs working in the language education field have been accorded Participatory Status and contribute to projects.

Language Education Policy and Programmes

The first intergovernmental conference on language education was held in 1957, followed by a series of projects carried out over the following decades by the Modern Languages Section, subsequently the Language Policy Division/Unit in Strasbourg.

From the outset, projects emphasized a learner-centred approach and the democratization of language learning. One of the basic aims was formulated by John Trim, the Director of Modern Languages projects 1977–1997, to 'promote the personal development of the individual, with growing self-awareness, self-confidence and independence of thought and action combined with social responsibility as an active agent in a participatory, pluralist democratic society'.

A series of pioneering projects developed a European community of practice through teacher training workshops and reciprocal visits, hosted by member states, which facilitated the sharing of innovations in curricula, materials and teaching practices. The *Common European Framework of Reference for Languages: Learning, Teaching, Assessment* and the European Language Portfolio are among the many outcomes of this cooperation. States benefited from mutual assistance in reviewing their policies in keeping with Council of Europe guiding values and principles ('Language Education Policy Profiles'), while support has been provided to those states addressing post-conflict language policy challenges. The educational and linguistic needs of minorities and specific groups such as Roma, migrants and refugees remain a priority.

An account of foundational Council of Europe projects in Strasbourg can be found in *Modern Languages in the Council of Europe 1954–1997* by John L.M. Trim. Further details are also found in *Milestones* on the CoE website.[4]

Programmes of practical support for the implementation of Council of Europe language education policy are provided by the European Centre for Modern Languages (ECML) in Graz, Austria. The Centre, established in 1994, is an Enlarged Partial Agreement (EPA) with over thirty participating members. States which are not members of the Council of Europe can apply to join.

The Centre's programmes, which are complementary to language policy work in Strasbourg, promote innovation and excellence in language education, focus on the practice of language learning and teaching, training multipliers, promoting dialogue and exchange among practitioners, and supporting networks of language professionals.

The ECML website[5] offers a wide selection of practical resources relating, for example, to teacher and learner competences, plurilingual and intercultural education, new media in language education, content and language integrated education, curricula and evaluation, migrant education and employment, languages of schooling, and sign languages. An account of its work is presented in *Changing Contexts, Evolving Competences: 25 Years of Inspiring Innovation in Language Education.*

Notes

(1) www.coe.int
(2) https://www.echr.coe.int (photos © Council of Europe)
(3) https://www.coe.int/en/web/culture-and-heritage/european-cultural-convention#19677664_20886832_True
(4) https://www.coe.int/en/web/language-policy/home
(5) https://www.ecml.at/

Index

For Product Safety Concerns and Information please contact our EU Authorised Representative:

Easy Access System Europe

Mustamäe tee 50

10621 Tallinn

Estonia

gpsr.requests@easproject.com

www.ingramcontent.com/pod-product-compliance
Lightning Source LLC
Chambersburg PA
CBHW071853270326
41929CB00013B/2215